DICKSEE'S CONTRIBUTION TO ACCOUNTING THEORY AND PRACTICE

This is a volume in the
Arno Press collection

DIMENSIONS OF ACCOUNTING
THEORY AND PRACTICE

Advisory Editor
Richard P. Brief

See last pages of this volume
for a complete list of titles

DICKSEE'S CONTRIBUTION TO ACCOUNTING THEORY AND PRACTICE

Richard P. Brief, editor

ARNO PRESS

A New York Times Company
New York • 1980

Editorial Supervision: Brian Quinn

First Publication in Book Form 1980 by Arno Press Inc.
Copyright © 1980, Arno Press Inc.

DIMENSIONS OF ACCOUNTING THEORY AND PRACTICE
ISBN for complete set: 0-405-13475-4
See last pages of this volume for titles.

Manufactured in the United States of America

Library of Congress Cataloging in Publication Data

Dicksee, Lawrence Robert, 1864-1932.
    Dicksee's Contribution to accounting theory
and practice.

    (Dimensions of accounting theory and practice)
    1. Accounting--Addresses, essays, lectures.
2. Auditing--Addresses, essays, lectures.
I. Brief, Richard P., 1933-   II. Title.
III. Title: Contribution to accounting theory and
practice. IV. Series.
HF5629.D56   657   80-1454
ISBN 0-405-13476-2

PREFACE

The introduction to this anthology was presented as a paper at the Third World Congress of Accounting Historians in London on August 18, 1980. I would like to thank Ms. Rhonda Baum for helping me prepare this volume for publication. Without her invaluable assistance this book would have remained a hope. I also thank Ms. Lula Ingram for her fine work in typing the introduction.

Richard P. Brief

New York University

July 1, 1980

CONTENTS

INTRODUCTION

Lawrence Robert Dicksee (1864-1932) is the father of modern accounting and his place in accounting history compares to Alfred Marshall's in economics.[1] Auditing (1892) is Dicksee's best known book and has had the most influence on practice. This classic went into 19 English editions and was the model for Montgomery's 1912 text in the United States. Dicksee also was the first accountant to write books on goodwill and depreciation. Equally as significant, but not as widely recognized, Dicksee wrote an early text on business organization, and he predicted the revolution in information processing technology almost 50 years before it actually occurred.

The bibliography at the end of this paper shows Dicksee's breadth of interest. Some of his most thought provoking ideas are found in articles published in The Accountant and The Accountants' Journal. Many of them were originally presented as papers at meetings of the student societies throughout Great Britain or as lectures at the London School of Economics. Often, they also were reprinted in other journals and published as short monographs.

The publications are listed in chronological order and the publication history for each item is given.[2] Dicksee's contributions can be classified into roughly three phases which were not mutually exclusive. From 1892 to 1904 Dicksee devoted most of his efforts to traditional subjects in auditing and

---

[1] An excellent biography of Dicksee was recently published by Kitchen and Parker [1980].

[2] The bibliography is based on Institute of Chartered Accountants in England and Wales [1913], American Institute of Accountants [1921, 1924, 1928, 1932] and British Museum [1959].

financial accounting. The second phase, 1905 to 1930, was devoted mainly to
the area of information systems. In the third phase, 1920 to 1930, Dicksee
reconsidered some critical issues in financial accounting. Shortly before
his death, Dicksee also wrote a series of articles called "Popular Fallacies."
They addressed a number of more philosophical issues which undoubtedly preoccupied him throughout his life.

THE EARLY YEARS: 1892-1904

Following the publication of Auditing in 1892, Dicksee wrote 22 articles
and books in the next 12 years. This work deals with aspects of auditing,
bookkeeping, depreciation, goodwill, specialized accounting systems, foreign
currency and accounting theory. Three articles written during this period
stand out from the rest.

"Forms of Accounts and Balance Sheets" (1893) is an expanded version
of Chapter 5 in Auditing. This article is interesting because it is one of
the first on the subject and because it illustrates the kind of imaginative
logic that Dicksee would use in later years. Dicksee often attempted to
begin exploring an issue by using what he called "first principles," and an
early example of this technique can be found in his definition of an asset.

> If we go back to the first principles, I think it must be
> admitted that an asset may be fairly defined as "an expenditure
> on a remunerative object"; and, indeed, it may be taken as a
> test of whether any particular expenditure is an asset or a
> loss to enquire whether, as a matter of fact, such expenditure
> was (looking back on it) worth the amount expended on it .... if
> (looking back on it) we think that if we had the opportunity of
> making the investment a second time we should have made it upon
> the same terms, we may fairly say that there is value for the
> original outlay; .... If, on the other hand, it appears that the
> value remaining for such expenditures is less than the original
> amount ..., it is obvious that ... depreciation has occurred.

Dicksee's views on the problem of asset valuation and the related problem of depreciation underwent significant changes in later years.[3]

Another outstanding work in this period is a lecture, "Profits Available for Dividends," delivered to the Institute of Chartered Accountants in England and Wales and published in 1895. Dicksee initially referred to an earlier debate between Ernest Cooper and Thomas Welton. It concerned the question whether profit is measured by subtracting revenue from expenses or by comparing the change in the value of net assets over two periods?[4] In effect, Dicksee said this controversy was an "empty box."

> I must confess that, to my mind, a discussion conducted upon such lines as these could not be altogether profitable; for a very little consideration will suffice to show that if the Balance Sheet were indeed a "just" one, and the Profit and Loss Account indeed a "full" one, then by every law of double-entry it must necessarily follow that the result would in each case be the same ....

He then argued that

> The most convenient method of considering the question has always appeared to me to be to follow the order I have just indicated- to criticise each item in the Profit and Loss Account first, and then to see whether a Balance Sheet prepared from accounts so stated may fairly be said to fully and fairly disclose the true financial position of the company as at the date named.

Four sources of profits were analyzed and ordinary profits are divided into profit on transactions completed but not yet received in cash and profit on transactions not completed, whether received in cash or not. In

---

[3]Kitchen [1976 and 1979] gives an interesting review of Dicksee's thoughts on depreciation and related problems.

[4]See Brief [1976].

analyzing expenses a distinction is made between those expenses that may properly be spread over a term of years and those that must be charged to the period in which they are incurred.

> It is only when we have adequate evidence that such expenditure was not incurred for the sole benefit of the period we are considering, and, moreover, that such expenditure may reasonably be expected to result in benefits accruing during future years, that we are justified in allowing any portion of it to be held in suspense ....

Advertising expense is used as an example to discuss deferred charges.

In the next several years Dicksee wrote Goodwill and Its Treatment in Accounts (1897) and a number of other articles and books. Advanced Accounting was published in 1903 and it begins by explaining the essential nature of the problems of asset valuation and profit determination. To deal with the subject along "systematic lines," the example of a single ship is used because "One of the most ancient (and therefore one of the simplest) modes of transacting business in through the agency of a ship" (p. 3).

Dicksee's "ship model" is a simple but effective device for explicating these basic issues.

> The problem [of profit determination] is ... quite simple in that at the completion of each voyage it is possible to strike a balance of accounts, leaving practically no balances outstanding as representing uncompleted transactions .... this method of arriving at profit depends for its accuracy upon the assumption that such payments have been made and charged up against Revenue as will make good any wastage that may have taken place in the original equipment of the undertaking ... - consumption of specific stores which may be readily replaced by the purchases of others, and the indirect operations of wear and tear and the lapse of time ... known as "Depreciation" (p. 4).

But any change in the value of asset due to causes outside ordinary operations, i.e., exogenous causes, should be ignored because the assets were not acquired

> with a view to there being eventually realised at a profit in the
> ordinary course of business, but with a view to their being used
> for the purpose of enabling trading profit to be made in other
> ways .... in any event it is quite an open question whether,
> pending realisation (which is not contemplated), any more reliable
> basis of value could be adopted than the actual cost in the first
> instance(p. 5).

The basic idea embedded in the ship model is the distinction between
a completed and uncompleted venture, i.e., between a single-period accounting model and multi-period model. This idea is a fundamental one and
Dicksee made further use of it in a later section of Advanced Accounting,
"Nature and Limitations of Accounts" (pp. 281-283). This section is a
condensed version of a 1903 article having the same title and which begins
by making reference to a pure venture model.

> If a particular venture has been undertaken and carried to
> a conclusion before the accounts in relation thereto are balanced,
> and the ultimate result then reduced to a cash basis, the most
> concise means of showing the transactions involved is, of course,
> a simple summarised Account of Receipts and Payments, and such
> a Statement will be a statement of fact, showing what sums have
> actually been received, what sums have been actually paid in
> respect of the venture, and what (if any) balance remains in
> the hand of the accounting party in cash.

However, in the case of most commerical concerns, the single-period model is
of limited value for the following reason.

> It is manifestly inconvenient for a trader to wait until he has
> altogether retired from business, realised his assets, and paid
> off his liabilities, before attempting to form any idea of how
> he stands, and those who carry on their business upon such lines
> end, as experience shows, not infrequently in finding that their
> liabilities considerably exceed their assets. Consequently it
> is imperative that an attempt should be made at comparatively
> frequent intervals- and in any event not less often than once
> a year- to arrive as nearly as may be at the financial position;

and for this purpose the books are regularly balanced, and the
usual so-called "final" accounts (that is, the Balance Sheet and
Profit and Loss Accounts) are compiled. In the nature of things,
however, these so-called "final" accounts are not final, but are
merely interim accounts.

Dicksee elaborates further on the problem of interim reporting.

... it is absolutely impossible to draw a line at any particular
date without its intersecting or "cutting into" a large number of
transactions which at that moment remain uncompleted. The precise
effect and money value of these uncompleted transactions can only
be estimated, and consequently a large number of the transactions
that go to make up the Trading and Profit and Loss Accounts must
also be, in a greater or less degree, dependent upon the estimates.
In some businesses as, for example, that of a retail trader- the
pending transactions will probably be relatively unimportant in
amount, although doubtless extremely numerous. In other cases-
as, for example, with a large firm of contractors- the number
of pending transactions may be comparatively small, but their
individual importance may be relatively enormous, and the manner
in which they are treated very materially affect the financial
result.

The 1903 article is Dicksee's last major effort in financial accounting
theory. For the next quarter of a century, he focused most of his attention
on the theoretical and practical implications of viewing accounting as a
system of information processing. The foundation for this broader view of
accounting can be traced to a paper, "The Importance of Accurate and
Adequate Accounting" (1905).

THE SECOND PHASE: 1905-1930

The 1905 paper signals Dicksee's emerging interest in the subject of
information systems. Having understood the basic problem of interim reporting, Dicksee began to think about the nature and use of accounting data. To
do so, he again resorted to "first principles".

The Science of accounting, in all its numerous ramifications,
arises primarily out of the need that accounting parties should

from time to time render those to whom they are responsible an account of their stewardship- that, at least, we may take to have been the original idea in the early days when capitalists were either quite illiterate, or at all events indisposed to concern themselves with so plebeian an occupation as commerce of any description.

However,

Accounting is not a matter of arithmetic, or of mathematics of any kind .... Speaking generally, an account is ... a narrative of the doings of an accounting party .... the method with which we are so familiar ... of reducing every transaction to a money equivalent, is not the essence of the account, but merely one of its numerous mechanisms.

This intriguing idea is elaborated on.

... an account ... is not merely a collection of figures and calculation, but essentially a narration, or history, of events, the ascertained (or estimated) money value of which is by no means only the essential point. In the absence of an adequate amount of "narration" it would be absolutely impossible for anyone- no matter how skilled in figures- to form any useful opinion as to their absolute, or even approximate accuracy .... Figures unsupported by explanatory narrative must be either accepted on trust or rejected incredulously; and therefore, in the absence of such explanatory narrative ... they must ... be regarded as entirely useless.[5]

Dicksee also reasoned that the objective of accounting is to provide timely information which would improve business efficiency and therefore the allocation of resources. He put it this way.

Stated quite shortly, it may, I think be said that accurate accounting- and more particularly accounting arranged upon suitable lines, so as to give not merely a review of historical facts, but also a summary of current results which may be likened to "news"- is of direct advantage to all undertakings as making

---

[5]J.R. Hicks made this point 40 years later [1948, p. 564]: "... there is hardly any situation which could be adequately depicted by a mere table of figures; every statistical table needs to be annotated, and in a similar way the full meaning of an accounting statement can only be expected to emerge in its accompanying report."

for increased efficiency and economy .... In these days of
competition business moves too quickly for anyone to rest content
with a Balanced Sheet and Trading and Profit and Loss Accounts
once every six or twelve months: he must be placed in possession
of all detailed information which these accounts imply systematically, continuously .... the importance of providing not
merely accurate, but also adequate, systems of accounts will
receive an increasing measure of attention at the hands of the
profession ....

In "Modern Accountancy Methods in Relation to Business Efficiency"
(1914), Dicksee goes deeper into the nature of financial information and
comments on the multi-dimensional aspects of accounting data.

The fallacy of the supposed perfection of the double-entry system,
as handed down to us by the Lombardy merchants of the fifteenth
century, is that, so to speak, it views everything in one plane.
It is about as true to nature as a system of geometry which regards
plane geometry as the only kind in existence, and ignores the fact
that there is such a thing as solid geometry.

Dicksee then asks and responds to the question, how should a simple human
action such as throwing a stone into a pond be recorded, an event which has
many consequences?

The object in drawing ... attention to this very simple example of
natural phenomena is to suggest ... that double-entry (as understood in the middle ages, and as to a large extent still practised
under modern conditions) is but an imperfect observation of all
the consequences of those events which are conveniently called
"business transactions."

In 1906 a book on office organization and management was published,
followed by several articles on depreciation. Business Organization appeared
in 1910 and a series of interesting lectures, "Business Methods and the War,"
came out in book form in 1915. The second decade in the twentieth century
also produced interesting papers on fraud, inventory and office machinery.

The paper on fraud (1911) argued that

> No business can be conducted- profit can be earned- without
> incurring some risk, and the risk of loss by fraud is just as
> much one of these inevitable risks as in the risk of loss by
> way of bad debt. It would seem, therefore, that it is not even
> desirable to attempt to obviate all risks of fraud; even if it
> were desirable, we may feel sure that it would be impracticable
> to do so on terms that left it possible to conduct a successful
> and profitable business.

The lecture on the auditor's responsibility for inventory valuation (1913),

ahead of his time, lamented that

> On the principle that it is useless to strain at the gnat,
> if one must perforce swallow the camel, it is at least open to
> question whether the auditor is not just as entitled to accept
> the certificates of the clerical staff that the clerical work
> has been accurately performed, as he is to accept the certificate
> of (say) the general manager that the valuation of the various
> items has been conducted on proper principles.

And an early analysis of the use of office machinery (1916) predicted that

> there is a great and increasing field for the use of machinery
> in connection with offices in directions in which at present it
> is not by any means generally utilised.

Dicksee also considered social and economics problems of fatigue, monotony,

unemployment and other effects of office automation. He was convinced that

this new technology would have important implications for the accountant.

> Unless the Accountant is content to be pushed aside, and
> to be dispensed with, it behooves him earnestly to grapple with
> this problem of the application of machinery to office conditions; as
> rapidly as possible to make good use of his opportunities- the
> wasted opportunities of the past; and to approach the subject
> with an enlightened and open mind, thinking only of the best,
> the quickest, and the most economical means by which the most
> desirable result can be achieved. If what I have put to you
> this evening has awakened you to the importance of a serious
> consideration of the matter, my time and your time will not
> have been wasted tonight.

Four other major papers on business efficiency and information systems

were written in the twenties. In "The True Basis of Efficiency" (1923),

Dicksee stresses the human factor and mentions that he "was disposed to think that the matter of colour affected people very much." The paper, "Some

Economic Aspects of Office Machinery" (1925), takes the position that economics

and human behavior are inseparable.

> Of course this view of economics is an utterly different
> one from the view that is sometimes put forward that economics is
> an absolutely cold-blooded and non-human science. It recognises
> that we are here dealing with the actions and re-actions of human
> beings upon each other, and it will be just as well, I think, for
> us all to realise that it is not possible to divorce economics from
> the humanities.

This paper also argues that "the whole object of accounting, of course, is to

build up information" and that

> the introduction of office machinery ... stimulates the demand for
> more information being compiled as an aid to management. It is in
> this way that we may reasonably assume that under all normal con-
> ditions there will be found enough work to be done to absorb all
> the workers already employed, so that the general effect of intro-
> ducing office machinery- and the introduction, of course, will be
> gradually- is that that the same number of workers are employed
> in producing more information, more records, and not a smaller
> number in producing the same quantity of information or records
> as before.

Dicksee then tried to answer some critics who felt, as some do today, that

modern technology would dull the mind.

> It may be that the introduction of calculating machines,
> instead of calculation being a mental process, may deprive
> present and future generations of the opportunities of develop-
> ing mentality that have been open to previous generations. If,
> however, there is anything in that argument, I think we must
> recognise that it might be applied equally well as an argument
> against the introduction of the metric system into this country.

In one of his final articles in the area of information systems,

Dicksee made the following prediction (December 21, 1929).

> ... future improvements in accounting methods must lie along the
> lines of employing perforated cards as full and detailed records
> of original transactions, subsequently handled by mechanical

sorting, counting and tabulating machines, so that any described
result may be reached at any desired moment with a minimum expenditure of time and trouble. It is clear that, so long as
we retain the ability to build up our transactions in any desired
form with any desired volume of detail, whenever we want information
from any particular view-point, that is really all that is necessary.
The laborious construction of ledger accounts merely for the sake
of enabling them to be listed into a trial balance is surely but a
relic of medieval superstition. Such an assertion may seem revolutionary to some. If so, it may be pointed out that not every form
of revolution is undesirable. Many of the most important forms of
movement are essentially revolutionary. In a mechanical age to veto
revolution would be almost the same thing as vetoing motion itself![6]

SECOND THOUGHTS ON FINANCIAL ACCOUNTING ISSUES: 1920-1930

Dicksee never lost interest in more traditional financial accounting

problems and he wrote several papers and a series of articles in this area

during the 1920s. Although his theoretical position had remained unaltered

by time, he had several new and interesting ideas.

The 1920 paper, "Published Balance Sheets and Accounts," restates the

view that a balance sheet is a list of "uncompleted transactions" and that

if assets were revalued each year

> ... to produce a Balance Sheet which will get into close touch with
> actual facts, we found that we have entirely defeated our purpose
> and have got right away from the true facts of the position, the
> essential fact being that the business is a going concern which
> we are going to carry on so far as we can anticipate, and which
> we have every reason to suppose that we shall be able to continue.

---

[6]Fifty years later, Burton [1980] described this revolution and its effects.
"In the last quarter century, the accounting profession has experienced
phenomenal growth, fueled primarily by a revolution in information processing
technology, a dramatic expansion in the regulatory environment and an increas-
recognition of the need for reliable financial information in the capital
markets."

Thus, Dicksee's position on asset valuation did not change in 30 years.

> ... theoretically at least, we ought to ascertain what benefits
> will be received from this outlay in each accounting period during
> which it is any advantage to us whatsoever, and charge the corre-
> sponding portion of the cost against each accounting period. That
> is what is commonly done in practice, with such items as plant
> and machinery and the like ....

But Dicksee did formulate some new ideas about the purpose of a balance sheet.

> In ordinary practice Balance Sheets seem to be used, ... not
> merely as a means ... [to] test the degree of success with which
> a board of directors has conducted the affairs of the undertaking,
> but also as a means ... to determine what is the true value of
> the company's share from time to time. It is very doubtful whether
> a Balance Sheet can be of much use for this latter purpose. The
> true value of the shares in a company depends, no doubt, to a cer-
> tain extent upon what return would be likely to be made to share-
> holders in the event of the company being wound up, but it depends
> certainly to a greater extent upon the income derived from the
> possession of the shares and the degree of probability of that
> income being maintained. The Balance Sheet as ordinarily prepared
> gives very little idea as to what shareholders may expect to receive
> if the company were wound up. It will give some idea as to the
> probability of the business being successful in the future, and
> it should enable us to determine whether the resources of the under-
> taking are sufficient to enable it to meet its debts as they fall
> due. We may, by looking at a Balance Sheet which has been prepared
> with reasonable honesty, satisfy ourselves that it is not likely
> that the company will be obliged to discontinue operations because
> it is unable to pay its debts, or may form the conclusion from
> looking at the Balance Sheet that there is a greater or less
> probability that it will be obliged to stop for want of money; but
> we can form no very useful idea from looking at any Balance Sheet
> as to whether the profits of the next few years will be as great
> as those of the last few years.

The final paper in the area of financial accounting, "Auditor's Responsibility for Balance Sheet Values," was published in 1927, 41 years after
he became a chartered accountant. After a lifetime of writing, teaching and
practicing accounting, Dicksee made seven recommendations for accounting
practice.

... the very common practice of directors, when issuing accounts to the shareholders, of enclosing a stamped form of proxy in favor of some of their own number should be forbidden by law.

... companies should [not] be allowed to frame a provision in the articles of association as a result of which the holders of certain classes of shares are deprived of all voting power.

... when a company goes into compulsory liquidation ... every director of that company should submit to a public examination somewhat analogous to a public examination in bankruptcy, and, until he has obtained the Registrar's certificate that he has passed that examination, it should not be competent for him to sit as a director on the board of any other company.

... in a very large number of cases ... no real difficulty would be experienced in prescribing a statutory form of published accounts that would be a very great improvement upon the vast majority of published accounts that one gets under present conditions.

... in all cases, [companies should] publish something in the nature of a Revenue Account or a Trading and Profit and Loss Account-something which shows, however inadequately, how the profit has been arrived at, instead of merely giving us the bare figure and leaving us to guess as to its source.

... many companies might with advantages follow a practice of issuing accounts more frequently than once a year.

... if it be thought desirable to meet in some way what is undoubtedly a rather insistent public demand, even if it is not a very well informed demand, for balance sheets that are really statements of affairs- revaluations of assets from time to time- that might, I think, best be met by the publication, not necessarily every year, but, say, every five years, of something in the nature of a valuation report like that which life assurance companies provide, quite independently of the annual balance sheet and not necessarily in any way linked up with it, but a quinquennial statement which would aim at showing the true position at the then current values as far as is reasonably practicable.

Dicksee ended his illustrious career with a series of 18 articles, "Popular Fallacies," published in The Accountants' Journal during 1930 and 1931. The topics range from the nature of goodwill to fatigue and unemployment. The issues raised are obviously those in which Dicksee had strong interest and personal conviction.

CONCLUDING COMMENT

Most students of accounting recognize Dicksee's contribution to auditing but few seem to know that he enriched other areas of accounting as well. His ideas were almost always original and many of them, especially in the area of financial accounting, have withstood the test of time. And the revolution in information processing predicted by Dicksee over 50 years ago already has occurred.

A large number of Dicksee's books and articles have been reprinted in recent years. Students, teachers and practitioners will enjoy Dicksee's style and find his ideas stimulating.

REFERENCES

American Institute of Accountants, Accountants' Index 1920 (New York: AIA, 1291).

———————————, Accountants' Index 1921-1923 (New York: AIA, 1924).

———————————, Accountants' Index 1923-1927 (New York: AIA, 1928).

———————————, Accountants' Index 1928-1931 (New York: AIA, 1932).

Brief, R. P., ed., The Late Nineteenth Century Debate over Depreciation, Capital and Income (New York: Arno Press, 1976).

British Museum, General Catalogue of Printed Books (London: Trustees of the British Museum, 1959), Vol. 52.

Burton, J. C., "Where Are the Angry Young C.P.A.s?" The New York Times, April 13, 1980, C 16.

Hicks, J. R., Book Review of F. S. Bray, Precision and Design in Accountancy in Economic Journal (December 1948), pp. 562-564.

Institute of Chartered Accountants in England and Wales, Library Catalogue 1913 (London: ICAEW, 1913).

Kitchen, J., "Lawrence Dicksee, Depreciation, and the Double-Account System," in Edey, H. and Yamey, B. S., eds., Debits, Credits, Finance and Profits London: Sweet & Maxwell, 1974).

———————————, "Fixed Asset Values: Ideas on Depreciation 1892-1914," Accounting and Business Research (Autumn 1979), pp. 281-291.

——————————— and Parker, R. H., Accounting Thought and Education: Six English Pioneers (London: ICAEW, 1980).

BIBLIOGRAPHY: ROBERT LAWRENCE DICKSEE

o   Auditing (London: Gee & Co., 1892).

Nineteenth English edition, 1959. Authorized American edition, 1905, edited by R.H. Montgomery. Second American edition, 1909. Reprinted by Arno Press, 1976.

o   "Investigations: Their Object and Extent," The Accountant (March 11, 1893), pp. 228-234.

Published in the Accountants' Journal (1892-93) and Leeds Chartered Accountants Students' Society Transactions (1892-93). Reprinted in M. Chatfield, ed., The English View of Accountant's Duties and Responsibilities: 1881-1902 (New York: Arno Press, 1978).

o   "Forms of Accounts and Balance Sheets," The Accountant (November 11 and 18, 1893), pp. 954-959, 973-981.

Published in The Accountants' Journal (1893-94) and London Chartered Accountants Students' Society Transactions (1893). Reprinted by Arno Press, 1980.*

o   Bookkeeping For Accountant Students (London: Gee & Co., 1893).

Seventh English edition, 1913.

o   "Profits Available for Dividends," in Four Lectures Delivered to the Institute of Chartered Accountants in England and Wales During the Years 1894 and 1895 (London: Gee & Co., 1895), pp. 33-59.

Reprinted by Arno Press, 1980.*

o   Comparative Depreciation Tables (London: Gee & Co., 1895).

Third English edition, 1925.

o   Goodwill and Its Treatment in Accounts (London: Gee & Co., 1897).

Fourth English edition, 1920. Published in The Accountant

(1897). Also published in <u>The Accountants' Journal</u> (1896-97)
and <u>Birmingham Chartered Accountants Students' Society</u>
<u>Transactions</u> (1896-97). Third edition, co-authored by F.
Tillyard in 1906. Reprinted by Arno Press, 1976.

o "Bookkeeping with Special Reference to Joint Stock Companies," <u>The</u>
<u>Accountant</u> (January 23, February 13, February 27, March 2 and April 10,
1897), pp. 116-119, 182-192, 210-214, 235-240, 339-344, 397-401.

Published in the <u>Accountants' Journal</u> (1896-97, 1897-98) and
<u>Secretary's Journal</u> (1897).

o <u>Student's Guide to Accountancy</u> (London: Gee & Co., 1897).

Second English Edition, 1907.

o <u>Bookkeeping For Company Secretaries</u> (London: Gee & Co., 1897).

Fifth English edition, 1914.

"The Liabilities of Auditors Under the Companies Acts," <u>The Accountant</u>
(May 14, 1898), pp. 500-511.

Published in <u>The Accountants' Journal</u> (1898-99) and <u>London</u>
<u>Chartered Accountants Students' Society Transactions</u> (1898).
Reprinted in M. Chatfield, ed., <u>The English View of Accountant's</u>
<u>Duties and Responsibilities: 1881-1902</u> (New York: Arno Press,
1978).

o <u>Bookkeeping Exercises for Accountant Students</u> (London: Gee & Co., 1899).

Fourth English edition, 1925.

o <u>Auctioneers' Accounts</u> (London: Gee & Co., 1901).

Published in George Lisle, ed., <u>Encyclopaedia of Accounting</u>
(Edinburgh: William Greens & Sons, 1903), v. 1, pp. 157-163.

o Solicitors' Accounts (London: Gee & Co., 1902).

        Third English edition, 1931.

o Advanced Accounting (London: Gee & Co., 1903).

        Seventh English edition, 1932. Reprinted by Arno Press, 1976.

o "The Nature and Limitations of Accounts," The Accountant (April 4, 1903),
pp. 469-74.

        Published in The Accountants' Journal (1903-04) and Birmingham
        Chartered Accountants Students' Society Transaction (1902-03).

        Reprinted by Arno Press, 1980.[*]

o Depreciation, Reserves and Reserve Funds, (London: Gee & Co., 1903).

        Sixth English edition, 1934. Reprinted by Arno Press, 1976.

o "Cost Accounts Suitable to Jobbing Tradesmen," in George Lisle, ed.,
Encyclopaedia of Accounting (Edinburgh: William Green & Sons, 1903).
v. 2, pp. 252-258.

o "Bookkeeping: Its Adaptability to the Requirements of Every Class of
Undertaking," in George Lisle, ed., Encyclopaedia of Accounting
(Edinburgh: William Green & Sons, 1903), v. 1, pp. 496-501.

o "Secretary," in George Lisle, ed., Encyclopaedia of Accounting
(Edinburgh: William Green & Sons, 1903), v. 6, pp. 36-62.

o "Auditing," in George Lisle, ed., Encyclopaedia of Accounting
(Edinburgh: William Green & Sons, 1903), pp. 163-193.

        Reprinted in R. Brief, ed., Selections from the Encyclopaedia
        of Accounting (New York: Arno Press, 1978).

o "Foreign Currencies and the Accounts of Foreign Branches," The Accountant
(February 4, 1904), pp. 281-291.

        Published in The Accountants' Journal (1903-04). Reprinted in

R. Brief and B. Merino, "An Early Contribution to Accounting for Foreign Exchange," Accounting Journal (Autumn 1978).

o "Presidential Address: Annual Dinner," The Accountant (November 19, 1904), pp. 626-631.

o Hotel Accounts (London: Gee & Co., 1905).

Second English edition, 1912. Published in The Accountant (1912).

o "Importance of Accurate and Adequate Accounting," The Accountant (February 4, 1905), pp. 146-151.

Published in The Accountants' Journal (1904-05) and Joint Transactions (1905). Reprinted by Arno Press, 1980.*

o Office Organization and Management, Including Secretarial Work (London: Sir Isaac Pitman & Son, 1906). Coauthored by Herbert Edwin Blain.

Fifthteenth English edition, 1951.

o "Depreciation; with Special Reference to the Accountants of Local Authorities," The Accountant (April 13, 1907 and Jule 1, 1907), pp. 482-492, 733-735.

Published in The Accountants' Journal (1906-07), Joint Transactions (1907) and Secretary (1907).

o "Accountant on Depreciation," The American Gas Light Journal (May 20, 1907).

Published in The Journal of Gas Lighting (1907).

o "Local Authorities and Depreciation," The Journal of Gas Lighting (April 16, 1907).

Published in Electric Review (1907).

o "Depreciation," The Municipal Journal (April 19 and 26, 1907).

o Modern Commerical Text-Books for Use in Schools and Colleges and for
   Men of Business (London: MacDonald and Evans, 1908).

o "Balance Sheets of Limited Liability Companies and Private Partnerships,"
   Associated Accountants' Journal (1908).

o ABC of Bookkeeping (London: Longmans Green & Co., 1908).

o "Auditing, with Special Reference to the Accounts of Local Authorities,"
   The Accountant (August 13, 1910), pp. 201-205.

o Business Organization (London: Longmans Green & Co., 1910).

          New edition, 1924. Reprinted by Arno Press 1980.

o Modern Methods of Accounting (London, 1911).

          See Book-Keeping Pamphlets, v. 4, n. 10.

o "Loose-Leaf Systems," The Accountant (November 11, 1911) pp. 652-656.

          Published in The Incorporated Accountants' Journal (1910-11)

          and The Accountants' Journal (1911-12).

o "Business Organization, with Special Reference to Fraud," The Accountant
   (December 2 and 9, 1911), pp. 761-767, 802-808.

          Published in The Incorporated Accountants' Journal (1910-11).

          Reprinted by Arno Press, 1980.*

o "Some Suggestions on Stock Accounts and Stockkeeping" The Accountant
   (May 3, 1913), pp. 668-73.

          Reprinted by Arno Press, 1980.*

o Mines Accounting and Management (London: Gee & Co., 1914).

o   "Modern Accountancy Methods in Relation to Business Efficiency," <u>The</u>
<u>Accountant</u> (November 14, 1914), pp. 581-586.

> Reprinted by Arno Press, 1980.*

o   <u>Business Methods and the War</u> (Cambridge: University Press, 1915).

> Published in <u>The Accountant</u> (1915). Reprinted by Arno Press,
> 1980.

o   <u>Machinery as an Aid to Accountancy</u> (London: Gee & Co., 1916).

> Published in <u>The Accountant</u> (1916) and <u>South African Accountant</u>
> <u>and Auditor</u> (1916). Reprinted by Arno Press, 1980.*

o   <u>Fundamentals of Manufacturing Costs</u> (London: Gee & Co., 1917).

> Second English edition, 1928. Published in <u>The Accountant</u>
> (1917). Second edition reprinted by Arno Press, 1980.

o   <u>Office Machinery and Appliances</u> (London: Gee & Co., 1917).

> Third English edition, 1928.

o   "Efficient Administration: A Prime Essential to Britian's Economic
Recovery," <u>The Accountant</u> (October 30, 1920), pp. 479-481.

> Reprinted as Chapter I in L.R. Dicksee, <u>The True Basis of</u>
> <u>Efficiency</u> (London: Gee & Co., 1922). Reprinted by Arno
> Press, 1980.*

o   "Published Balance Sheets and Accounts," <u>The Accountant</u> (November 20,
1920), pp. 561-564.

> Published in <u>The Accountants' Journal</u> (1921). Reprinted by
> Arno Press, 1980.*

o   <u>The Fundamentals of Accountancy</u> (London: Gee & Co., 1921).

> Published in the <u>Accountants' Journal</u> (1920-1922).

o   <u>The True Basis of Efficiency</u> (London: Gee & Co., 1922).

o "Goodwill and its Valuation in Accounts, The Accountants' Journal (August 1922), pp. 196-200.

> Published in Public Accountant (1923).

o "Costing," The Accountants' Journal (November 1922), pp. 388-97.

> Reprinted by Arno Press, 1980.*

o "The True Basis of Efficiency," The Accountants' Journal (November 1923), pp. 437-442.

> Reprinted by Arno Press, 1980.*

o "Accountancy," Accountant's and Secretary's Yearbook (1912-25), pp. 1-4.

o "Fraudulent Accounting," The Accountants' Journal (May-December, 1924; January-April 1925), pp. 5-7, 85-89, 166-169, 241-244, 321-324, 404-407, 492-494, 566-569, 646-650, 721-725, 801-804, 885-889.

> Reprinted by Arno Press, 1980.

o How to Install a Proper Accounting System (London· Chapman & Hall, 1925).

o "Published Balance Sheets and Window Dressing," The Accountant (April 17, 1926), pp. 567-571.

> Published in the Canadian Chartered Accountant (1926), Indian Accountant (1926), Public Accountant (1926, 1927), and Incorporated Accountants' Journal (1926),

o "Some Economic Aspects of Office Machinery," The Accountants' Journal (June, 1925), pp. 195-199.

> Reprinted by Arno Press, 1980.*

o Published Balance Sheets and Window Dressing (London: Gee & Co., 1927).

> Published in The Accountants' Journal (1925-1926). Reprinted by Arno Press, 1980.

o "Auditor's Responsibility for Balance Sheet Values," The Accountants' Journal (May 1927), pp. 57-66.

Published in <u>Public Accountant</u> (1927) and <u>Canadian Chartered Accountant</u> (1928). Reprinted by Arno Press, 1980.*

o "Should an Auditor Resign," <u>Australian Accountant and Secretary</u> (April 1928).

o "Staff Problems Arising Out of the Mechanisation of Bank Accounting," <u>The Accountant</u> (September 14 and 28, 1929), pp. 316-317, 375-376.

o "Accounting Methods - Yesterday, To-day and Tomorrow," <u>The Accountant</u> (December 7, 14 and 21, 1929; January 18 and 25, 1930), pp. 715-716, 756-757, 789-790, 75-76, 109-110.

Reprinted by Arno Press, 1980.*

o "Mechanisation of Bank Accounting," <u>The Accountant</u> (February 2, 1929), pp. 133-135.

o <u>Garage Accounts</u> (London: Gee & Co., 1929).

Published in <u>The Accountant</u> (1929).

o "Fifty Years of Chartered Accountancy; Origin and Growth of the Institute; Registration Hopes." <u>Financial News</u> (May 14, 1930).

o <u>Securities and Their Transfer</u> (London: Gee & Co., 1930).

o "Audit of Share Registers," <u>The Accountant</u> (June 14, 1930), pp. 765-766.

Published in <u>Commonwealth Journal of Accountancy</u> (1930).

o "Popular Fallacies," <u>The Accountants' Journal</u> (January-December 1930; January, March - July, 1931), pp. 641-644, 718-722, 803-806, 873-875, 8-10, 108-111, 157-159, 233-236, 297-299, 383-386, 458-460, 537-539, 600-602, 745-747, 817-819, 11-14, 92-94, 167-170.

Reprinted by Arno Press, 1980.*

o <u>Gas Accounts</u> (London: Gee & Co., 1931).

---

*Richard P. Brief, ed., <u>Dicksee's Contribution To Accounting Theory and Practice</u> (New York: Arno Press, 1980).

FORMS OF ACCOUNTS
AND BALANCE SHEETS

Lawrence R. Dicksee

The Chartered Accountants Students' Society of London.

FORMS OF ACCOUNTS AND BALANCE SHEETS.

By Mr. Lawrence. R. Dicksee, F.C.A.

At a meeting of the above Society held on the 25th October, 1893, the following lecture was delivered by Mr. L. R. Dicksee, F.C.A.:—

In suggesting for your consideration a few points in connection with the forms in which Accounts and Balance Sheets should be stated, I may mention at the outset that it is my intention to confine myself to those accounts which are ordinarily certified by the Auditor, i.e., the Balance Sheet and Trading and Profit and Loss Accounts of private traders, firms, joint-stock companies, and other public institutions; and the particular object of my address is to place before you what I consider to be the chief considerations that should guide us in a selection among numerous different forms in which such accounts can be drafted, in order that we may best achieve the objects for which they are prepared.

The accounts which we now have to consider will usually consist of a Revenue or Profit and Loss Account and a Balance Sheet. In some undertakings—as for instance Municipalities, Building Societies, and Charitable Institutions—it is perhaps more usual for us to find a Cash Account rather than a Revenue or Profit and Loss Account; but although this is the usual practice, and, indeed, in the first two cases is the practice sanctioned by the Legislature, I do not think it can be regarded as an altogether satis-

factory one, and I would therefore suggest that you should always advocate the practice which is now becoming very general, of supplementing the Cash Account with a proper Revenue Account.

Turning now to the account which in different undertakings is variously called the Trading Account, the Manufacturing Account, the Profit and Loss Account, and the Revenue Account, let us ask ourselves first of all the real object of preparing this account, and I think upon consideration that you will agree with me that this account is prepared for the purpose of showing

Firstly, the amount of business done in each of the various branches in which business is carried on;

Secondly, the amount of expenditure in each of the branches necessary for the carrying on of that business; and

Thirdly, the amount of surplus or profit or loss, as the case may be, which arises from the carrying on of the particular business.

The object of this information is doubtless, primarily, to ascertain the amount of ultimate profit or loss, as the case may be; but beyond this there is also the further object, which perhaps is only fully appreciated by those skilled in accounts, of comparing the corresponding items of various periods, with a view to ascertain how income may be increased and expenditure reduced, or, on the other hand, so far as possible, why income has become reduced and why expenditure has increased.

It will thus be seen that the efficiency of this account depends very materially upon the skill with which the income and expenditure have been distributed over the various headings employed; and consequently, if we are to profitably consider the question, it becomes necessary for us to discuss the nature of the various headings under which the items of this account should be divided.

It follows that, inasmuch as this account details for our consideration the summarised result of the transactions recorded in the books, the nature of the account itself will very materially depend upon the precise business which is being carried on, and it therefore becomes necessary for us to further consider the subject under the heading of various classes of business.

Taking first commercial concerns (which undoubtedly represent the great majority of the undertakings which we are now considering) we find that the transactions consist in the buying of goods and the selling thereof, either in the precise form in which they were purchased (as in the case of traders), or in an altered form (as in the case of manufacturers); in both cases there being the further expenditure incidental to the carrying on of the undertaking.

Dealing first with the Accounts of Traders, which are naturally of a simpler nature than those which require to be kept by manufacturers, the first circumstance which strikes us is the method usually in vogue by which a trader computes the amount of advance upon purchase price which it is necessary for him to charge for his goods in order to obtain a remunerative return for his labour, and this excess is very generally known by the term of "Gross Profit."

It would be very difficult to find an exact definition of the term "Gross Profit," inasmuch as the items from which it is calculated will be found to vary in different undertakings; but seeing that the whole business of a trader is based upon the calculation of a fixed percentage of gross profit upon each different class of goods dealt with, I think it necessarily follows that any form of accounts which does not recognise the existence of such a thing as "Gross Profit" fails to afford the trader that assistance which he is entitled to look for from his accounts, and consequently to a very great extent fails to justify its existence.

I have heard it argued by many experienced Accountants that Gross Profit cannot be considered to arise until such things as rent of warehouse, salaries of warehousemen, &c., have been debited to the Trading Account; but as it is the almost universal custom of traders to reckon their percentage of Gross Profit entirely from the cost price of their goods (although as a matter of convenience they actually make the calculation backwards from their selling price) it seems to me that, however correct it may be in theory, it is in practice nothing more than pedantic to include in this first section of the Profit and Loss Account anything more than Sales and the Closing Stock upon the credit side, and Purchases and the Opening Stock upon the debit. It is of course quite possible to argue that the resultant credit balance means absolutely nothing at all; but, even if this

is so, the fact remains that unless we so prepare an account it is impossible for us to see, or for the trader himself to see, whether the aggregate transactions of a period actually result in the percentage of gross profit which he had been calculating upon throughout that period; and therefore I think that, whether we choose to call the balance of this first section "Gross Profit," or whether we merely employ the indefinite term "Balance," the overwhelming weight of advantage lies in our bringing our account, in this respect at least, into accord with the custom of every trader, and so enabling him to ascertain whether during any period he has actually achieved the results which he anticipated.

In the next section of the "Profit and Loss Account" I would include all those items of income and expenditure relating to the business except such as may be said to be of a financial nature, such as discount interest and income-tax, which latter I would relegate at the third and last section of this account, which also shows the disposal of the profit among the proprietors or shareholders as the case may be, Interest upon borrowed capital or upon partners' capital I would also include under this last section, and also directors' fees; but the salary of a managing director or of a working partner I should consider more properly belonged to the second section, which bears the bulk of the general expenses.

And here perhaps I may be allowed to diverge for a moment with a view to consider the justification of debiting the Profit and Loss Account of a business with either interest on partners' capital or salaries of working partners. It is, I think, unusual to find both these items charged in the same set of accounts, and that for the simple reason that in such a case it would be difficult to say clearly what the remaining balance of profit expressed; it is open to us either to adopt the view that a partner is entitled to a fixed interest on the amount of his capital, and that the remaining balance of profit represents his remuneration for carrying on that business; or, on the other hand, we may assess the value of a partner's supervision at what we think to be a fair salary, and describe any remaining excess of income over expenditure as the remuneration belonging to the partner as a capitalist; but if in our accounts we provide the proprietors with what we consider to be a fair interest for the use of their capital and also a fair remuneration for their services as workers, it would appear that there ought, as a matter of fact, to remain no further surplus—unless, indeed, it were in the nature of a reserve to be devoted to a fund for the purpose of equalising the results of trading.

This, however, is a question of theoretical interest perhaps, rather than of practical importance; and we will therefore return to the consideration of the relative advantages of debiting partners' salaries, and debiting interest on capital. I think, perhaps, from a practical point of view, there is less real difference between the two methods than would at first sight appear, for it is obvious that the ultimate results in each case must necessarily be the same; but where partners devote different amounts of time to the business, or where they risk different amounts of capital, the question certainly assumes some importance. Upon the

whole, I think that where partners devote equal capital but
different amounts of time, it is simpler to disregard interest
upon capital, and to charge partners' salaries; but in the
case of partners devoting unequal amounts of capital and
equal time, that interest upon capital should be charged,
rather than salaries. Under both these circumstances, however, the assumption is that the ultimate net profits are
divided equally; but where this is not the arrangement of
the partners, of course it is more than likely that the
inequality of their respective contributions will have been
duly taken into consideration when arranging their
respective shares.

Be this as it may, however, the fact remains that such
questions of the adjustment of profits between partners
inter se do not actually arise out of our present consideration
(which is solely that of the form in which accounts should
be drafted), and it is, therefore, perhaps hardly necessary
that I should discuss the matter further than to suggest
what I consider to be the best form of treatment in each case.

Returning now to our typical Profit and Loss Account of
Traders, I may remark that the utility of a division between
the second and third sections comes in in this way—that if
the amount of business and the rate of expenditure have
been fairly constant, the balance shown at the foot of the
second section will also be constant, irrespective altogether
of any fluctuation in the amount of capital which the firm
may have had at its disposal; and this I consider extremely
useful, both for the purpose of seeing how far the net profits
of a concern have been affected by purely financial reasons,
and how far by commercial reasons, and also on account of
the convenience it affords if it should at any future time be
decided to convert the venture into a limited liability company. Schedule A shows what I consider to be a
good form of Trading and Profit and Loss Account for a firm
of traders. Schedule A A. shows the form of the last
section thereof, in the case of a joint-stock trading company.

Passing on to the accounts of manufacturers, I think it is
first necessary for us to subdivide this heading in accordance
with the various classes of business that fall hereunder.
Under the first class is the manufacturer who is but
slightly removed from the trader; that is to say, the manufacturer who does not require to sink a large proportion of
his capital in expensive plant and machinery—the most
typical examples of which are, perhaps, that of the small
manufacturing jeweller and the small manufacturing tailor,
both of whom, by the way, are fast dying out. In this class,
as with traders pure and simple, we find the selling price
based upon a percentage of so-called Gross Profit, the outlay
in this case being the cost of materials together with the
wages spent upon manufacturing; and, therefore, although
the method is clearly indefinable from a theoretical point of
view, I here again advocate the division between the first
and second sections being drawn exactly where it is drawn
by the manufacturer himself in his mental calculations.
Those who wish to have their accounts as complete as possible may prefer, in addition, to make a further subdivision
of this account in the second section, separating the
expenses of manufacturing (such as rent of factory, wages

paid for supervision of workers, depreciation of plant, etc.)
from those expenses which relate more particularly to the
storing of goods and the selling thereof; but inasmuch as
the balance shown by this break would correspond with
nothing in the mind of the manufacturer it appears to me
to be superfluous, and personally I prefer to merely show
separate totals for these classes of expenditure in the same
section, as shown in Schedule B.

The manufacturers belonging to the next class are those
whose transactions consist in the manufacture of one or
more classes of goods involving expensive plant, which
goods are first manufactured and then warehoused before
being sold. These undertakings are naturally upon a much
larger scale than those which I have just considered, and
we consequently find that the accounts are, as a rule, more
scientifically kept and the method of costing more complete.

The first section of the account thus becomes divided into
two parts, upon what I may call parallel lines, viz.:

The Manufacturing Account, which deals with the con-
version of raw material into manufactured articles, and
shows us the profit upon manufacture and the stock of new
materials on hand, and

The Trading Account proper, drawn upon the same lines
as first section of a trader's Profit and Loss Account.

The second and third sections of the account do not show
us any new features that call for our consideration.

Schedule C shows what I consider to be the most suitable
form for this class of accounts, but, of course, the precise
wording will depend entirely upon the particular industry
carried on.

The next class of manufacturers with which we have to
deal consists of those whom I may conveniently summarise
under the head of Contractors, *i.e.*, those manufacturers who
only make articles which have already been sold (if I may
use the term) for an agreed price. To this class belong
builders and many engineers.

It is perhaps more in this class than anywhere else that
the absolute necessity of proper Cost Accounts is so evident:
I would therefore regard all Contractors' Accounts as
incomplete which did not provide, in addition to an ordinary
Profit and Loss Account, a Summary of Cost Account showing the same result. This being done, the chief interest
centres around the Cost Account rather than the Profit and
Loss Account itself, and I therefore think that there is less
necessity for the latter to be unduly elaborate; I usually
prefer to state this latter account in two sections only, the
first section corresponding to sections one and two in the
classes of accounts that we have already considered, and the
second dealing only with the financial items, (as shown in
Schedule "D." The Summary of Cost Account I would show
in a tabulated form, the totals of the vertical columns agreeing
with the various items of the Profit and Loss Account (but
perhaps somewhat more summarised in form), while the
details of the columns headed "Profit" and "Loss" would
show the actual amount of profit realised, or loss incurred
over the execution of each separate contract, as shown in
Schedule D D.)

Another very important class of accounts, which can

hardly be said to come under any of the previous headings, are those relating to mines. These accounts I think are best dealt with in a manner somewhat similar to that indicated in the case of contractors; that is to say, in one section I would include all the items relating to the actual working of the undertaking, and in a second section those appertaining more particularly to finance : Cost Accounts would be made weekly or monthly, but they would usually form no part of the annual accounts.

With regard to non-commercial accounts, I think the system of dividing the account into two sections only conveniently applies.

I may add that the introduction of a separate section for the financial items possesses this further advantage that, in those cases where it is deemed inadvisable to publish full accounts, the published account may conveniently consist of the last section of the Profit and Loss Account only; of course this consideration will only apply in the case of the accounts issued by a company to its shareholders, and in such cases I think when only the final section of the Profit and Loss Account is published it should contain not only the Directors' Fees, Interest on Debentures, Contributions towards Reserve Fund, etc., but also the amount set aside for Depreciation of Plant, Investments, etc.

This is perhaps the proper place to offer a protest against the method adopted by many companies of stating in their published accounts a so-called "Net Profit," out of which it is proposed to set aside a certain sum for Depreciation and Directors' Fees. Of course if the Articles of Association provide that the accounts shall be so stated, there is, for the moment no other course to be adopted; but for my own part I would suggest that an opportunity could not be taken too early of altering Articles which produced so clearly misleading a result. ——

In the foregoing remarks I have of course not considered those undertakings whose form of accounts is specially provided for by Act of Parliament, these accounts are :—

Such Railways and Tramways as come under the provisions of the Regulation of Railways Act, 1868.

Such Gas Companies as come under the provisions of the Gas Works Clauses Act, 1871.

Life Assurance Companies, which come under the provisions of the Life Assurance Companies Act, 1870, and a few other undertakings with which we need not at present concern ourselves.

I may mention, however, that inasmuch as the form of accounts provided in each of these cases is probably as excellent a one as could well be conceived (due exception being always taken to the transposed form of Revenue Account provided for Life Assurance Offices), it is clearly advisable to adopt it whenever appropriate, even in such cases as it is not absolutely compulsory; and this, I think, also applies to a certain extent at all events—to the accounts of Water Companies, which possess many features in common with those of Gas Companies, although strangely enough there is no statutory form for the accounts of such undertakings.

It is not a little curious that many Gas and Water Companies are constituted under the provisions of the Gas Works Clauses Act, 1871, and this occasionally without expressly requiring them to keep separate accounts for Gas and Water. In such cases it will usually be found quite impossible to do more than provide separate Revenue Accounts for "Gas" and "Water," but in such a case the statutory form of accounts will, of course, be followed as nearly as possible.

Turning now to the question of Balance Sheets (which I consider should invariably be published), perhaps the first point to be disposed of is the rival advantages of the Single and Double-Account systems.

In undertakings whose accounts are based upon the latter system, it is assumed that the capital of the undertaking is sunk in the purchase and the construction of definite permanent works, and the Balance Sheet is divided into two portions, one showing on the one hand the expenditure on such works, and upon the other the Capital raised wherewith to meet such expenditure ; while the second section, or General Balance Sheet, contains what may be conveniently called the "floating" assets and liabilities arising incidentally in the course of carrying on the undertaking. It has been thought by some that this method of stating the accounts absolved the company from making any provision to meet the depreciation of its permanent assets, and, to a certain extent (e.g., with regard to preliminary expenses), this would appear to have been the intention of the Legislature ; but I think what was really intended was that Fluctuation, rather than Depreciation, was to be disregarded ; and I wish to call your attention to the fact that it is not only possible, but also perfectly easy, for provision for depreciation to be made, and stated, in accounts kept upon the Double-Account System.

If we go back to first principles, I think it must be admitted that an asset may be fairly defined as "an expenditure upon a remunerative object"; and, indeed, it may be taken as the test of whether any particular expenditure is an asset or a loss to enquire whether, as a matter of fact, such expenditure was (looking back at it) worth the amount expended upon it. This applies whether the expenditure is in the nature of capital spent in the purchase or construction of any particular property, or whether in the purchase of property or labour which was subsequently sold to another. In the former case, if (looking back upon it) we think that if we had the opportunity of making the investment a second time we should have made it upon the same terms, we may fairly say that there is value for the original outlay ; and in the latter case, if we may say that—looking back upon it in the light of our present experience — we would again sell upon trust to any particular individual property upon which we had expended time or money, we may fairly say that value is still remaining for the amount with which he at present stands charged. If, on the other hand, it appears that the value remaining for such expenditure is less than the original amount of such expenditure, it is obvious that, as a matter of fact, depreciation has occurred.

With regard to those few classes of undertakings whose accounts the law requires to be kept upon the Double

Account System, it would appear that in view of the permanence of the undertaking (and the subsequent remoteness of realisation and an *ascertained* loss) the Legislature does not require any provision to be made to meet such depreciation, except in the case of leaseholds ; but, on the other hand, it indirectly sanctions (where it does not expressly enforce) the provision of a prudent reserve to meet any outlay that may in future be required to keep the property in a state of working efficiency equal to that in which it at first stood.

On the other hand, it is a very generally accepted principle with regard to those undertakings which are not specially provided for by legislation, that before reckoning profits an adequate sum should be set aside to meet any loss arising from the depreciation of property : curiously enough, however, it would appear doubtful as to whether the law compelled any company to make provision for depreciation before declaring dividends out of its earnings.

In both cases, therefore, we see, firstly, that the question of depreciation is rather one of prudence or of internal administration than of compulsion ; and, secondly, there is no essential difference in this respect between accounts kept upon the Single-Account system and those kept upon the Double-Account system. In both cases, however, it is usual to provide for depreciation, although the method employed under the two systems naturally varies.

Upon the Double-Account system, it being impossible to deduct the depreciation from the amount shown in the Capital Expenditure Account, the method adopted is to accumulate the amount set aside from time to time upon a Depreciation Account which is included as a liability in the General Balance Sheet, although not necessarily stated separately. On the other hand, the more usual course to adopt with accounts kept upon the Single Account system is to deduct the amount written off for depreciation from the amount at which the value of the asset is stated, and this whether the Assets Account and Depreciation Account are kept separate in the Ledger or not.

I think, therefore, it will be seen that the question as to whether a certain set of accounts should be kept upon the Double or the Single Account system, however interesting it may be in other respects, does not really in the least affect the question of the desirability or necessity of making an adequate provision for the depreciation of wasting assets. There is this, however, to be said, that while, with accounts stated upon the Double Account system, it will naturally be assumed (in the absence of evidence to the contrary) that no such provision has been made, it will, in the case of accounts kept upon the Single Account system, be as naturally supposed that the values assigned to the various assets are actual, and not fictitious, amounts. Consequently, I think that, in those undertakings where it is difficult, if not impossible, to assign an accurate value to a company's assets (and where those assets are of a permanent nature and represent the bulk of the working capital), the Double Account system is that which is most applicable, as being the less likely to create a misapprehension upon the part of the shareholders. For example, in the case of a single-ship company it is usual to make no allowance for depreciation of

the value of the vessel, which naturally represents practically the whole of the company's capital. Such a case is, I think particularly suitable for the Double Account system, and that for the simple reason that this system would best record the actual facts of that particular case, which are as follows :

A certain number of persons, having collectively subscribed a certain sum, purchased therewith a ship with which they proceeded to earn profits to be distributed among them. Upon the Double Account system the distinction between these two points is very clearly defined ; in the Capital Account is shown the amount subscribed by the shareholders on the one side, and upon the other the cost of the vessel together with the balance of working capital (if there be any) ; while in the General Balance Sheet are shown only the floating assets and liabilities. Under these circumstances no shareholder who possessed any knowledge of accounts could reasonably complain, if in the event of the vessel being sold at a subsequent date it should be found to have deteriorated in value, for he would know that the question of depreciation had never been considered, and that throughout the career of the company the net proceeds of each voyage had been divided among the shareholders.

On the other hand, with companies which venture the bulk of their capital in any trade, the question is widely different ; for in such cases the permanent assets naturally form a much smaller proportion of the total capital, and consequently the Double Account system (which pre-supposes the investment of practically the whole capital of the undertaking in permanent assets with which the business of the company is carried on) does not apply, and in these cases, therefore, it is, I think, essential that all assets which are not taken into account at what may fairly be assumed to be their value at the date of the accounts should be definitely stated to be "at cost."

We will now proceed to recapitulate the various items which one ordinarily finds upon a Balance Sheet and consider what is the best form of wording under various circumstances. For this purpose (confining ourselves at present to the accounts of limited companies) we cannot do better than take as our model the form of Balance Sheet provided in "Table A" of the Companies Act, 1862, which, as you are well aware, sets the liabilities upon the left-hand side, and the assets upon the right-hand side, commencing upon both sides with the most permanent items and leaving those which are most constantly varying to the last.

Some years ago it was not unusual to find Balance Sheets stated with the assets upon the left-hand and the liabilities upon the right-hand side. The circumstance is doubtless at first sight curious, but—like many other things—there was good reason underlying this apparent anomaly. Under the Italian system of bookkeeping, which is still practised in some old-fashioned merchants' houses, it is the custom at every period of balancing, after the Nominal Accounts have been closed, to transfer the balances of the Real and Personal Accounts into one account, usually called in England the "Balance Account," and in France the "*Balance de Sortir*," or Closing Balance : under such circumstauces the Ledger would be actually closed, which in fact is never the case under the ordinary English system. The Balance Account so raised would practically be a detailed Balance Sheet, but with the assets upon the " Dr.," and the liabilities upon the " Cr. " side, as shown in the old-fashioned Balance Sheets to which I refer. The re-opening of the Ledger for the next period's transactions would necessitate the writing back of the balances of the Real and Personal Accounts to their respective headings, which would involve (for the sake of completing the Double-entry) a *second* Balance Sheet, but with the sides trans-posed, viz., the liabilities on the " Dr.", and the assets upon the " Cr." side.

Why this latter, rather than the former, should be the form which is now generally adopted, it is not very easy to see; but perhaps the best reason that can be given is that insomuch as a set of books must be formally closed before they can be closed, the first Balance Sheet will naturally be in the form of an Opening Balance Sheet in the modern form; and that consequently, when the abbreviated methods of modern bookkeeping dispensed with the actual closing of the books at each balancing, it would be natural to adhere to the form of Balance Sheet which was used in the first instance. Inasmuch, however, as our modern Balance Sheet is not a Ledger account, but merely a summarised extract from the Ledger, I think that the headings " Dr." and " Cr." must be considered as out of date, and I do not, therefore, employ them in Balance Sheets, although of course their use is not yet quite obsolete.

Upon the liability side of a Balance Sheet the most prominent item, in the case of a limited company at least, is the shareholders' capital, which, as you are aware, can only be increased beyond its original limit, or reduced, after due compliance with important legal technicalities. In stating the Capital Account it is, I think, desirable to show, firstly, the Nominal Capital, *i.e.*, the limit sanctioned by the Memorandum of Association; secondly, the number and value of each class of shares issued and the amount called up thereon, from which should be deducted the amount of Calls in Arrear, stating the number of shares upon which such calls are due. In France, and I believe also in South America, it is usual to state the full amount of the Capital Issued as a liability, and the Amount Uncalled as an asset; I do not think this is a very desirable form to adopt, as it can hardly be said that uncalled capital is more than a contingent asset.

FORMS OF ACCOUNTS
AND BALANCE SHEETS

Lawrence R. Dicksee

The Chartered Accountants Students' Society of London.

FORMS OF ACCOUNTS AND BALANCE SHEETS.

By Mr. Lawrence R. Dicksee, F.C.A.

(Concluded from our last issue.)

The next item to be stated is, I think, the amount paid up upon Shares Forfeited when such shares have not been re-issued by the company; when they are re-issued this item may appropriately be absorbed in the Reserve Fund.

The next item which we come to is the amount due upon Debentures, the amount extended being the nominal amount, or in the case of Debentures issued at discount, the amount actually received. In the latter case, however, the nominal amount should also be stated, and in both cases the rate of interest should be mentioned. I may here state that the appropriate place for premiums received upon issues of either Shares or Debentures is, I think, in the Reserve Fund.

The next item upon the Balance Sheet will be the amount due upon Mortgages, which, like Debentures, constitute a preferential liability, and ordinarily speaking, are practically permanent; the rate of interest should be stated here also.

Next we come to the ordinary liabilities of the company, which, according to "Table A," are separated under the following sub-headings :—

(a) Debts for which acceptances have been given.
(b) Debts to tradesmen for supplies of stock-in-trade, and other articles.
(c) Debts for law expenses.

(d) Debts for interest upon Debentures, and other loans.
(e) Unclaimed Dividends.
(f) Debts not enumerated above.

It has become a very general practice for the item (d) "Debts for interest on Debentures and other loans," to be shown as an addition to the loans themselves. There is, of course, no possible objection to this proceeding from an accountant's point of view, but I do not think its advantages particularly obvious.

The next item upon the Liability side is "Reserve Fund, showing the amount set aside from profits to meet contingencies." This, perhaps, is as good a definition of a Reserve Fund as has been offered, and although special Reserve Funds may be created for the purpose of providing for specified contingencies, I think we may take it as an axiom that no sum which is not set aside *from profits* can properly be called a Reserve Fund. Nevertheless, under the heading of "Reserve," all sorts of items are frequently included which under no possible circumstances can be considered to have been set aside out of the profits. This, perhaps, raises the somewhat large question as to what are actual profits; but I think that, if I enumerate the items which one sometimes finds under this heading, you will agree with me that the term "Reserve" or "Reserve Fund" is by no means invariably applicable:

(a) A sum set aside to meet depreciation of property, and to provide for its future renewal, is a charge against profits rather than a sum to be set aside out of profits:

(b) A sum set aside for the purpose of equalising the charge against Profit and Loss for repairs and replacement of machinery, etc., would also appear to be a charge against profits.

(c) A reserve to provide for loss upon bad debts or depreciation of investments would likewise appear to be a charge against profits—unless, indeed, the amount so set aside was more ample than the circumstances of the case necessitated—and in this case it would, I think, be the proper course to charge against profits what might be considered a fair reserve for loss, and to accumulate any further reserve that might be thought prudent in the form of a Reserve Fund pure and simple.

(d) Investment Fluctuation Account.—This is an item which, unless further explained, should never appear upon the face of a Balance Sheet; and that for the simple reason that its meaning is by no means clear. It may mean that investments have been revalued at a higher figure than cost price, and the proceeds carried to this account rather than credited to Profit and Loss or to Reserve Fund; or, on the other hand, it may mean that the investments are stated in the Balance Sheet at a higher figure than their actual value, and that the amount of the Investment Fluctuation Account is an amount set aside in anticipation of future loss. The former is a perfectly legitimate form of Special Reserve Fund. The proper place for the latter (which is, in fact, merely a Depreciation Account) appears to be in reduction of the stated value of the assets.

(e) Sinking Fund, or an amount set aside (and specifically invested) for the purpose of meeting a future loss upon redemption of debentures issued at a discount, renewal of leases, etc.

(f) The so-called "Reserve Fund" of a Life Assurance Company, which really amounts to a fund set aside out of the surplus premiums paid by the assured in the earlier years of their insurance to meet the deficiency of such premiums to cover the increased risk of later years, when the expectation of life is shorter. To a very large extent the Reserve Funds of our Life Assurance companies are "premiums paid in advance" rather than "accumulated profits."

There can, I think, be no doubt but what it is improper to state as a Reserve Fund any sum which has not been actually set aside out of profits, not for the sake of meeting an anticipated future loss, but rather solely for the purpose of providing against unforeseen contingencies.

The last item upon this side of the Balance Sheet is the Balance of Undivided Profit. It is, I think, preferable to show this balance without elaboration upon the Balance Sheet, and in a Profit and Loss Apportionment Account (or the last section of the Profit and Loss Account) to show the connection between this account and the balance shown upon the last Balance Sheet and the balance of the Profit and Loss Account for the current period. There is, however, no more serious objection to the former method than that it does not appear to be so clear as the latter.

With the question of Contingent Liabilities I need hardly trouble you now, beyond stating that all such liabilities must be noted upon the Balance Sheet, even if it is anticipated that they will not ultimately result in a claim against the company.

Turning now to the Assets, we find that "Table A." deals first with "freehold land, leasehold land, and leasehold buildings," which it requires to be stated separately, and apparently without deduction for depreciation. I say "apparently," for depreciation is not here mentioned, although it is specifically provided for in the case of stock-in-trade and plant. This tends, I think, to show that even in

accounts stated upon the Single Account system the Legislature did not intend to make it compulsory for the permanent assets of a company to be revalued periodically; and this, it will be remembered, is a question with two sides to it, viz., the possibility of a rise in value and the possibility of a fall. Had "leaseholds" been excepted I think we might reasonably have assumed that it was not intended that companies should allow either a rise or fall in their permanent assets to modify their trading profits: but it is impossible to suppose that the depreciation of leaseholds was intended to be ignored, and therefore the whole point remains (as it must remain until the question is definitely settled by a further enactment) extremely uncertain so far as the legal obligations of a company are concerned, although there need be no uncertainty as to what is the most prudent course to adopt.

Next in order "Table A." states "Stock-in-Trade and Plant: the cost to be stated, with deductions for deterioration in value as charged to Reserve Fund or Profit and Loss." It would have seemed more natural to have placed Plant before Stock-in-trade, as being the more permanent of the two items; and it seems strange to talk of a "deduction for deterioration in value as charged to the Reserve Fund." I take it that, inasmuch as the Reserve Fund has already been defined as "an amount set aside from profits to meet contingencies," the deductions—in so far as they are to be charged against Reserve Fund—are supposed to be for unforeseen deterioration rather than for regular depreciation.

We now come to the "Debts owing to the company," which for some inexplicable reason appear to be stated under separate headings, instead of being under sub-headings, as in the case of the debts owing by the company. The headings are as follows:—

Debts considered good, for which the company holds bills or other securities;

Debts considered good, for which the company holds no security;

Debts considered doubtful and bad.

It is also provided that "any debt due from a director or any other officer of the company is to be separately stated." I do not think that it would be considered generally desirable to separately state the amount of the doubtful and bad debts, but the provision for the separate statement of any debt due from a director or other officer is one, I think, that should not be lost sight of: we may take it that it is not intended to apply in the case of debts for small amounts in the regular course of business, but cases will readily occur to you in connection with some recent failures where the compliance with this provision might have materially affected the course of events.

The next item on the Balance Sheet is Investments, which should, I think, be stated in some detail, and if the investments are on account of Reserve Fund or Sinking Fund the circumstance should be clearly stated. The Life Assurance Companies Act 1870 provides the following sub-division of the item "Investments" upon the Balance Sheets of Life Assurance companies, and I think we may take it as being the least detailed form of specification that is admissible.

> British Government Securities;
> Indian and Colonial Securities;
> Foreign Government Securities;
> Railway and other Debentures and Debenture Stocks;
> Railway Shares, Preference and Ordinary,
> House Property;
> Other investments (to be specified).

Personally, I think that in all cases—except, perhaps, in the case of an Investment Trust company—the actual investments should be stated separately; for when we come to think that such an item as "Foreign Government Securities" may include investments so various as French Rentes, Turkish Bonds, and South American Republic Bonds, it is obvious—in this case, at least—the particular heading adopted is no indication whatever to the general desirability of the investment. Again, "Railway Shares" may mean anything between Great Western Stock and Grand Trunk Stock, to say nothing of Mexican and other similar railways.

The accruing interest due upon investments should, I think, always be included up to the date of the accounts, although not confused with the capital nature of the investments themselves; but in the case of dividends upon ordinary shares, and some preference shares, the amount is too indefinite to be estimated, and in these cases I think that only dividends that have been declared and are still unpaid can be taken as assets.

Last upon the assets side is the item of Cash, which is, I think, best separated into

Amount at bankers on deposit (including accrued interest);
Amount upon current account; and
Amount in hand.

It is hardly necessary that I should enter into detail into the forms of Balance Sheets required for different classes of undertakings; the same rules will apply in almost all cases, and although modifications of detail will appear desirable in almost each particular case, these naturally must be considered and modified according to the particular circumstances that obtain; the general principle in all cases being that the accounts must be not only correct, but also so clear as to render misapprehension impossible even among those who do not profess to be skilled accountants.

In this respect it is, perhaps, well to bear in mind the particular classes of persons who are likely to be interested in the accounts that we are considering. Thus, in the case of a friendly society, lucidity will be the great thing to be aimed at; while in the case of such an institution as a bank, we must bear in mind that the main object of the Balance Sheet is, perhaps, less to inform shareholders as to the amount of their profits than to allow the public to form a reliable estimate upon the bank's stability.

In Schedules E., F., and G., I have stated three general forms of Balance Sheets for use under different circumstances, to which I invite your careful attention.

In considering these matters, however, we must not lose sight of the fact that it is very exceptional for the form in which accounts are stated to be actually under the control of the auditor. As a rule, articles of association provide that the accounts shall be rendered in such form as the directors shall think fit; and in such cases it is, of course, impossible for the auditor to dictate as to the precise form to be adopted.

This, however, does not release him from the responsibility of judging as to the fitness of the form in which the accounts are rendered by the directors: in this respect he is placed in a position, and furnished with information which is withheld from the general body of the shareholders, for the express purpose of enquiring into the conduct of the directors and other officials, and to satisfy himself that the accounts submitted by the directors to the shareholders are such as will reasonably disclose the position of the company. Considerations with regard to the form which the accounts should take are frequently of a nature which the auditor must of necessity weigh for himself; for inasmuch as the shareholders have no knowledge of the transactions or position of the company other than that which they gain from a perusal of the directors' accounts and the auditor's report, it stands to reason that, if the accounts do not sufficiently disclose these things, it may frequently happen that the shareholders themselves would have no reason to suspect that the accounts were not all that they should be.

It therefore follows that although we, as auditors, have not the drafting of a company's accounts, it is necessary for us in all cases to consider the form in which they are submitted for our approval, and not merely to content ourselves with an examination of their technical correctness. It has been stated that the accounts submitted to the shareholders, being the accounts of the directors, they and they only are responsible to the shareholders for the form. This is true to the extent that the auditor has no power to compel the directors to modify the form of their accounts; but it is not true in the sense that if the accounts submitted are, so far as they go, correct, the auditor is under no responsibility to specially report in such cases as they are insufficient to enable anyone examining them to obtain a correct idea of the company's position. Were this the case it would, indeed, be difficult to see in what respect the shareholders gained by an audit of their accounts, for it is obvious that it would be possible to conceal almost anything in the shape of fraud or unjustifiable extravagance.

The shareholders have, however, a clear right to such accounts as will enable them from time to time to judge of the value of their investment, and it is for the purpose of making these accounts reliable for the purposes of such valuation that an auditor is appointed: and while there rests with him the serious responsibility of concealing such matters of internal detail as would, if divulged, tend to damage the position of the business, yet, on the other hand, he must not fail to remember that it is the shareholders and not the directors who are the masters of the fortune of the company, and that—except in such matters of internal detail—they have an indisputable right to the fullest and clearest information.

The Chairman (Mr. E. E. PRICE, F.C.A.) stated :—

He was glad Mr. Dicksee had called attention to the old-fashioned plan of placing "Dr." and "Cr." at the head of the Balance Sheet. He thought these headings should always be struck out—assets and liabilities were what was wanted; or better still, the words "Capital and Liabilities," and "Property and Assets."

He then referred to the question of debentures and mortgages. He thought it was a very essential thing that whenever there was a charge of any kind it should be clearly stated, as also the nature of the charge and what property it affected; and with regard to interest in arrear it should be added to the loan, because in cases where there was a mortgage or charge it extended to interest in arrear as well as to the principal.

With reference to Depreciation, he said it seemed to him that a Reserve Fund might, for the sake of convenience, be placed among the liabilities rather than write the amount off the assets on the other side, as, for instance, in the case of loss on exchange. The books might be kept in rupees at 1s. 4d., and the present value being below that sum, provision of course must be made to meet the loss. The assets could not be written down because the value of the rupee was fluctuating daily, but a Reserve Fund should be made, and the amount of such reserve should appear on the liability side of the Balance Sheet.

Mr. C. R. TREVOR, F.C.A., said he was glad to have been present and heard the paper read. There was plenty of material in it for thought and consideration. It was necessary for them to reflect and consider on what they heard, and reason the points out in their minds, and not follow in the beaten track of listening without considering. He referred to the forms of accounts of institutions, and stated that he considered a Revenue Account the more useful form because it necessarily covered the same ground as a Cash Account, and also included outstanding income or expenditure. There was great diversity in the forms of accounts of institutions. He often met with titles which did not correspond; for instance, where the form was headed "Receipts and Expenditure," which should, of course, be "Income and Expenditure," or "Receipts and Payments," the latter including only actual sums received and paid, whilst the former included outstanding items as well. "Receipts and Payments" might be treated as a *Cash Account*. In that case it would be necessary to debit cash with the receipts and credit it with the payments.

As regards statements of affairs he found there were firms of accountants who still adhered to the plan of placing the assets on the debit side and the liabilities on the credit side. One reason which he considered conclusive for arranging Balance Sheets in the form now generally adopted was that where the Balance Sheet showed a surplus it was at the credit of the concern or the individual whose Balance Sheet it was, and the surplus must, therefore, appear on the right-hand or credit side of the account.

In Life Assurance Accounts the sides of the Revenue Account were reversed, in the form rendered compulsory by the Life Assurance Companies Act. He had seen a Profit and Loss Account of a fire insurance company following the form of the Revenue Account in the Act, and consequently debited with the balance of profit brought from the previous year, and also with the profit accrued during the current year. In the total the Profit and Loss Account had at the debit £28,000, while the intention was to show that the amount was a credit available for distribution.

Mr. A. D. BARBER asked whether, in the case of debentures issued at a discount, the amount would be written off to Profit and Loss.

Mr. DICKSEE stated that, as regards debentures issued at a discount, if the debentures were not redeemable the only practical effect was that the company would be paying a slightly increased rate of interest. If they were redeemable, it would, of course, be necessary to set aside, during the period which the debentures had to run, the amount of the discount, in the same way that sums were set aside for the renewal of a lease, or on the instalment principle, by writing off an equal amount each year.

With reference to Reserve Funds, he read the following extract from a letter he had received, with reference to the reserve funds of Life Assurance Companies. "The Level " Premium System, so much condemned by the advocates of " these assessment companies, is really the truly Natural " Premium System, for it is the natural premium for the " first year at the age of entry, i.e., the premium for that " one year's risk, plus the similar premium one year older " for the second year's risk, plus the like premium a further " year older for the third year's risk, and so on throughout " the term of expectation of the given life. The equivalent " annuity or equalised annual payments, to the summation " of these premiums, constitutes the level premium ; and " hence an assurer pays far less than the true or natural " premium as his policy becomes old, owing to his having " paid more than the exact value of the risk in the earlier " years of its existence—the reverse of the operation of the " assessment plan, whereby if such companies were to live " long enough, the necessary premiums to be charged when " the policies became of long duration would prove pro-" hibitive.

" It is by the Level Premium Companies laying by funds " out of these premiums in the early years of the existence " of their policies that they make the reserves so fallaciously " condemned by the assessment or natural premium com-" panies, and which are absolutely necessary to meet the " claims of policies now on the books. These reserves were " not accumulated out of policies which have long ceased to " exist, but are the accumulations of the present generation " of policy-holders, and each policy will draw its own full " share of such reserves as it becomes a claim. It is these " reserves that give a policy-holder, either in this or any other " solvent insurance office, the certainty that his policy is " provided for and will be paid in due course ; whereas in an " assessment or natural premium office, he has the comfort " of knowing that as the premiums he has paid have been " spent, his relatives are dependent on the caprice of the " surviving policy-holders to pay the proceeds of his " policy ! "

A vote of thanks having been accorded to the chairman for presiding, and to Mr. Dicksee for his valuable paper, the meeting terminated.

SCHEDULE A.

TRADERS' ACCOUNTS.

Dr. TRADING ACCOUNT (FIRST SECTION) for the year ended 31st DECEMBER, 1892. Cr.

	Stock on 1st Jan. 1892	Purchases for the Year	Gross Profit	Total		Sales for the Year	Stock on 31st Dec. 1892	Total
	£ s d	£ s d	£ s d	£ s d		£ s d	£ s d	£ s d
Grocery Dep'rtm'nt	2,250 0 0	17,750 0 0	2,000 0 0	22,000 0 0	Grocery Department	20,000 0 0	2,000 0 0	22,000 0 0
Wines and Spirits Department ..	20,000 0 0	13,500 0 0	1,500 0 0	35,000 0 0	Wines and Spirits Department	10,000 0 0	25,000 0 0	35,000 0 0
Drapery Dep'rtm'nt	7,500 0 0	34,500 0 0	4,000 0 0	46,000 0 0	Drapery do.	40,000 0 0	6,000 0 0	46,000 0 0
Tailoring do.	4,750 0 0	4,625 0 0	625 0 0	10,000 0 0	Tailoring do.	5,000 0 0	5,000 0 0	10,000 0 0
Mantle do.	5,000 0 0	10,375 0 0	2,625 0 0	18,000 0 0	Mantle do.	15,000 0 0	3,000 0 0	18,000 0 0
Fancy Goods do.	3,500 0 0	3,625 0 0	875 0 0	8,000 0 0	Fancy Goods do.	5,000 0 0	3,000 0 0	8,000 0 0
Furniture do.	12,000 0 0	26,500 0 0	2,500 0 0	41,000 0 0	Furniture do.	25,000 0 0	16,000 0 0	41,000 0 0
	£55,000 0 0	£110,875 0 0	£14,125 0 0	£180,000 0 0		£120,000 0 0	£60,000 0 0	£180,000 0 0

Dr. PROFIT AND LOSS ACCOUNT (SECOND SECTION) FOR THE YEAR ENDED 31ST DECEMBER, 1892. Cr.

	£ s d	£ s d		£ s d
To Rent, Rates and Taxes	2,000 0 0		By Gross Profit for the year, as per Trading Account	14,125 0 0
„ Salaries of Assistants, etc., viz. :				
Salaries .. £4,000 0 0				
Cost of Board.. 2,500 0 0				
	6,500 0 0			
„ Trade Expenses	1,500 0 0			
„ Carriage	1,000 0 0			
„ Depreciation	250 0 0			
		11,250 0 0		
„ Balance carried down	..	2,875 0 0		
	£	14,125 0 0		£ 14,125 0 0

(THIRD SECTION.)

	£ s d	£ s d		£ s d
To Interest on Capital	2,500 0 0		By Balance brought down	2,875 0 0
„ Income Tax	125 0 0		„ Discounts upon Purchases ..	2,325 0 0
		2,625 0 0		
„ Balance, being net profit for the year, viz.:				
A., one-half share	1,287 10 0			
B., one-third share	858 6 8			
C., one-sixth share	429 3 4			
		2,575 0 0		
		£5,200 0 0		£5,200 0 0

SCHEDULE AA.

Showing the Third Section of the previous example re-drafted for the use of a Trading Joint Stock Company in cases where the first two Sections of the Account are not published.

Dr.   PROFIT AND LOSS ACCOUNT FOR THE YEAR ENDED 31ST DECEMBER, 1892.   Cr.

	£ s d	£ s d		£ s d
To Amount written off for depreciation	250 0 0		By Gross Profit for the year (less general expenses)	3,125 0 0
„ Income Tax	125 0 0		„ Discounts upon purchases	2,325 0 0
„ Directors' Fees	1,000 0 0			
„ Auditors' Fees	105 0 0			
		1,480 0 0		
„ Interest on Debentures, at 4 per cent. (less income tax)..	..	975 0 0		
„ Balance carried down, being net profit for the year	..	2,995 0 0		
		£5,450 0 0		£5,450 0 0
To Interim Dividend, paid on 10th August, 1892, viz.:			By Balance brought forward from last year	555 0 0
Preference Shares, at 8% per annum (less income tax)	390 0 0		„ Net Profit for the current year, as shown above	2,995 0 0
Ordinary Shares, at 10% per annum (less income tax) ..	731 5 0			
		1,121 5 0		
„ Balance, available for dividend	..	2,428 15 0		
		£3,550 0 0		£3,550 0 0
Proposed Apportionment of balance:				
Preference Shares, at 8% per annum (less income tax) £390 0 0				
Ordinary Shares, at 15% per annum (less income tax) 1,096 17 6				
Reserve Fund 750 0 0				
Balance to be carried forward to next year's account 191 17 6				
£2,428 15 0				

SCHEDULE B.

MANUFACTURERS' ACCOUNTS (CLASS I.).

Dr.   TRADING ACCOUNT (FIRST SECTION) FOR THE YEAR ENDED 31ST DECEMBER, 1892.   Cr.

	£ s d	£ s d		£ s d	£ s d
To Stock on hand, 1st January, 1892:			By Sales		12,000 0 0
Materials..	1,000 0 0		„ Stock on hand, 31st December, 1892:		
Goods unfinished ..	250 0 0		Materials	1,500 0 0	
Manufactured Goods ..	1,750 0 0		Goods unfinished ..	2,750 0 0	
		3,000 0 0	Manufactured Goods ..	1,250 0 0	
„ Purchases	8,000 0 0				5,500 0 0
„ Wages	2,000 0 0				
		10,000 0 0			
„ Gross Profit, carried to Profit and Loss Account	..	4,500 0 0			
		£17,500 0 0			£17,500 0 0

Dr.   PROFIT AND LOSS ACCOUNT (Second Section) for the Year ended 31st December, 1892.   Cr.

	£ s d	£ s d		£ s d
To Manufacturing Expenses, viz.:			By Gross Profit for the year, as per	
Rent, Rates, Taxes, etc. ..	100 0 0		Trading Account	4,500 0 0
Salaries	250 0 0			
Depreciation	50 0 0			
General Expenses ..	100 0 0			
		500 0 0		
„ Warehouse Expenses, viz.:				
Rent, Rates, Taxes, etc.	200 0 0			
Salaries	400 0 0			
Depreciation	50 0 0			
General Expenses ..	250 0 0			
		900 0 0		
„ Balance, carried down	..	3,100 0 0		
		£4,500 0 0		£4,500 0 0

(Third Section.)

	£ s d	£ s d		£ s d
To Interest upon Capital	500 0 0		By Balance, brought down	3,100 0 0
„ Discounts upon Sales	300 0 0		„ Discounts upon Purchases ..	200 0 0
„ Income Tax	62 10 0			
		862 10 0		
„ Balance, being net profit for the				
year, viz.:				
A, three-fifths' share.. ..	1,462 10 0			
B, two-fifths' share	975 0 0			
		2,437 10 0		
		£3,300 0 0		£3,300 0 0

SCHEDULE C.

MANUFACTURERS' ACCOUNTS (Class II.).

Showing the same figures as those employed in the first section of the Account stated in SCHEDULE B., re-drafted for the purpose of separating the results of manufacturing from those of trading.

Dr.   MANUFACTURING ACCOUNT (Section 1A) for the Year ended 31st December, 1892.   Cr.

	£ s d	£ s d		£ s d	£ s d
To Stock on hand, 1st January, 1892:			By Amount transferred to Trading		
Materials..	1,000 0 0		Account (being the trade-price		
Goods unfinished	250 0 0		of goods manufactured dur-		
		1,250 0 0	ing the year)		7,700 0 0
„ Purchases	6,000 0 0		„ Stock on hand, 31st December,		
„ Wages	2,000 0 0		1892:		
		8,000 0 0	Materials	1,500 0 0	
„ Gross Profit, carried to Profit			Goods unfinished	2,750 0 0	
and Loss Account	..	2,700 0 0			4,250 0 0
		£11,950 0 0			£11,950 0 0

Dr.   TRADING ACCOUNT (Section 1B) for the Year ended 31st December, 1892.   Cr.

	£ s d		£ s d
To Stock on hand, 1st January, 1892 ..	1,750 0 0	By Sales	12,000 0 0
„ Transfer from Manufacturing		„ Stock on hand, 31st December,	
Account	7,700 0 0	1892	1,250 0 0
„ Purchases of Ready-made Goods ..	2,000 0 0		
„ Gross Profit, carried to Profit			
and Loss Account	1,800 0 0		
	£13,250 0 0		£13,250 0 0

NOTE.—THE PROFIT AND LOSS ACCOUNT (*i.e.*, the second and third sections) will be the same as those shown in SCHEDULE B., except that the Gross Profit credited in the second section will appear in two lines, viz.: Manufacturing £2,700; Trading, £1,800.

SCHEDULE D.

MANUFACTURERS' ACCOUNTS (CLASS III.).

Dr.　　PROFIT AND LOSS ACCOUNT FOR THE YEAR ENDED 31st DECEMBER, 1892.　　**Cr.**

	£ s d	£ s d		£ s d
To Wages	50,000 0 0		By Contracts	200,000 0 0
„ Stores consumed	40,000 0 0			
„ Materials	70,000 0 0			
„ Depreciation of Plant ..	2,500 0 0			
„ Special Expenses on Contracts ..	2,500 0 0	165,000 0 0		
„ General Expenses, viz. :				
Rent, Rates, Taxes, etc. ..	3,000 0 0			
Depreciation of Machinery ..	1,250 0 0			
Repairs to do. ..	500 0 0			
Do. Buildings ..	200 0 0			
Motive power	750 0 0			
Salaries	1,500 0 0			
Incidental Expenses ..	300 0 0	7,500 0 0		
„ Balance carried down ..	..	27,500 0 0		
		£ 200,000 0 0		£ 200,000 0 0
To Interest upon Loans	1,250 0 0		By Balance brought down	27,500 0 0
„ Do. upon Capital ..	1,500 0 0		„ Discounts upon Purchases	2,500 0 0
„ Income Tax	750 0 0	3,500 0 0		
„ Balance, being net profit for the year, viz. :				
A, one-third share	8,833 6 8			
B, five-twelfths share ..	11,041 13 4			
C, one-fourth share	6,625 0 0	26,500 0 0		
		£ 30,000 0 0		£ 30,000 0 0

SCHEDULE DD.

MANUFACTURERS' ACCOUNTS (CLASS III).

Dr.　　SUMMARY OF COST ACCOUNT, for the year ended 31st DECEMBER, 1893.　　**Cr.**

Number of Contract	Forward from last Account	Hours of Time*	Wages Amount	Stores Issued.	Materials Purchased	Plant Issued.	Special Expenses	General Expenses	Discount and Interest	Net Profit on Contract	Total	Number of Contract	Amount of Contract	Stores returned cr or sold	Plant returned or sold	Total Loss on Contract	Total Cost of Contract carried forward (if uncompleted)	Total
	£		£	£	£	£	£	£	£	£	£		£	£	£	£	£	£
1,285	10,000	10	400	500	250	..	10	62	9	650	11,881	1,285	10,000	81	1,800	..	..	11,881
1,286	5,000	50	2,000	1,500	4,750	750	40	312	42	..	14,394	1,286	12,500	194	700	1,000	..	14,394
1,287	..	100	4,100	2,500	7,500	1,250	120	625	83	950	17,128	1,287	16,000	28	1,000	..	..	17,128
etc.	etc.	etc.	etc.	etc.	etc.	etc.	etc.	etc.	etc.	etc.	etc.	etc.	etc.	etc.	etc.	etc.	etc.	etc.
	£20,000	1200	£50,000	£46,000	£72,000	£25,000	£2,500	£7,500	£1,000	£27,500	£251,500	..	£200,000	£6,000	£22,500	£1,000	£22,000	£251,500

Sundry Debtors .. £16,000　　*Omitting "ooo's"　　Sundry Debtors .. £15,000
Stores .. .. 2,000　　　　　　　　　　　　　　　Stores 4,500
Plant .. .. .. 2,000　　　　　　　　　　　　　　Plant.. 2,500
　　　　　£20,000　　　　　　　　　　　　　　　　　　　　£22,000

SCHEDULE E.

PRO FORMA BALANCE SHEET OF A GAS AND WATER COMPANY
(DOUBLE-ACCOUNT SYSTEM.)

Dr.   **C**   CAPITAL ACCOUNT ON 31ST DECEMBER 1892.   *Cr.*

	Expenditure to 31st Dec. 1891.	Expended this year.	Total to 31st Dec. 1892.		Certified Receipts, 31st Dec. 1891.	Received during year.	Total Receipts to 31st Dec. 1892.
	£ s d	£ s d	£ s d		£ s d	£ s d	£ s d
GAS.				By "A" Shares of £10 each	40,000 0 0	—	40,000 0 0
To Expenditure to 31st Dec. 1891:—				„ "B" Shares of £10 each including premiums received on issue of			
„ Lands acquired (including Law charges) ..	432 0 0	25 0 0	457 0 0	same	27,500 0 0	17,500 0 0	45,000 0 0
„ New buildings, manufacturing plant, machines, storage works, & other structures connected with manufacture ..	26,807 0 0	4,395 0 0	31,202 0 0	„ Debenture Stock at 5 per cent.	12,500 0 0	—	12,500 0 0
„ New mains and pipes, including laying of same, paving, & other works connected with distribution	14,161 0 0	859 0 0	15,020 0 0				
„ New meters, including fixing	600 0 0	130 0 0	730 0 0				
„ Cost of promoting special Act	2,000 0 0	591 0 0	2,591 0 0				
Total Gas	£44,000 0 0	£6,000 0 0	£50,000 0 0				
WATER.							
To Expenditure to 31st Dec. 1891:—							
„ Lands acquired (including Law charges) ..	216 0 0	—	216 0 0				
„ New buildings, storage, & filtration works, & other works connected with collection of water	12,886 0 0	4,637 0 0	17,523 0 0				
„ New mains, including laying of same, paving, and other works connected with distribution	19,706 0 0	1,939 0 0	21,645 0 0				
„ Cost of promoting special Act	2,067 0 0	1,739 0 0	3,806 0 0				
Total Water ..	£34,875 0 0	£8,315 0 0	£43,190 0 0				
„ Balance of Capital A/c.	1,125 0 0	3,185 0 0	4,310 0 0				
	£80,000 0 0	£17,500 0 0	£97,500 0 0		£80,000 0 0	£17,500 0 0	£97,500 0 0

I   GENERAL BALANCE SHEET ON 31ST DECEMBER 1892.

	£ s d		£ s d	£ s d
CAPITAL ACCOUNT:—		CASH AT BANKERS		3,239 0 0
Balance to credit thereof (Account C)	4,310 0 0	COALS, for Stock on hand 31st Dec. 1891 ..	365 0 0	
PROFIT AND LOSS ACCOUNT:—		COKE, TAR, etc.	118 0 0	
Balance to credit thereof (Account E)	4,179 0 0	GENERAL STORES..	1,445 0 0	
RESERVED FUND:—				1,928 0 0
Balance to credit thereof (Account F)	2,225 0 0	GAS AND METER RENTAL, balance of this Account due to the Company on 31st		
DEPRECIATION FUND (for Works on Leasehold Lands):—		December 1891	4,281 0 0	
Balance to credit thereof (Account F*)..	775 0 0	GAS FITTINGS, ditto ditto ..	444 0 0	
INTEREST ACCRUED AND UNPAID ON DEBENTURE STOCK to 31st December 1891	312 0 0	COKE AND OTHER RESIDUALS, ditto ..	436 0 0	
SUNDRY TRADESMEN AND OTHERS:—				5,161 0 0
For amount due for Coals, Stores, &c., to 31st December 1891	2,900 0 0	WATER RENTAL, ditto ditto ..	700 0 0	
WAGES AND SUNDRIES	299 0 0	WATER FITTINGS, ditto ditto ..	825 0 0	
				1,525 0 0
		RATES AND TAXES, paid in advance		147 0 0
		INVESTMENTS (specified)		3,000 0 0
	£15,000 0 0			£15,000 0 0

SCHEDULE F.]   *PRO FORMA* BALANCE SHEET OF A MANUFACTURING COMPANY
(SINGLE-ACCOUNT SYSTEM).

BALANCE SHEET, 31st DECEMBER, 1892.

LIABILITIES.	£ s d	£ s d	ASSETS.	£ s d	£ s d
Nominal Capital (10,000 shares of £10 each)	100,000 0 0		Leasehold Buildings at——, (at cost)	10,000 0 0	
			Less, Depreciation	1,248 0 0	
Capital Subscribed (5,000 shares of £10 each, £8 per share called up)	40,000 0 0				8,752 0 0
Less, Calls in arrear	250 0 0		Stock in Trade (at cost), viz.:		
		39,750 0 0	Materials	6,000 0 0	
Debenture Stock (at 4½ per cent.) .	..	25,000 0 0	Goods unfinished	9,000 0 0	
Bills Payable	..	8,000 0 0	Manufactured Goods ..	15,000 0 0	
Sundry Creditors	..	8,750 0 0			30,000 0 0
Interest on Debentures	..	548 8 9	Plant and Machinery:		
Unpaid Dividends	..	12 10 0	Value, 1st January, 1892 ..	20,000 0 0	
Reserve Fund	..	4,000 0 0	Additions during the year ..	1,800 0 0	
Profit and Loss Account (balance available for dividends, etc.) ..	..	5,691 0 0		21,800 0 0	
			Less, Depreciation	2,000 0 0	
					19,800 0 0
			Warehouse and Office Fittings:		
			Value, 1st January, 1892 ..	250 0 0	
			Less Depreciation ..	31 5 0	
					218 15 0
			Bills Receivable	..	7,500 0 0
			Sundry Debtors	..	20,000 0 0
			Investment of Reserve Fund— £3,168 6s. 4d., Great Northern Railway 4 per cent. Debenture Stock, at 131¼ ..	..	4,000 0 0
			Cash:		
			At Bank	1,281 3 9	
			In hand	200 0 0	
					1,481 3 9
		£91,751 18 9			£91,751 18 9

SCHEDULE G.]   *PRO FORMA* BALANCE SHEET OF A TRADING FIRM (*c.f.* SCHEDULE A).

BALANCE SHEET. 31st DECEMBER, 1892.

Liabilities.	£ s d	£ s d	£ s d	£ s d	Assets.	£ s d	£ s d
Capital Account, viz.:					Freehold and Leasehold Premises ..	8,700 0 0	
A., Balance 1 Jan., 1892 ..	25,000 0 0				Less Depreciation	150 0 0	
Interest thereon ..	1,218 15 0						8,550 0 0
	26,218 15 0				Fixtures and Fittings: value 1 Jan. 1892	1,500 0 0	
Share of year's profits .. 1,287 10 0					Additions during the year ..	450 0	
Less Drawings 1,000 0 0						1,950 0 0	
	287 10 0				Less Depreciation	100 0 0	
		26,506 5 0					1,850 0 0
B., Balance 1 Jan., 1892 ..	15,000 0 0				Stock-in-Trade (at cost)	..	60,000 0 0
Interest thereon ..	731 5 0				Cash: At bank	3,975 0 0	
	15,731 5 0				In hand	425 0 0	
Share of year's profits .. 858 6 8							4,400 0 0
Less Drawings 750 0 0							
	108 6 8						
		15,839 6 8					
C., Balance 1 Jan., 1892 ..	10,000 0 0						
Interest thereon ..	487 10 0						
	10,487 10 0						
Share of year's profits .. 429 3 4							
Less Drawings 500 0 0							
	70 16 8						
		10,416 13 4					
			52,762 5 0				
Trade Creditors..			20,000 0 0				
Sundry Creditors			750 0 0				
Customers' Deposit Accounts			1,287 15 0				
			£74,800 0 0				£74,800 0 0

PROFITS AVAILABLE
FOR DIVIDEND

Lawrence R. Dicksee

PROFITS
AVAILABLE FOR DIVIDEND.

BY LAWRENCE R. DICKSEE, F.C.A.

THE subject that has been chosen for my lecture to you to-night may aptly be described as one of the most important that arise in connection with the auditing of companies' accounts; and, indeed, one may go farther than this, for a very little reflection shows that the whole object and end of every audit is to ascertain the company's position, primarily with a view to determining the amount of profit that has been earned, and upon which a dividend may be declared.

In view, then, of the far-reaching importance of my subject, it is hardly to be expected that, in the time now at our disposal, I shall be able to afford you an insight into more than a few of the various considerations that suggest themselves, but in so far as the time serves us I propose to deal shortly, first, with the legal side of the matter, showing the principles upon which this question has already been decided upon various occasions; and, secondly, in dealing with the practical, or accountancy, side.

Before going thoroughly into the legal aspect of the case it will be well for us to pause for a moment to consider the exact nature of dividends themselves.

Any number of persons, consisting of seven or more, are enabled under the Companies Acts to associate together in a corporate form for the purpose of carrying on any legal occupation or trade. Generally, the companies so formed are primarily for the acquisition of gain ; that is to say, the members constituting the company do not engage in these operations from any philanthropic or humanitarian motive, but rather in order that they may thereby amass profits which, from time to time, may be distributed among them in the form of dividend. With the exception, then, of those few companies which are not formed for the acquisition of gain, the earning of profits available for dividend may be said to be the chief reason for the existence of every registered company, and that being so, the importance of the question, " What are profits available for dividend?" must be readily conceded.

In the case of companies limited by guarantee (that is to say, companies without paid-up share capital) this problem is comparatively simple, for after the payment of all liabilities or provision for the payment thereof, any surplus remaining must necessarily be profit, and available for distribution among the members ; but in the case of a company having a paid-up capital the problem is further complicated by the requirement, concerning which I shall have something to say further on, that under ordinary circumstances the capital fund subscribed by the shareholders must be kept intact, and the balance, after providing for the maintenance of such capital, only is available for dividend.

The question as to when it is necessary and when it is not necessary for the capital fund to be kept intact is the principal one upon which legal decisions have as yet been given, and a consideration of the various cases can only suggest to the enquirer that even yet the question is extremely indefinite, while it is not always easy to reconcile the decisions that have already been given.

It is, in the first place, to be remembered that there is nothing in the Companies Acts which expressly prevents any company from paying dividends otherwise than out of profits ; while, on the other hand, Table A, which is not compulsory, provides under Article 73 that " no dividends shall be payable

" except out of the profits arising from the business of the
" company."

The earlier cases exhibit a considerable amount of uncertainty as to whether a dividend paid out of capital was
necessarily illegal, but in later cases it has been clearly
established that the application of a company's capital to the
payment of dividend is *ultra vires* and a breach of trust. This
principle will be found very clearly stated in the course of
Lord Justice Cotton's judgment in *Lee v. Neuchatel Asphalte
Company, Lim.* His Lordship there states that " it is a well-
" established principle of company law that the capital assets
" of a company must not be applied for any purpose not one
" of the objects of the company, and though there is nothing
" in the Companies Acts which says that dividends are not to
" be paid except out of profits—for the article to that effect in
" Table A in the schedule to the Act of 1862 is merely a
" matter of internal regulation—yet it is well-established that
" the paying of a dividend is not one of the objects of a com-
" pany, and therefore that the capital assets of a company
" must not be applied in that way. If the directors were to
" sell what was a permanent property of the company and
" then to declare a dividend, that would come within the
" principle laid down in *Guinness v. Land Corporation of Ireland*
" (L.R. 22, Ch.D. 349) that the capital of a company cannot
" be applied for purposes not authorised. But that is not the
" case here, and we must take a reasonable and sensible view
" of the circumstances of this case."

It may at first sight seem that we have now advanced
very definitely towards a true solution of the matter, but in
truth we are very much where we were at first, for the question
still remains to be solved, " What are dividends paid out of
capital, and what are dividends paid out of profits ?" The
difficulty of forming any general rules upon such decisions as
have already appeared upon the matter is in consequence
of the fact that the solution of this question must necessarily
vary very much with the peculiar circumstances attendant

upon each individual case. This fact is stated in *Buckley* as follows:—"The profits of an undertaking are the excess of " revenue receipts over expenses properly chargeable to " Revenue Account. It is impossible to lay down any " general rule as to what expenses are chargeable to revenue " and what to capital." It is singular how little real information is to be conveyed from such a statement as this, but it is noteworthy that even this meagre definition requires further qualification, for not only is it impossible to lay down any general rules as to what expenses are chargeable to income and what to capital, but a like difficulty will frequently be experienced with regard to the apportionment of receipts.

With regard to the case of *Lee v. Neuchatel Asphalte Company*, upon which so much has been said and written, I think that the difficulty which some seem to have experienced in accepting the views of the judges concerned is chiefly in consequence of their failing to appreciate the very peculiar circumstances relating to the accounts of this particular company. It will be remembered that this was an action brought to restrain the company from declaring a dividend without having set aside any portion of its profits to provide for the loss of capital arising from the effluxion of its concessions. In this particular case the company's articles expressly provided that it should not be necessary for the directors to provide a sinking fund to meet the waste of the assets before declaring a dividend, and further it appeared that as a matter of fact the wasting assets belonging to the company had increased rather than diminished in value; by reason of certain favourable arrangements that had been made with the granters of the concessions. It therefore seems that the bare decision that, under all the circumstances, the company was entitled to pay the dividend in question amounts to little or nothing that can be considered of general application; for it seems that there was, as a matter of fact, no depreciation to be provided for.

I believe this to be a fair, although a short, statement of

the facts relating to this particular case, and under these circumstances I think it must be admitted that there is very little therein which can be said to be of general application ; but the case seems to suggest that directors in the case of such companies as this—the bulk of whose capital is sunk in assets of a wasting nature—will not, in the absence of special articles to the contrary effect, be required to provide for depreciation before computing profits ; while, at least, it seems very clear that so long as the aggregate value of the assets is not diminished the Courts will not require depreciation to be provided—even although it be evident that, as a matter of fact, the property be of a wasting nature.

Although there is undeniably something very unsatisfactory in the uncertainty aroused by this decision, it must not be forgotten that the Courts will not lightly interfere with the deliberate action of a company in the payment of dividends, unless it be in order to protect the rights of creditors, or of different classes of shareholders. These two points being apparently the chief, if not the sole consideration of the Courts, it seems hardly surprising that we should not find its decisions based upon trains of reasoning that are capable of being reduced to general principles of such a nature as would commend themselves to the accountant, but it seems to be fairly clear that there is nothing in the Companies Acts that requires a company constituted for some ephemeral purpose (*e.g.*, the working of a mine, or the running of a single ship, or any other property that must inevitably become valueless at some future time) to accumulate a sinking fund that will enable it to return the shareholders their capital in full when the company's span of life has run its allotted course. If there should be any doubt upon this point it seems to be dispelled by the following extract from the judgment of Lord Justice Lindley in the case we have just been discussing. " If," said his Lordship, " a company be formed to acquire or " work property of a wasting nature—*e.g.*, a mine, quarry, or " patent, the capital expended in acquiring the property may

" be regarded as sunk and gone, and if the company retains
" assets sufficient to pay its debts, any excess of money
" obtained by working the property over the cost of working
" it may be divided among the shareholders ; and this is true,
" although some portion of the property itself is sold, and in
" one sense the capital is thereby diminished. If it is said
" that such a course involves payment of dividends out of
" capital, the answer is that the Acts nowhere prohibit such a
" payment as is here supposed. The proposition that it is
" *ultra vires* to pay dividends out of capital is very apt to
" mislead, and must not be understood in such a way as to
" prohibit honest tradings. It is not true, as an abstract pro-
" position, that no dividends can be properly declared out of
" moneys arising from the sale of property bought by capital.
" But it is true that if the working expenses exceed the
" current gains, profits cannot be divided, and that if in such
" a case capital is divided and paid away as dividend, the
" capital is misapplied, and the directors implicated in the
" misapplication may be compelled to make good the amount
" misapplied. This was the case in *Rance's* case (L.R. 6 Ch.
" App. 104); in the *Oxford Benefit Building Society's* case
" (L.R. 35 Ch.D. 502); in *Leeds, &c., Investment Company v.*
" *Shepherd* (L.R. 36, Ch.D. 787) ; and in *Stringer's* case (L.R.
" 4 Ch. App. 475). In the present case the articles say that
" there need be no sinking fund ; consequently, capital lost
" need not be replaced ; nor, having regard to these articles,
" need any loss of capital by removal of bituminous earth
" appear in the Profit and Loss Account of the working of
" the company's property."

We may, therefore, probably take it as settled law that a
company formed for a purpose which, in the nature of things,
cannot be permanent, may by its articles specially provide
that the excess of current receipts over current expenses
(disregarding depreciation) shall be treated as profit available
for dividend. Ordinary industrial undertakings, however,
could hardly be said to come under the above decisions.

Before turning from the legal to the practical side of our subject, I should like to refer you to another decision, which seems to me of the greatest importance. I refer to the case of *Bolton v. Natal Land and Colonisation Co., Lim.*, in which it was decided that a company dealing in land ought not to take into its Revenue Account either estimated increases or decreases in the value of such land while it still remained unsold, but that its having done so once in years gone by was no cause for prohibiting a dividend now proposed to be declared out of the surplus of current receipts over current expenses. This decision of Mr. Justice Romer's seems at first sight a most strange one, and I am inclined to doubt whether it would be upheld by the Court of Appeal; but it may be mentioned, as being somewhat in mitigation, that in this particular case the increase credited to revenue was not actually distributed among the shareholders, but merely placed there as a set-off against a like amount of bad debts upon the debit side; the object being that in future the company might be able to declare such dividends as should be earned from year to year. Moreover, I believe it was known that even the increased value placed upon the assets did not exceed the actual market value at the time, and indeed some of the more recent reports of this company tend to show that the valuation placed upon its assets was well within the mark. Still, however, the fact seems to remain that the Court has given its countenance to a method of declaring dividends upon the face of a deficiency in capital caused by a loss on Revenue Account by permitting an anticipation of profits to be derived from the sale of articles in which a company deals. With every respect to Mr. Justice Romer's decision, I submit that we, as auditors, should not pass accounts in which the profits to be derived from the carrying on of the company's business are anticipated in the manner described.

The last legal decision that I propose to refer to at the present time is in the case of *Verner v. Commercial and General Trust Lim.*, in which it was decided that a *pure* trust company may, with the consent of its articles of association, distribute as dividends the income received from its investments, notwithstanding the fact that a shrinkage has occurred in the aggregate value of such investments.

Later on I shall have to call your attention to one or two other cases, but we have now dealt with all the principal recent decisions that may be said to be of general application.

Up to the present we have only arrived at one really general conclusion, namely, that ephemeral companies may—if their articles of association so provide—divide an excess of current revenue over current expenditure which, as accountants, we cannot justly hold to be pure profit.

Such cases are, however, the exception rather than the rule; and, in the absence of express authority to the contrary, we must take it that true profits, and true profits alone, are available for dividend. We may, therefore, narrow down our enquiry to a consideration of the nature of true profits.

What is profit of a company?

Some five or six years ago this question was very fully discussed by two of our most eminent Chartered Accountants, and I do not think I should be doing either an injustice were I to suggest that up to the close of the discussion each thought that his view of the matter was opposed to the other's. The first held that true profits could only be arrived at by drawing up a just Balance Sheet, containing on the one hand a full statement of the capital and liabilities, and upon the other a fair valuation of all the assets; the excess of the latter over the former being profits available for dividend. The other view was that the true profits of a company could only be ascertained by drawing up a full Profit and Loss Account, to which should be credited all the income or gross profits fairly earned during the period; while on the debit side was entered every expense or loss incurred that could be fairly attributed to the earning of such income or gross profits. I must confess that, to my mind, a discussion conducted upon such lines as these could not be altogether profitable; for a very little consideration will suffice to show that if the Balance Sheet were indeed a "just" one, and the Profit and Loss Account indeed a "full" one, then by every law of double-entry it must necessarily follow that the result would in each case be the same. It has always seemed to me that each of the disputants held in his hand one-half of the truth. Surely the real object of double entry is that, when we have prepared our Profit and Loss Account upon the lines that commend themselves to us upon the score of fairness and fulness, crediting all sources of profit that appear to be due to the period's transactions, and debiting all expenses and losses incidental thereto, we may review and reconsider the correctness of the resultant profit in the light of a Balance Sheet prepared upon these lines, seeing whether our views of profit and loss have resolved themselves into a just and reasonable statement of the company's liabilities and assets; for it will be then, and then only, that our statement of profits can be justified. The great advantage of double-entry is that it allows us to view this most important question of profits from two points of view, and it is only when our statement of profits available for dividend appears tenable from both standpoints that it can be said to be reasonable and fair.

The most convenient method of considering the question has always appeared to me to be to follow the order I have just indicated—to criticise each item in the Profit and Loss Account first, and then to see whether a Balance Sheet prepared from accounts so stated may fairly be said to fully and fairly disclose the true financial position of the company as at the date named.

Let us proceed to put this plan into practice; and turning from the general to the particular, let us now proceed to consider each of the more unusual items in a Profit and Loss Account in turn.

Dealing first with sources of profit, or income, we may divide the various classes that it is necessary to now consider under the following headings :—

(1) Profit on transactions completed but not yet received
    in cash.

(2) Profit on transactions not completed, whether re-
    ceived in cash or not.

(3) Profits arising from rise in value of fixed or floating
    assets.

(4) Receipts not properly incidental to the business
    carried on.

Now let us consider under what circumstances each of the
above may properly be described as "profits available for
dividend."

(1) *Profit on transactions completed but not yet received in
cash.*—This head will probably include the bulk of the items
composing the revenue credits of any particular company. The
transactions are in the ordinary course of business, and the
sole surviving indication of their incompleteness is the
presence of a debit to the customer, representing the amount
of his indebtedness. It is indisputable that it is not
necessarily imperative that the profit should be held in
suspense until the amount is actually received, but before we
can certify to the correctness of the accounts it is desirable
that we should consider (*a*) whether it may be fairly and
reasonably anticipated that the debt will be discharged in due
course; (*b*) whether any allowance or discount is likely to be
claimed when the debt is discharged; and (*c*) whether it is
not necessary to allow for the loss of interest incidental to the
deferred payment of the debt. These contingencies must all be
fairly and squarely weighed and duly provided for, but I may
mention that it is customary to provide for the usual cash
discount off trade debts, even in the case of debtors who
never avail themselves thereof; while, on the other hand,
except in exceptional cases, it is unusual for commercial
companies to consider the loss of interest incidental to the
deferred payment of an account. Financial companies, whose
profit is, to a great extent, made up of interest, are of course
obliged to consider this question, and consequently you will

find that banks always provide for rebate of interest upon current bills; but in commercial houses the matter is not ordinarily of sufficient magnitude to require consideration. When considering whether profits coming under this heading may fairly be distributed, all that requires to be considered is whether it is reasonably certain that such profits will not have suffered shrinkage in the course of realisation. On the other hand, of course, any expected shrinkage must be provided fo:.

(2) *Profit on transactions not completed, whether received in cash or not.*—The class of transactions coming under this heading is a very numerous one, but I shall fairly cover the ground if I consider three varieties :—

(*a*) Interest on loans or investments still outstanding.

(*b*) Commissions earned, but not yet receivable.

(*c*) Commissions earned and received, but subject to contingencies.

(*a*) *Interest on loans or investments still outstanding.*— There is no doubt whatever that interest received on investments (except in so far as it may have been received in advance) is fairly profit; but when the investment is still outstanding, we have always to face the possibility of an ultimate loss, and this must fairly be considered and provided for. It has been decided (*Verner v. Commercial and General Trust, Lim.*), that a trust company may by its articles provide that the whole of its receipts, less expenses, shall be distributed as dividend, no matter what the market value of its investments, but such a decision as this would hardly apply to any company that carried on a mixed business. A shrinkage in the value of reserve fund investments might properly be held to be a shrinkage in the reserve fund itself, and not a charge against the year's profits, but inasmuch as every true reserve fund is neither more nor less than undivided true profits, there is nothing in this view to contradict the general principle that a shrinkage in the value of temporary investments is a revenue charge. Interest received in advance must, of course, be held in suspense, and only credited when actually earned. The interest earned upon loans repayable by instalments (as in the case of building societies) must also be carefully apportioned, so that each year may be credited with the interest earned upon the balance from time to time outstanding. It is a good rule that no interest should be credited to revenue if the repayments are twelve months or upwards in arrear; but each case must be taken upon its own merits—if the security be ample, the rule may be relaxed, and on the other hand, if the security be speculative, a contingent loss of capital may have to be provided against.

In the midst of so much uncertainty it is worthy of notice that, in the case of building societies, the law knows no distinction between loss of capital and loss on revenue. A trust company may declare dividends, notwithstanding a heavy loss upon its investments; but the directors and auditor of a building society have been held personally liable to refund dividends paid by them under precisely similar circumstances.

(b) *Commissions earned but not yet receivable.*
(c) *Commissions earned and received but subject to contingencies.*

We may consider these two sources of profits together, inasmuch as they are subject to the same conditions, save that in the latter case we have not to allow for the further contingency of possible bad debts. Such commissions as these may be, of course, of many kinds, but it will be sufficient for me to instance two varieties. The first is that of an agent who is entitled to a commission upon either his gross sales or the net profits arising therefrom, but subject to deduction in the event of bad debts arising. In this case, I think it may be taken that the actual commission to date, if ascertainable, may fairly be considered as a net profit; provided such reasonable allowance for bad debts be made as would be prudent were the debts payable to the agent instead of to his principal.

The second case I propose to lay before you is that of an

underwriting company who, having underwritten certain
shares or debentures, and having paid for and received the
same, have earned the commission due upon such underwriting,
but are still holders of the shares or debentures in question.
It will, probably, be within the recollection of my hearers
that an instance of this kind arose incidentally in the libel
case of *Foster v. Newnes*, which was tried in the early part of
the present year. The Court before which this action was
heard could not, of course, pronounce any decision upon this
point that would be regarded as a legal precedent; but the
effect of the verdict given seems to have been that a commission payable to the managing director, upon the assumption
that such commissions upon underwriting were profits
available for dividend, had not actually been earned. Whatever may at first sight appear to be the correct view of the
case, it seems to me that the more one examines the various
circumstances the more convinced one must become that such
commissions as this cannot profitably be regarded as profit at
all, so long as the shares or debentures underwritten remain in
the company's possession.

Whatever may be the actual course of procedure with
regard to such transactions, the actual facts of the case are
that underwriters—where an allotment is made to them at
all—buy the shares allotted at a price less than their face-
value; and, consequently, it cannot be seriously argued that
they have ever cost to the company the amount of such face-
value. If, then, such shares are taken into the Balance Sheet
at par, the effect of such a proceeding is to state them at a
higher price than they have actually cost; and this is, I think,
a course of action that should be most strongly deprecated by
the auditor. *Primâ facie*, and in the absence of definite
evidence to the contrary, it would certainly appear that the
mere fact that such shares are still in the underwriter's
possession is an indication that they are unsaleable, or at
least unsaleable at par; and seeing that they cannot be
regarded as fixed assets, but must rather be looked upon as

stock-in-trade, there can, I think, be no excuse for their being inserted in a Balance Sheet at a higher value than they would fetch in the open market at the date of the accounts.   I am, of course, not unmindful of the fact that, in the case of unquoted securities, the greatest difficulty may be experienced in ascertaining what the actual value of such shares may be, nor do I think it necessarily follows that the auditor should be required to hold himself responsible for the value at which they are stated in the Balance Sheet; but he may, at least, be sure that, if there exists any uncertainty concerning the value of such assets, there is, at least, an equal uncertainty as to whether the commission upon underwriting will ever be realised in cash; and, upon the face of such an uncertainty, I cannot but think it is most imprudent that such commission should be credited to Profit and Loss Account.

(3) *Profits arising from a rise in value of fixed or floating assets.*—It is probably here that we come to the chief difficulty experienced by auditors in dealing with the verification of profits available for dividend, and this on account of the extreme uncertainty of the legal decisions to which I have already alluded.   There can be no question but that it is against the rules of sound finance to take credit for any assumed rise in value of either fixed or floating assets until such rise in value has been converted into cash; but, on the other hand, it seems very doubtful whether an auditor would be able to support this view as against the directors and shareholders of a company.

With regard to the floating assets there is, I think, very little doubt but that the directors would be legally justified in inserting them in a Balance Sheet at their current market value (that is to say, the value at which they could be purchased by the directors at the date of the Balance Sheet), and this, notwithstanding the fact that such value was in excess of the price that had actually been paid for them.   Such a practice is undoubtedly objectionable, but in the case of floating assets it may be advanced in mitigation of such a proceeding that the trade profits, although anticipated, are not in the long run disturbed thereby; but with fixed assets the case is clearly different, for, however real the assumed rise in value might be, it is indisputable that it could not have arisen directly from the carrying on of the business of the company, and so could not properly be credited to profit and loss. I may incidentally mention here that profits attributed to a rise in the value of fixed assets do not appear to be "profits available for dividend" within the meaning of Table A. I think, as a matter of account, that any profits attributed to an assumed rise in the value of fixed assets could only be properly brought into the accounts by being credited either to a reserve fund, or to an Investment or Property Fluctuation Account, and I believe that this is a view which receives the general support of the profession; but, on the other hand, it must be borne in mind that there is nothing illegal in paying dividends out of reserve, and consequently the crediting of such assumed profits to a Reserve or a Suspense Account will in itself do nothing towards preventing their being subsequently distributed as dividend.

Now, there are two instances that I should like to consider in this connection. The first is the case of the business premises of a bank or insurance office, which, under normal circumstances, usually stand in the Balance Sheet at a figure greatly below their actual market value, and which have occasionally been inflated for the purpose of showing a sufficient profit to enable a customary dividend to be paid. Such a procedure as this is certainly not to be recommended, and is not very easily justified; but the fact remains that such a course has been pursued in the case of more than one company of established soundness, and so long as the facts are clearly stated upon the face of the accounts, I do not think that any actual responsibility could be incurred by the auditor in certifying as to their correctness.

The other class of transaction to which I wish to refer is in the case of an assumed rise in value of property, which it

is now sought to take credit for at a figure in excess of its
original cost. Here, I must confess, I think a very different
set of conditions obtains. This is not a case in which the
company merely falls back upon a secret reserve created in
former years by excessive depreciation, but clearly an anticipation of profits which, it may be, can, in the nature of
things, never be actually realised so long as the company
remains in existence ; and I think that in such cases as this
auditors would do well to bear in mind the ruling of Mr.
Justice Romer in the case of *Bolton v. Natal Land and
Colonisation Company, Lim.*, that " it was not correct, in
" estimating the profits of a year, to take into account the
" increase or decrease in the value of the capital assets of the
" company." Personally, I must confess that I am unable to
see how his Lordship justifies his decision in this particular
case by this general ruling stated in the course of his judgment ; but it seems so clear to me that the profits arising from
an increase in the market value of the land upon which a
company's works are built are for all trading purposes absolutely fictitious, that I cannot but think that auditors would
be only wise were they to decline to sanction accounts in
which credit is taken for an assumed rise in the value of fixed
assets—at least, until some more authoritative decision has
been given. On the other hand, for my own part, I do not
anticipate that even our judges would so far depart from the
rules of sound accountancy as to ever pronounce that such
profits as this are profits available for distribution, but should
a Royal Commission be appointed to enquire into such matters,
in accordance with the suggestion made at Liverpool a few
weeks since, it is possible that this, and many other matters
mentioned in this paper which are now unsettled, might
be arranged upon a sound and satisfactory basis.

(4) *Receipts not properly incidental to the business carried
on.*—I have before reminded you that Table A expressly
provides that the only profits available for dividend are those
arising from the carrying on of the company's business, and I

think we must give these words their full effect to the extent
of supposing that any sums received by a company, save in
the regular course of its business, would not be divisible unless
the articles of association provided that they should be so
treated.   Examples of such receipts are the premiums received
upon an issue of shares or debentures, and cash that had been
paid up upon shares forfeited.   It is very generally agreed
that these items ought properly to be credited to the reserve
fund; but, as I have already pointed out, in the absence of
special articles providing to the contrary, it is competent for
the directors to apply the reserve fund for the payment of
dividends, and consequently the only practical advantage
gained from treating these receipts in the manner I have
described is that the attention of shareholders is naturally
more or less called to the circumstances of the case thereby.

Now let us turn to the debit side of our Profit and Loss
Account, and consider what expenses it is necessary to include
before arriving at a figure of net profits available for distribution.   Leaving upon one side the ordinary expenses incidental
to every business or company, we may divide the points that
require special consideration into the following classes :—

    (1) Payments that may properly be spread over a term
         of years.
    (2) Liabilities not disclosed, and contingent liabilities.
    (3) Depreciation.
    (4) Losses arising by fluctuation of floating assets.
    (5) Losses arising by fluctuation of fixed assets.
    (6) Reserves for losses.
    (7) Preliminary expenses.

    (1) *Payments spread over a term of years.*—With regard
to this point it is to be remembered that, in the absence of
adequate evidence to the contrary, any expenditure incurred is
chargeable against the profits earned during that period, and
it is only when we have adequate evidence 'that such expenditure was not incurred for the sole benefit of the period we are
considering, and, moreover, that such expenditure may

reasonably be expected to result in benefits accruing during future years, that we are justified in allowing any portion of it to be held in suspense. Examples of these items are sums expended in opening up a mine, in laying down plant, and (to a certain extent) in renewing and improving existing plant. The actual consideration of what may properly be spread over a term of years, and what ought to be charged in the year during which it is incurred, raises the question of the distinction between capital and revenue expenditure, which I can hardly be expected to go into at the present time ; but I may mention that the practice—which is, unfortunately, very general—of spreading repairs over a term of years is hardly to be justified. Where it is desired to equalise the charge to profit and loss, it is not unusual, and is quite permissible, to debit a fixed sum to profit and loss and pass a corresponding credit to Repairs Account, against which the repairs actually executed are debited, and where this is done and the amount of the annual charges to profit and loss is, upon the average, sufficient, there can, under ordinary circumstances, be no debit balance to be carried forward ; but in the case of an accident or any other unforeseen contingency, there would, I think, be no objection to carrying forward a moderate debit balance upon the Repairs Account as an asset, but I do not think it is justifiable for a company to merely debit the actual repairs incurred during earlier years of its existence, and then as soon as a heavy bill comes in to seek to spread the expenditure over a term of years.

Another point in this connection which requires to be very carefully considered is that of advertising. Up to a certain point it may be said that the expenses of advertising are incurred in advance of any benefits that can be received therefrom, and may consequently properly be carried forward so as to be charged against the future period wherein those benefits are to be experienced, but care must be taken not to allow the Suspense Account to become unwieldy. And I may give it to you as my experience that in many cases where advertising is systematic and a heavy item, the amount carried forward—either as representing advertisements supposed to be in advance of orders that will be received thereon, or as representing plant (probably of a more or less depreciated nature)—is out of all proportion to the actual value that can reasonably be expected to be made good out of future business. My own opinion is that the current profits of any business ought to be sufficient to pay for any advertising expenses incurred during that period that are not of an exceptional nature; and although, as auditors, we cannot always prevent a reasonable amount being carried forward, still I would warn you that the existence of a continually increasing balance to Advertising Suspense Account must be regarded as evidence of financial weakness.

(2) *Liabilities not disclosed, and contingent liabilities.*— With regard to these I need now say but little, for nothing arises in connection with the subject we are now considering that would not arise in the ordinary course of audit. Naturally the auditor must satisfy himself that all liabilities, either directly or indirectly shown by the books, are included, and he must further reasonably satisfy himself that the liabilities so disclosed are actually exhaustive. With regard to contingent liabilities he must enquire into the circumstances, and approve the estimate placed on each by the directors; and if in his opinion this estimate is insufficient, it is clearly his duty to express his conviction upon the face of his report. Still the existence of a contingent liability naturally affects the question of profits available for dividend, but exceptional cases may arise in this connection. Take, for instance, the case of a single ship company. Supposing the accounts showed a balance to the credit of profit and loss of £5,000, and it came to the knowledge of the auditor that an action had been brought against the company claiming £10,000 damages in respect of a collision, I am not satisfied in my own mind that the company could be restrained from dividing its £5,000 profit, no matter how clear the case was against them; but,

at the same time, I feel clear that the auditor would not be
doing his duty if he refrained from calling the attention of the
shareholders to all the circumstances of the case.

(3) *Depreciation.*—So far as anything may be learned
from the legal decisions that have been given, it seems fairly
clear that depreciation need not be provided against the fixed
assets of a company which, in the nature of things, cannot
continue its operations indefinitely; as, for example, a leasehold mine, a single ship, or a land development company.   In
the case, however, of companies which, in the nature of
things, may be assumed to be carrying on their business in
perpetuity, as, for example, an ordinary industrial concern
owning leasehold property, there seems to be no decision
which leads us to suppose that an auditor would be justified
in certifying profits as correct which did not provide an
adequate amount for depreciation; so that when it became
necessary to eventually renew these wasting assets it might
not be found that the company was without the funds
necessary to enable it to do so.

With regard to the distinction that has been drawn
between fixed and floating assets, it must, however, be stated
that some considerable uncertainty exists.   From an accountancy point of view, it may be stated that the floating assets
of a company consists of its cash, its debtors, and the goods
in which it trades; while its fixed assets are those which it
holds in order to enable it to trade, or in order to facilitate its
trading.   Within limits, this distinction will enable us to draw
a line successfully between fixed and floating assets in most
undertakings; but there are certain classes of assets which
appear to be perpetually upon the border land, and concerning
these considerable uncertainty must be felt; while the decision
of Mr. Justice Romer, in the case of *Bolton v. Natal Land and
Colonisation Co., Lim.*, is directly opposed to the distinction
I have just laid down, inasmuch as his Lordship describes the
land held by the defendant company (which was virtually its
stock-in-trade) as being part of the capital assets of the com-

pany. In the face of this uncertainty, therefore, it becomes especially desirable to carefully consider each question of depreciation upon its own merits; for even if we may take it as settled law (which can hardly be the case at present, inasmuch as no decision has yet been delivered by the House of Lords) that the fixed assets of a company need not be subjected to depreciation, yet, in each case, we shall require to carefully consider the question as to what are, and what are not, fixed assets for this purpose.

(4) *Losses arising from the fluctuation of floating assets.*— Keeping to our definition that floating assets consist of a company's cash, debtors, and the property in which it trades, it will be seen that the object of every company is, with all convenient speed, to convert its debtors and stock into cash— the latter at a profit; consequently, in the valuation of these floating assets, it is essential that a figure not exceeding the current market price should be the basis of such valuation; and this, I think, applies not only to the goods—which must be taken at cost, or at the market price, if that market price be less than cost—but also to the debtors, which must be taken at a figure which it is honestly believed they will actually realise without undue delay; and even to the cash itself, which—in so far as it may be represented by foreign currencies—must be converted for Balance Sheet purposes, not at the average rate ruling for the period under review, but at the actual rate upon the date of taking the accounts. In a like manner, all floating assets in foreign countries must be taken first at a fair valuation in the local currency, and subsequently converted into sterling at the market rate of the day.

(5) *Losses by fluctuation of fixed assets.*—Again keeping to our definition of fixed assets as the property owned by a company for the purpose of enabling it to carry on, or of facilitating its carrying on business, it may be taken that so long as this property continues to be useful for this purpose it retains its value as an asset; and although, of course, this

statement may require to be modified by considerations of depreciation, there being in the nature of things no necessity to consider what might or might not be the result of an immediate realisation, we are not called upon to consider, or to carry into effect, temporary fluctuations in the value of such fixed assets. So long as these assets are maintained in such a condition as will enable the company to utilise them to the extent originally contemplated, they remain, so far as the company is concerned, to be of a value equal to their cost price, and consequently we are not called upon to disturb the trade profits by any consideration of fluctuations in their value. On the other hand, it may be noted that this argument as to the manner in which fluctuations downward should be treated is *a fortiori* an argument in favour of a similar treatment in the case of fluctuations upward.

(6) *Reserves for losses.*—If the values of the various assets have already been duly considered upon the lines I have laid down, there is no occasion for any special consideration to be directed to the question of reserves for losses, inasmuch as these reserves must already have been provided so far as they are necessary. It is, however, desirable to call attention here to one point of the very greatest importance, and this is that any reserve which has been created for the purpose of providing against a loss, and not for the purpose of providing against mere contingencies, must not at any subsequent period be applied to the payment of dividends, except in so far as it can clearly be shown that this reserve is more than ample for the purpose for which it was created. In view of the fact that many reserves for depreciation and other like losses are required by articles of association to be styled Reserved Fund, and in view of the further fact that a true reserve fund may at any time be divided as dividend, it is especially important that this point should not be lost sight of.

(7) *Preliminary Expenses.*—Under ordinary circumstances, preliminary expenses may be disposed of under the class of expenses which we considered first, namely, those

which may properly be spread over a term of years, but it is desirable to note further that there is nothing, either in the Companies Acts or in any legal decision that has yet been given, to compel a company ever to make good its preliminary expenses out of revenue before declaring dividends upon its trade profits.

Having now considered the various classes of receipts which cannot properly be credited to Profit and Loss Account, and having further considered the question of those expenses which should properly be debited to that account before we can arrive at profits available for dividend, we may now turn to some more general considerations. Foremost among these is the general rule that a company cannot declare a dividend so long as there remains a debit balance upon its Profit and Loss Account; but should a company which in its earlier years has proved unprofitable subsequently succeed in making a trading profit, it is provided by section 9 of the Companies Act 1867 that " Any company limited by shares may by " special resolution so far modify the conditions contained in " its memorandum of association, if authorised so to do by its " articles as specially framed or as altered by special resolu- " tion, as to reduce its capital; but no such resolution for " reducing the capital of any company shall come into opera- " tion until an order of the Court is registered by the Registrar " of Joint Stock Companies as is hereinafter mentioned." The effect of this provision is that a company having a capital of say £100,000 in fully paid-up shares of £1 each, and a balance to the debit of its Profit and Loss Account of £5,000, may, subject to certain restrictions for the protection of creditors and others, reduce its capital to 100,000 shares of 19s. each, representing a capital of £95,000, which proceeding would enable it to transfer £5,000 from the credit of its Share Capital Account to the credit of its Profit and Loss Account, and so clear up the debit balance standing upon the latter, leaving the company free to distribute any future profits that might be earned among its shareholders. It seems by no means clear that these provisions as to the reduction of a company's capital were not intended to apply to all companies, and consequently there is some difficulty in reconciling them with the legal decisions that have been given with reference to the ability of a company to declare dividends, notwithstanding the fact that its paid-up capital is not represented by available assets ; but this is a discrepancy which it would be waste of time for us to seek to reconcile, and we must accordingly take matters as we find them, and so long as the existing precedents are upheld, regard them as a correct interpretation of the existing law.

Having now as fully as the time at my disposal permitted, considered the various questions that suggest themselves in relation to the subject we have been discussing, I propose in conclusion to briefly draw your attention to two further points.   Firstly, the liability of an auditor who certifies profits as available for distribution, when, as a matter of fact or of law, no such profits are available ; and secondly, the practical position that may sometimes result from an auditor finding himself at disagreement with the directors upon the question of what are true profits.

Firstly, with regard to the liabilities of an auditor for what must in practice come under the head of either negligence or incapacity, the two leading cases bearing upon this are the case of *The Oxford Building Society*, decided by Mr. Justice Kay in 1886, and the case of *The Leeds Estate Building and Investment Society, Lim. v. Shepherd* decided before Mr. Justice Stirling in the following year.   In the *Oxford* case it was decided that the auditor was responsible in damages for dividends improperly paid out of capital, and that his liability was not affected by the acquiescence of shareholders to the payment of such dividends ; while in the *Leeds* case it was further held that the auditor's liability was not affected by the fact that the Balance Sheet which he had certified was in accordance with the books, it being stated that "it was the " duty of an auditor not to confine himself merely to the task of

" ascertaining the arithmetical accuracy of the Balance Sheet,
" but to see that it was a true and accurate representation of the
" company's affairs ; it was no excuse that the auditor had not
" seen the articles of association when he knew of their
" existence." It may be added that in this latter case the
Statute of Limitations was pleaded on behalf of the auditor,
and the plea not being resisted his liability was limited to the
dividends paid within six years from the commencement of
the action.   So far as these decisions go, they establish very
clearly the liability of an auditor for negligence; but they can
hardly be considered as exhaustive, as there was practically
no defence in either case, it being beyond dispute that the
accounts were grossly false.   Whether the Court would arrive
at a like decision in a case that depended upon some question
as to which differences of opinion might reasonably be
entertained is a matter which still remains to be decided, and
in this respect I much regret that the decision of Mr. Justice
Vaughan Williams in the case of *The London and General
Bank, Lim.*, has not yet been made known, as when I
suggested the title of this lecture I had quite hoped that the
result of this case would have been published in time for us to
review the older cases in comparison with this one, which is
at once more recent and immeasurably more important.
Since this lecture was first delivered his Lordship's decision
has—as you are all doubtless aware—been given against the
auditors; but inasmuch as this decision is the subject of an
appeal that is still pending it is obviously undesirable that I
should discuss the matter at the present time.

Another instance of the liability of auditors was afforded
in the criminal proceedings instituted against the directors of
The Portsea Island Building Society.   These proceedings
resulted in the discharge of all the defendants ; but it was, I
think, expressly stated by Mr. Justice Hawkins, that a civil
liability upon the part of the auditor had been established.
Another case of failure to establish a criminal liability against
an auditor occurred in connection with the failure of *The*

Lancaster Building Society, when it was stated that, no matter how scandalous the negligence of an auditor might be, a jury would not be justified in returning a verdict of guilty, unless they were satisfied that there was evidence of not only criminal negligence but also of fraudulent intent. The only recent case of a criminal liability being established in connection with an auditor that I have been able to find reported is in connection with the failure of an Australian bank, and here it was shown that the auditor had not only passed fraudulent transactions, but had himself derived pecuniary benefit from at least some of these transactions. Although, therefore, there is still some room for uncertainty as to the extent of an auditor's civil liabilities, I think the question of his criminal responsibility may be taken to be clearly established. It must be clearly shown that he benefited by the transactions which are concealed from the knowledge of the shareholders; or it must, at least, be shown that he had criminal knowledge of the existence of such transactions, before any liability can be fixed upon him for a criminal offence.

Let us now turn to the other side of the question, and consider, in conclusion, the position of the auditor who disapproves of the statement of profits declared by the directors. His first duty is, of course, to endeavour to induce the directors to see the matter from his point of view, and in order to gain this end he should spare no pains and take no account of the trouble involved, for if it be possible to convert the directors to his own convictions, he may rest assured that by this course he will have saved himself much trouble, which would otherwise be necessarily involved. Should it, however, occur that a hopeless disagreement of opinion remains, the auditor should carefully reconsider his position with a view of making sure that what he is asking the directors to do is a matter within his province, involving questions of right and wrong, and not in any way fringing upon questions of administrative expediency which are rightly in the discretion of the directors. Having reconsidered the question, and being

still of the same opinion, it remains open to the auditor either
to refuse to certify the accounts or to report to the shareholders
in what respects he finds them inaccurate or misleading.
The latter, I think, is clearly the position that he should take
up, and recent legislation has shown that this is the
attitude favoured by Parliament. Whether the duties of the
auditor close here is, however, a matter upon which some
difference of opinion seems to exist. For my own part I think
that the auditor should see that the shareholders become
acquainted with his views, and he may satisfy himself
of this either by ascertaining that his adverse report has
been printed with the published accounts, or that it is
read at the meeting of shareholders. Where the articles
of association require the auditor's report to be printed, he
should not, however, be satisfied if it is merely communicated
to the shareholders at the meeting. It seems impossible,
however, to lay down any general rules upon this point that
are likely to prove of practical value, for, of necessity, much
must depend upon the circumstances of each particular case.
The only point I wish to emphasise in this connection is that
the auditor can hardly be said to have completed what was
required of him if he does not take reasonable steps to ensure
that any adverse criticism that he has to make is communicated to the shareholders in at least as public a manner as
the articles of association required that his certificate of
approval should be communicated.

It has been stated by a County Court Judge that an
auditor has no right to attend a meeting of shareholders, but
this statement seems so contrary to the reasonable requirements of the case that one may perhaps be excused from
accepting it unconditionally. It seems to me that, where
there is any likelihood that shareholders may reasonably
require more information than that afforded them by the
published report and accounts, the auditor ought to make a
point of being present at the meeting in order to answer any
questions that may be put to him; and although, of course,
unless he be a shareholder, he has no right of speech, yet I do

not think it could be contended that the chairman could prevent his speaking if the sense of the meeting were in favour of a further explanation. The extent to which an auditor may consider it desirable or expedient to supplement the information afforded by the directors is, however, a matter requiring grave consideration, and the exercise of no little tact and discretion; but these are qualities which from first to last are required by every auditor in the discharge of his duties, and it may be assumed, I think, that the accountant who is competent to audit the accounts of a company is at least capable of discriminating as to how far it is expedient that the information afforded by such accounts should be supplemented by further information upon the auditor's responsibility.

In the foregoing remarks, I have endeavoured to call your attention to the leading principles upon which a just account of profits must be based, and to the leading decisions that have been given thereon during recent years. I would warn you, however, that the subject is not one that can be definitely measured up either with a foot-rule or any other rule, but is one that exercises the very highest capacities of the auditor, as one versed in every ramification of accountancy, as one possessing some knowledge of the legal decisions bearing upon the matter, and—perhaps most of all—as a man of the world. We should be failing in our duty to the public were we to cry "Peace" when there is no peace; but we should be equally failing in our duty if by any indiscretion of ours, a company that had met with temporary reverses were brought to the ground. Somewhere between the rocks and the shallows shall we find the deep water through which we may pass not merely in safety but also with credit; and we have the authority of our esteemed President for asserting that as long as we "feel reasonably satisfied" that the Balance Sheet we have signed "conveys to its shareholders a true and accurate statement of the position of the company," we cannot have gone far astray in our attempt to solve the question of what are "profits available for dividend."

THE NATURE AND LIMITATIONS
OF ACCOUNTS

Lawrence R. Dicksee

The Birmingham Chartered Accountant Students' Society.

The Nature and Limitations of Accounts.

By Lawrence R. Dicksee, F.C.A.

A paper read at a meeting of the above Society, held on February 16th 1903, Mr. J. H. Heaton, F.C.A., presiding.

When I received the appointment of Professor in Accounting at your University in July last, one of the earliest, and one of the most pleasing, communications that I received was that from your Honorary Secretary, asking me to deliver a lecture at a meeting of your Society. In view of the considerable amount of work which this appointment, and a similar one in London, involved, I unfortunately found myself unable to accede to this request at once, but, having now got matters a little more into shape, I have lost no time in giving myself the pleasure of meeting you here to-night.

The difficulty which I experienced at the outset was to choose a subject which, without having already been worn threadbare by previous lecturers, would be one that might prove equally interesting—and, I hope, equally profitable—to both junior and senior members—those of you who have yet to go up for your Intermediate and Final Examinations, and also those who are, happily, beyond the reach of these formidable ordeals. In choosing as my subject "The Nature and Limitations of Accounts," I hope that I have succeeded in making such a selection. A great deal has already been written and said upon it in general terms, but little, so far as I am aware, from the precise point of view which I wish to present to you to-night; while it must, I think, be generally admitted that the matter is at least one of very considerable importance.

The work of an accountant in general practice is of a very various nature, but unquestionably the backbone of our calling consists in the verification of statements which accounting parties are called upon from time to time to submit to those to whom they are accountable. These accounts somewhat vary in form, according to the nature of the undertaking, and the transactions which it conducts; but their object is in every case to show in as concise a form as possible the general effect of those transactions, and the general position of the undertaking up to that point. It is a very common thing to find these accounts spoken of as "final accounts," and the term is perhaps not ill-chosen in contrast to the accounts recording transactions from day to day, as ordinarily made in the books of a going concern; but the special point which I invite you to consider with me this evening is as to how far these accounts *can* under normal circumstances be regarded as "final," and as to how far they must be regarded as of a tentative character.

This point does not appear to have been fully appreciated by the older generation of practitioners, who were in the habit of certifying all accounts as "Audited and found correct." I propose to show you to-night that this form of expression is often inapplicable, and why that is the case.

One of the chief objects of every system of accounts is to so record the various transactions that at any desired date the position of affairs can be ascertained by collecting into one general account those Ledger balances which represent losses or expenses and profits, and into another general account those Ledger balances which represent outstanding assets and liabilities, the former being usually called the Revenue (or Profit and Loss) Account, and the latter the Balance Sheet. A good and practical system of accounts will be one that enables these periodical accounts to be compiled when required with a minimum amount of labour, or disturbance of the general trend of the business transactions; and from a theoretical point of view, with a properly organised system of accounts, it is a perfectly simple matter to prepare both Profit and Loss Account and Balance Sheet, because when one is dealing with *pro formâ* transactions the exact nature of the facts which it is intended to record can be readily assumed. In practice, however, these facts are to a large extent *not* capable of being actually ascertained, but have to be estimated, and the head of one of the largest firms of Chartered Accountants (Mr. Frederick Whinney, F.C.A.) has stated it as a matter of experience that he has never yet signed the Balance Sheet of a commercial undertaking without its subsequently transpiring that *some* items included therein have proved to be incorrect. This statement may appear to you to be

a little startling, but it is no doubt literally true; and because there is a great deal of misapprehension as to the exact nature of a Balance Sheet and its necessary limitations, it is, I think, desirable that I should invite you to consider dispassionately to-night the actual position of affairs.

If a particular venture has been undertaken and carried to a conclusion before the accounts in relation thereto are balanced, and the ultimate result then reduced to a cash basis, the most concise means of showing the transactions involved is, of course, a simple summarised Account of Receipts and Payments, and such a statement will be a statement of *fact*, showing what sums have actually been received, what sums have been actually paid in respect of the venture, and what (if any) balance remains in the hands of the accounting party in cash. Such a statement is, of course, capable of absolute verification, and, however complicated its details may be, no insuperable difficulty need arise in compiling an account which will consist exclusively of items in respect of which there is no room for either estimate or conjecture.

In the case of most commercial concerns, however, the position of affairs is by no means so simple. One of the chief objects of keeping accounts at all is to be able to ascertain the financial position of affairs from time to time. It is manifestly inconvenient for a trader to wait until he has altogether retired from business, realised his assets, and paid off his liabilities, before attempting to form any idea of how he stands, and those who carry on their business upon such lines end, as experience shows, not infrequently in finding that their liabilities considerably exceed their assets. Consequently it is imperative that an attempt should be made at comparatively frequent intervals—and in any event not less often than once a year—to arrive as nearly as may be at the financial position; and for this purpose the books are regularly balanced, and the usual so-called "final" accounts (that is, the Balance Sheet and Profit and Loss Account) are compiled. In the nature of things, however, these so-called "final" accounts are not final, but are merely *interim* accounts, it being quite impossible to prepare really final accounts until the business venture is at an end. It is a fact that cannot be too carefully borne in mind that, so long as the business is being continued, most of the Ledger balances which go to make up the Balance Sheet are records of *pending matters*, and as such of necessity by no means final.

In order to make this clear I may draw your attention to the fact that whereas the accounts relating to a completed matter (as, for instance, a consignment or joint-venture of any kind) can, when the goods have been sold and paid for, be conveniently reduced to a single summarised cash statement, the accounts relating to a pending matter (such as those of any commercial business that is being still carried on) cannot be completely disclosed by any Cash Account, no matter how ingeniously devised. A Cash Account, like every other form of account, has its limitations, and although it is still the only account that is ordinarily asked for by the Court of Chancery (which is still worked upon the same lines that obtained in mediæval times), it has long ago been realised by commercial men that something further is required from accounting parties in order to set forth the position of affairs in relation to matters still pending. The generally accepted idea among business men is that the position of affairs in connection with a going concern can be best shown by means of a Balance Sheet, which is more or less a statement of the assets and liabilities of the undertaking as at the date thereof, and by a Revenue (or Profit and Loss) Account, showing its earnings and expenses since the date when the last periodical account was taken.

With regard to the Balance Sheet, this is a summarised statement of Ledger balances at any particular date that represent assets or liabilities. A little reflection must, I think, convince you that, if only for the reason that these Ledger balances relate to the uncompleted transactions of a going concern, they are—or at least the majority of them are—in the nature of things incapable of absolute verification. This idea is so little understood that it will not be lost time if I explain it to you in somewhat further detail, and, to enable this to be done upon a convenient basis, I will draw your attention to the items that would appear upon the Balance Sheet of most ordinary commercial undertakings:—

BALANCE SHEET,	19
Capital and Liabilities.	Property and Assets.
1 .Nominal Capital	1 Freeholds
2 Issued Capital	2 Leaseholds
Called up	3 Goodwill
Less Calls in arrear	4 Plant and Machinery
Paid up	5 Stock
Add Paid in advance	6 Bills Receivable
3 Mortgages	7 Trade Debtors
4 Debentures	8 Other Debtors
5 Bills Payable	9 Investments
6 Trade Creditors	10 Cash
7 Other Creditors	
8 Unclaimed Dividends	
9 Reserve Fund	
10 Profit and Loss Account	
11 Disputed Claims	
12 Contingent Liabilities	

These are the headings under which the Balance Sheet of a limited company carrying on an ordinary commercial business would usually appear.

Taking these item by item: In the case of a company the amount of subscribed Capital (less Calls in arrear and including money received in anticipation of Calls) can, of course, be absolutely verified, as these figures merely represent totals of cash received; and this remark applies also to Calls in Arrear, which represent Capital called up but not received, so that the net figure of Capital paid up is an actual fact. It may, of course, be doubtful whether these arrears will ever be actually received in cash, but as they are not treated in the Balance Sheet as an asset this is of comparatively little importance for our present purpose. Passing on to the next six items (the liabilities due by the undertaking), a moment's reflection will show you not merely that some of the liabilities actually due may have been omitted from the books, and therefore not included under this heading in the Balance Sheet; while, on the other hand, the transactions of the undertaking may be so complicated as to make it absolutely impossible for *anyone* to say for certain what its total liabilities are at the date of the Balance Sheet. Such a position of affairs frequently arises where there are disputes, or where the undertaking is liable contingently, as, for example, in the event of a third party failing to meet a liability. In all these cases it is not humanly possible to do more than, after diligent inquiry, make the best possible estimate of the sum that the undertaking will eventually be called upon to pay.

Passing now on to the assets' side of the account, you will observe that the items Freeholds, Leaseholds, Plant and Machinery, and Stock relate to visible property owned by the undertaking. Under ordinary circumstances no difficulty will arise upon the question of ownership, although even here in some instances there may be doubts existing and actions at law pending. The chief difficulty, however, in determining the actual position of the undertaking will consist in placing a proper money value against each of the various items. Questions of depreciation and the like will, of course, have to engage the most careful attention; but so as not to break the thread of my present argument, I will at the moment content myself with saying that *whatever* figures may be placed against each one of these items, they cannot in the nature of things be really seriously expected to represent its actual value *so definitely as to preclude all likelihood of any loss or profit being realised should these assets be sold.* In so far, therefore, as the figures of value attached to these items may influence the final result shown by the accounts, it must be clear that this result is necessarily very largely a matter of opinion rather than a question of absolute fact.

Now, if these remarks apply to the visible property of an undertaking, they apply with greatly increased force to the invisible property represented by Goodwill and by debts due to the business, and such rights and interests as it may possess. The value of Goodwill is always a matter of opinion, rather than a question of fact, and it naturally fluctuates continuously. It is impossible to determine its value at any interim period.

In placing a value upon Bills Receivable and Trade and other Debtors, one has to consider, not merely the amount that is legally due to the undertaking (which will not always be capable of exact statement, as the amount due may be contingent upon events that have not yet happened—as, for example, when one is dealing with sums due under uncompleted contracts), but one has further to consider, in arriving at a figure of money actually receivable, whether it will ever be received— and, if so, when. That losses frequently occur in business through Bad Debts is a mere common-place; but provision therefor, no matter how carefully considered, can never be anything better than an estimate. While, again, if payment is likely to be delayed any appreciable period of time, questions of interest or discount arise, and it cannot be truthfully said that the "present value" of a debt receivable at a future date is equal to its face value; while it must be equally obvious that, if the date when the amount will be received is a matter of conjecture, the discount that must be deducted in order to arrive at the present value of the debt is also a mere matter of estimate rather than a question of fact.

Passing on to the item "Investments," one is again faced with a serious difficulty in arriving at a correct basis of values. Market prices are, of course, to some extent an index of value, but in many cases official quotations are purely nominal—that is to say, if any considerable quantity of that particular class of stock or shares were to be placed upon the market for sale, or if an order were received for the purchase of any considerable quantity, the market price would be at once affected. And if these difficulties arise in connection with the valuation of those investments that can be regularly dealt with on the Stock Exchange, how much greater are the difficulties in connection with the valuation of those investments that are *not* quoted, or in which there is no free market! At the best, it is only possible to arrive at a close, approximate valuation; and, at the worst, any figure of value attached to such an asset may be a mere matter of conjecture or guesswork.

Indeed the only item upon this side of the Balance Sheet that is really capable of absolute verification is the Cash in Hand, which may, of course, be tested by actual enumeration, and which is of a definite unalterable value, inasmuch as every other asset has to be reduced to this particular unit of money. For practical purposes it is possible to verify the bank balance with equal accuracy; but this, of course, is subject to the solvency of the bank with which the money is lodged, a bank balance being really nothing more nor less than a book debt.

Turning now, again, to the liabilities' side of our Balance Sheet, the next item that we have to deal with is the Reserve Fund. This raises a number of very important questions. For our present purposes, however, it will suffice to remember that a Reserve Fund is an accumulation of net profits made in past periods, which might have been distributed in the form of dividend, but which it has been thought expedient to retain in hand. The accuracy of this item depends, therefore, upon the accuracy of all the previous accounts upon which statements of profits have been based, and also upon the fact that the profits which have been put upon one side must still be intact if the balance of this account is to represent an actual fact.

The last item upon the liabilities' side of the Balance Sheet is the Profit and Loss Account, and inasmuch as this item is merely the difference between the valuation of the assets upon the one hand, and the valuation of the liabilities (including paid up Capital and Reserve Fund) on the other, it is obvious that its accuracy must depend absolutely upon the accuracy with which each single one of the other items has been stated.

As to contingent liabilities, I need not now say more than that, if any contingent liability which has been omitted from the effective money columns of the Balance Sheet afterwards matures, the accuracy of that Balance Sheet is of necessity at once impugned.

If I were to take you in detail through the various items that go to make up the Trading and Profit and Loss Accounts of an ordinary commercial business, you would find that there, as in the Balance Sheet, only a very limited number of the items are capable of being stated as matters of actual fact so long as the business remains a going concern. The division into years (or half-years) is an entirely arbitrary one, the balancing dates selected being sometimes dependent upon the date when the undertaking commenced business, and at other times being arranged at a date when, for one reason or another, it is more convenient to take stock. But by whatever means the date of balancing may have been arrived at, it must be obvious that the business does not *stand still* even for a moment of time; and that, so long as the concern continues to carry on business, it is absolutely impossible to draw a line at any particular date without its intersecting or "cutting into" a large number of transactions which at that moment remain uncompleted. The precise effect and money value of all these uncompleted transactions can only be estimated, and consequently a large number of the transactions that go to make up the Trading and Profit and Loss Accounts must also be, in a greater or less degree, dependent upon the estimates. In some businesses—as, for example, that of a retail trader—the pending transactions will probably be relatively unimportant in amount, although doubtless extremely numerous. In other cases—as, for example, with a large firm of contractors—the number of pending transactions may be comparatively small, but their individual importance may be relatively enormous, and the manner in which they are treated very materially affect the financial result. For example, it is quite conceivable that a large contractor may not have more than a dozen or so contracts in the course of a year, and at balancing time perhaps as many as two-thirds of these may be in various stages of incompleteness. Until each contract is actually completed, and the contract price received, it is impossible to absolutely determine the profit or loss that may have been realised upon the job; but in the meanwhile large sums will have been spent upon materials and wages, which *primâ facie* must be charged up against profits, and in order, therefore, to avoid the profits for the period being under-estimated it becomes essential that some amount should be credited to Profit and Loss Account as representing the estimated value of that portion of the work which has been done. In the nature of things, estimates of this description can never be more than approximately correct, and, indeed, no serious attempt can be made to actually determine the profits earned in each separate period. All that can be done is to take reasonable precautions against *over*-estimating these profits, and the result is that under a prudent system of accounting the annual (or half-yearly) profits of a business of this description would invariably be deliberately under-estimated.

So far we have neglected to take cognisance of a very important factor, which must at all times distinguish practical from theoretical bookkeeping. The theory of double-entry is that the Profit and Loss Account shows the financial result of the period, and that this result is also independently shown by a Balance Sheet, which is a statement of assets upon the one side and capital and liabilities upon the other, the difference between the two being also the profit, and agreeing with the figure arrived at by means of the Profit and Loss Account. In practice, however, a very important consideration arises—namely, that profits or losses may accrue to a business from causes other than those properly incidental to the carrying on of that business. In the case of an ordinary joint-stock company, profits of this description would not ordinarily be legally divisible among the shareholders, while losses arising from such causes need not necessarily be made good before the business profits are divided. It is, however, imperative that the accounts of a company should be so framed as to distinguish between profits that are divisible and profits that are not. It is of almost equal importance that the accounts of a private firm or trader should also observe this distinction, as every business man naturally requires his accounts to show the result of carrying on the business, quite irrespective of the manner in which it may have been affected by outside causes. The point to which I wish to draw your attention is the effect upon the accounts of realising the distinction that exists between these two different classes of profits and losses—namely, those which appertain to the carrying on of the business, and those which do not.

As it is necessary that the accounts should show the result of carrying on the business, it is equally necessary that only those items which are really profits arising therefrom, or expenses incurred in the earning of these profits, should come into the Profit and Loss Account; as, if any other items be also included, the results of the trading are naturally obscured. On the other hand, if all extraneous items are excluded from the Profit and Loss Account, it is clear that they must also be excluded from the Balance Sheet, or (failing that) they must be compensated for in the Balance Sheet by raising a special "Suspense Account," so that the totals of both sides of the Balance Sheet may still agree, for of course the balance of the Profit and Loss Account shown in the Balance Sheet must at all times agree with the result shown by the Profit and Loss Account itself.

As an example of what I mean I may say that if a company, for the purposes of its business, owns certain freehold land, any increase that there might be in the value of that land would not be a profit arising out of the business carried on, and ought not, therefore, to be credited to Profit and Loss Account. If this increase be ignored altogether, of course no entry need occur in the accounts at all; but in that case, the figure at which the freehold land is stated in the Balance Sheet will be less than its true value. In practice this is the plan generally adopted, the result being that there is not necessarily any connection between the value placed upon such assets in the Balance Sheet and their intrinsic value at that date.

Sometimes, however, it is thought desirable to state the assets upon the face of the Balance Sheet at their true value, as nearly as that can be ascertained. In that event it becomes necessary to open an account, which must be credited with the increase that is debited to the Real Account, and this new account (which is in the nature of a Suspense Account) must appear upon the liabilities' side of the Balance Sheet. The only example of this treatment that is at all general is in connection with investments. It is sometimes thought desirable to show investments approximately at their market value; but if an appreciation of investments is not "profit" that is legally divisible, it becomes necessary to open an "Investment Fluctuation Account," and to credit to that account whatever may have been debited to the Investment Accounts in order to write them up to their present value.

Dr.	INVESTMENT ACCOUNT.		Cr.
To Balance (cost of Investments)...	£10,000	By Balance down...	£11,500
„ Investment Fluctuation Account (appreciation of investments) ..	1,500		
	£11,500		£11,500
To Balance down (value at this date)	£11,500		

Dr.	INVESTMENT FLUCTUATION ACCOUNT.		Cr.
		By Investment Account (increase to date) ..	£1,500

BALANCE SHEET.			
Investment Fluctuation Account ..	£1,500	Investments (at value) ..	£11,500

Per contra losses may occur, which it is unnecessary should be made good before dividing current profits in the form of dividend. Sometimes there may be no objection to assets standing in the books at a nominal figure which is admittedly in excess of their true value at that particular date; but in other cases this plan may be objectionable, as not showing the true position of the undertaking. In such a case the Asset Account must be written down, or written off altogether; and, as the loss is not to be charged against trading profits, it cannot be debited to Profit and Loss Account, but must remain on the Ledger as a debit balance, and therefore appear somehow upon the assets' side of the Balance Sheet.

You will thus see that, apart from the practical impossibility of constructing a Balance Sheet in connection with a going concern that will state with absolute accuracy the exact amount of its assets and liabilities, it is frequently necessary to include in Balance Sheets, upon the assets' side, items that possess no intrinsic value, or upon the liabilities' side items that do not in any real sense represent liabilities. But just because a Balance Sheet is not a statement of facts, but rather an expression of opinions, is it important that every possible effort should be made to secure its being a really reliable statement—and not merely a loose estimate—of the true position of affairs. The ultimate responsibility rests, of course, with the directors, whose duty it is to cause true and proper accounts to be kept; but none the less is it our duty, as auditors, to in all cases do our best to secure the publication not merely of honest, but also of fair and full, accounts. And it is just because there must always be many points arising that are matters of opinion, rather than of fact, that there is scope for the expression of the expert opinion of a Chartered Accountant as auditor.

THE IMPORTANCE OF ACCURATE AND ADEQUATE ACCOUNTING

Lawrence R. Dicksee

The Northern Chartered Accountants Students' Society.

The Importance of Accurate and Adequate Accounting.

By Lawrence R. Dicksee, M.Com., F.C.A.
(*Professor of Accounting at the University of Birmingham.*)

A lecture delivered at a meeting of the above Society on
Wednesday, 11th January 1905, Mr. Thos. Bowden, F.C.A.
(the President of the Society), in the chair.

When I intimated to your Secretary my selection of
" The Importance of Accurate Accounting " as the subject
of my address to you this evening, I explained that I did
so because, in the event of my finding it impossible to
devote the time necessary to a regular lecture, I thought
the subject was one which might afford scope for me to
make a few useful and instructive remarks to you
extempore. This choice has proved fortunate, in
the sense that the pressure of other engagements
has made it impossible for me to give such time
and consideration to the preparation of my paper
to you this evening as I should have liked; but,
on the other hand, it is perhaps a little unfortunate,
in that I *have* been able to find time to devote some
little attention to the preparation of my remarks, and the
subject is one that appears to hardly lend itself to half

measures. Had I been compelled to speak to you
entirely without preparation, you would, no doubt, have
received my remarks—whatever they might have been—
in an indulgent spirit; but the subject is one which, as
I have said, does not lend itself to half measures, and
I am fully conscious that, in the time that has been at my
disposal, I have not been able to deal with it to advantage.

The importance of accurate accounting is, of course, the
foundation upon which our profession has been raised—
its very *raison d'être*, in fact—and from one point of view,
therefore, it would appear to be entirely unnecessary to
attempt in any way to demonstrate what you are doubtless already disposed to accept as an axiom. But, just
because the point is one that we are so apt to take for
granted, it occurs to me that possibly we may be a little

too inclined to take for granted all that it implies, and to give others—perhaps less well-informed than ourselves, or at all events others who have devoted less time to the special consideration of the subject of accounts—credit for fully appreciating the significance of this important and fundamental proposition. Paradoxical as it may seem, I cannot help thinking that most business men—and, indeed, many accountant students, and perhaps even some practitioners—are so inclined to take this proposition for granted as to run seriously into danger of neglecting it altogether; and this affords my chief justification for drawing your attention this evening to what might—superficially viewed—seem to be so elementary and so obvious a matter.

The science of accounting, in all its numerous ramifications, arises primarily out of the need that accounting parties should from time to time render to those to whom they are responsible an account of their stewardship—that, at least, we may take to have been the original idea in the early days when capitalists were either quite illiterate, or at all events indisposed to concern themselves with so plebeian an occupation as commerce of any description. (And it is significant in this connection that single-entry bookkeeping, which still survives, and is probably—even in this 20th century—more usual than double-entry bookkeeping, goes but little further than enabling a business undertaking to render accounts to those with whom it may have business relations from time to time, or to check accounts received from them in the ordinary course of business. Of late years, however, we have to a large extent reverted to the position that obtained in mediæval times.) The extension of the limited-liability system has so operated that those actually responsible for the keeping of accounts are as much—and as literally—accounting parties as were the stewards of the landowners in classic and mediæval days; and although there still remain a minority of cases in which the person keeping the accounts is not primarily accountable to anyone save himself, it would be well that we should not lose sight of the fact that the foundation of all accounts is a statement rendered by an accounting party to his principal.

Accounts may be roughly divided into three headings, which are known to lawyers as the " Account Current," the " Account Stated," and the " Account Settled." The Account Current is an open account, when the balance is not struck, or is not accepted by all the parties; the Account Stated has been expressly or impliedly acknowledged to be correct by all the parties; while the Account Settled has been agreed and discharged. The Account Current thus usually relates to transactions which are still in progress, or at all events have not been so agreed between the parties as to preclude the idea of

subsequent amendment if necessary ; and from this standpoint it will hardly fail to escape you that most of the forms of accounts with which we (as accountants) are primarily concerned come under this heading—a proposition which involves upon us the admission that these accounts are not final, and are subject to approval. As accountants, we are called upon, in the exercise of our profession, to examine these accounts in the interest of those for whose benefit or information they have been compiled, and to express an opinion as to whether or not, in view of all the ascertainable facts, they are entitled to acceptance. I put the proposition in this way because you will observe that the necessities of the case are such that, at all events in a great number of cases, anything in the nature of an absolute certification is in the very nature of things out of the question. An accountant's " certificate," in so far as it relates to pending matters, can, it seems to me, never be more than the deliberate expression of an expert's opinion as to the reasonable accuracy, or otherwise, of the account rendered by the accounting party.

There are, I think, few more general misconceptions than the idea—so very prevalent, not merely among laymen, but also among those who one might reasonably expect to be better informed—that an account is in all essentials a matter of figures. This, it seems to me, is a complete misunderstanding of the whole basis of the matter. Accounting is not a matter of arithmetic, or of mathematics of any kind. If it were, its results—whatever they might be—would be absolute ; whereas, in connection with all those classes of accounts which come under the heading of the Account Current nothing better than a tentative result can in the nature of things be expected. Speaking generally, an account is not merely—or even substantially—a collection of figures or calculations, but a narrative of the doings of the accounting party ; and, as such, the precise form of wording employed to explain each separate figure in that account is of at least as much importance as the actual figures themselves. The art of accounting, if not actually older than the art of enumeration itself, is at least far older than—and was in general use long before—the art of calculating with the Arabian system of numerals. It was also (we may be sure) in existence long before any such fixed medium of exchange as money was in general use. The employment of money has, of course, greatly simplified the art of accounting ; and, indeed, but for money, the complex transactions that are ordinarily engaged in in modern times would be quite incapable of any clear exposition in the nature of an account. But the fact remains that the method with which we are so familiar (and therefore so apt to take for granted as the essential basis of the whole matter) of reducing every transaction to a money equivalent, is not the *essence* of the account, but merely one of its numerous mechanisms. Theoretically at least it would be possible to explain the most complicated series of business transactions without placing paramount importance upon their value in actual money, and in days when commerce consisted merely of a system of barter or exchange that form of accounting would be the one naturally employed. At the present time, if by any chance a transaction in the nature of barter or exchange takes place, it is (quite conventionally) recorded in accounts as though each of the items of which it is composed represented an actual purchase or sale, as the case may be. Such a mode of record is, of course, entirely artificial; but the employment of a definite standard of value, such as that represented by money, is so extremely convenient that in spite of its essential unreality it has come to be not merely the usual, but even the only method of record now recognised. You will hardly fail to notice, however, that, granted the somewhat obvious conveniences of recording *all* transactions according to their known (or estimated) money value, the accuracy of the record so compiled depends absolutely upon the money value attached to each separate individual transaction of which that record consists; and, to enable the accuracy of these estimates to be judged, a reasonable amount of explanation (or narration) must of necessity be appended to each separate item.

I am inclined to think that we, as accountants, are, on the whole, inclined to take a little too much for granted in this direction. A well-known solicitor put it to me, I remember, some little time since in the form that " accountants are apt to overlook the importance of the middle column "—meaning the space for narration between the Date column on the left and the Money column on the right-hand side. Solicitors (whose only method of charging for accounts is at the rate of so much per folio) have, of course, no temptation to confine their narration within even reasonably concise limits; but this idea is, I think, well worth bearing in mind, as reminding us that an account—whatever its precise nature—is *not* merely a collection of figures and calculations, but essentially a narration, or history, of events, the ascertained (or estimated) money value of which is by no means the only essential point. In the absence of an adequate amount of " narration " it would be absolutely impossible for anyone—no matter how skilled in figures— to form any useful opinion as to their absolute, or even approximate, accuracy; and it is doubtless to this fact that we owe the somewhat cynical proverb that " Nothing is so misleading as facts, except figures." Figures unsupported by explanatory narrative must be either accepted on trust or rejected incredulously; and

therefore, in the absence of such explanatory narrative as may be reasonably necessary to enable us to apply an intelligent criticism, they must, it seems to me, be regarded as entirely useless. Yet, in spite of these points (which are hardly likely to be seriously contested), the fact remains that even at the present time much accounting is conducted in this altogether inadequate manner. How often does one find in Ledgers an entry supported by no more explanatory narrative than the mystic words " To Sundries," or " By Sundries "—words which mean absolutely nothing in themselves, and are therefore so much misplaced energy? In Journals, again, where the old-fashioned form of Journal still obtains, the practice of supplying an ample narration to each entry, fully explaining its justification, seems to be dying out, with the result that one finds in Journals entries the meaning of which we can guess at truly, but the justification for which we must guess at also, in that none whatever is actually put forward. Regarded as an account—that is to say, as such a narrative of transactions as is due from an accounting party to his principal—these methods are, it seems to me, altogether inadequate. The Journal is one of those books which affords us a fatal facility for making any desired entry, which reminds one of the definition of an accountant as " One who is competent to deal with accounts in any desired way." An ability to juggle with figures, or to juggle with entries in books, cannot be dignified by the name of accounting; and if we really get to the bottom of the whole matter, and duly appreciate the underlying object of all accounts, there is, I think, but little danger of any further misunderstanding in connection with the crying need for ample narration.

As accountants—or at all events as auditors—the particular forms of account with which we are especially concerned are the Balance Sheet, and those variously named summaries of nominal accounts which may, perhaps, be most concisely spoken of as the Revenue Account—that is to say, the accounts which, collecting together the various sources of income, expenditure, and loss, show as a result the true net profit for the period under review. Both of these accounts belong to the category of " Account Current "—that is to say, they are accounts rendered for the approval of the parties interested, and do not deal exclusively with ascertained and agreed facts. I have no intention of taking you this evening in detail through the various representative items that constitute either the Revenue Account or the Balance Sheet; but you will, I think, see my point clearly when I mention to you that neither a Revenue Account nor a Balance Sheet can be criticised in any independent way as a mere collection of figures. The narrative, or explanation, appended to the various items is indeed the very essence of the whole matter. It is to the narrative of the Revenue Account that we look for such information as will enable us to determine whether extraneous, unrealised, or even unrealisable, profits have been included upon the credit side; and whether due allowance has been made *per contra* not merely for all current expenses, but also for all expenditure and losses properly incidental to the earning of the revenue brought into credit. Similarly in the Balance Sheet we look to the narrative to enable us to determine substantially the financial position—that is to say, the extent of the floating (or circulating) assets available to meet claims of creditors due in the near future, and available to pay such dividends as the Revenue Account may claim to be justified by the circumstances. An adequate narration will also show us (so far as it is possible for any summary to enable us to form an opinion) the substantial soundness of the valuations attached to the various fixed assets, by contrasting the expenditure upon renewals separately shown in the Balance Sheet and the expenditure upon renewals and replacements shown in the Revenue Account, and the provision for depreciation (or obsolescence) shown in both, with the opening and closing balances on the Asset Account. We can then—within certain limits—form some sort of an idea as to the soundness of the financial policy that has been pursued. A mere statement of the present valuation of each asset would, in this connection, be absolutely unintelligible, more especially when we bear in mind that (for one excuse or another) the amount of real information given in such Revenue Accounts as are customarily published is absolutely *nil*.

On the other hand, I would not have you suppose that I have any intention of insisting that, under all conceivable circumstances, the whole of the known facts should be stated in all published accounts. Primarily—and in the absence of any special considerations that may tend to modify that view—it must, I think, be admitted that it is the duty of all accounting parties to submit accounts that are not merely accurate as a matter of mere figures and of ultimate results, but are also—not merely in name, but also in fact—a sufficient narration, or history, of the transactions that have been embarked upon by accounting parties, and of their effect to date. The accounts (being Accounts Current) are, it must of course be conceded, in no case final accounts, but merely provisional or interim accounts; but, as I have said, in the absence of special circumstances they should be entirely candid, and convey to the principal all the knowledge at the command of the accounting party. The accounts rendered by an agent to his principal, by an employee to his master, or by a trustee to his *cestuis que trustent*, should follow this rule, and should convey to the party entitled thereto all the information at the disposal of the accounting party, without any reserve whatever; but in connection with the application of accounts to companies a certain amount of modification becomes necessary, owing to the peculiar constitution of these undertakings. A company may be roughly regarded as an over-grown partnership; and because it *is* over-grown the management of the undertaking has to be deputed to a relatively small number of the partners, who (and who alone) are expected to make themselves conversant with the facts, and to be responsible to the others for the general success of the venture. In the majority of cases it is expressly provided that the remainder of the partners shall not be entitled to detailed information as to what has taken place, and in any event it is not practicable that *all* information should be placed at their disposal—if for no other reason, because they would not be willing to devote sufficient time to the matter to enable such information to be imparted. As a consequence, it seems to necessarily follow that the "rank-and-file" of the shareholders of a company are not entitled to so strict and so detailed an account as would be (say) an employer, or a beneficiary under a trust. I have no time this evening to go fully into this aspect of our inquiry; but we may, I think, admit in general terms that under these somewhat peculiar (although in these days very common) circumstances, the accounting party is to a certain extent absolved from his duty to account in detail for all his actions. This modification, however, so far from relieving the accounting parties (*i.e.*, the directors) from all responsibility, throws upon them the enormous added responsibility of deciding what must be withheld from each separate shareholder in the interests of the undertaking collectively, and of placing before them such accounts as they are entitled to in a form which, if not complete in every detail, is at least entirely adequate. The discretion conferred upon directors, to withhold information in the interests of the company itself, is no release from what I may call the "common-law" liability of the directors to account in the ordinary way.

And now, having considered at some length the importance of accurate accounting in the abstract, let us turn our attention to the practical advantages that are likely to ensue from its adoption, and the disadvantages of its neglect. Stated quite shortly, it may, I think, be said that accurate accounting—and more particularly accounting arranged upon suitable lines, so as to give not merely a review of historical facts, but also a summary of current results which may be likened to "news"—is of direct advantage to all undertakings as making for increased efficiency and economy; while its absence leads to inefficiency, general lack of control, loss, and eventually to insolvency. It may seem perhaps a somewhat extreme statement to attribute insolvency merely to bad or indifferent accounting, but an examination of available figures shows that in something over 80 per cent. of the bankruptcies that take place annually no proper books of account have been kept, such as enables the debtor to see his position with reasonable clearness; and in the majority of cases this absence of proper accounting may be regarded as one of the main causes —if not the primary cause—of the failure.

It is, however, by no means necessary to have recourse to such extreme cases in order to emphasise the importance of proper accounts, so kept that they may answer not merely the requirements of theorists, but also those of practical men, who want their information *quickly*, so that they may be readily able to utilise it to advantage. In the time that now remains to me I cannot attempt to deal at all exhaustively with this aspect of our subject, but I can give you a few hints which may prove suggestive, and may perhaps encourage some of you to follow the matter up further for yourselves. Thus unsystematic accounting in connection with debtors' accounts frequently leads to items properly chargeable being overlooked until perhaps it is too late to recover them at all, or at all events too late to raise the question without causing irritation to customers; or it may be that the bad accounting takes the form of frequent overcharges, and the damage caused by such carelessness is by no means entirely removed by a willingness to give credit for such overcharges whenever attention is drawn to them. Valuable connections may be permanently alienated through errors of this description. Then, again, indifferent accounting almost invariably means accounting that is not kept closely up to date, and is not used to the best advantage when available. As applied to a Sold Ledger, this means that insufficient attention is given to the collection of customers' accounts, with the result that an unnecessary amount of working capital has to be employed, or unnecessary charges in respect of interest incurred; and in many cases wholly preventable risks of loss through bad debts are incurred, either through dilatoriness in the writing-up of the books, or through inability to appreciate the use to be made of the record when it is available.

Then, again, in the absence of proper Cost Accounts, a manufacturer is completely in the dark. He may have his own idea of the manufacturing profits that he is making; but in the absence of any attempt to reconcile this mental estimate with the actual results, it would be extremely unsafe to attach too much reliance upon its accuracy. Experience shows that even the most careful can go strangely astray in these matters, and it is safe to assume that those who keep no proper accounts are no more likely to be accurate in these matters than those who do.

The use of Cost Accounts does not, however, by any means merely consist in the fact that they subdivide the results shown by the general financial accounts, and explain how much of the ascertained profit has been earned by each department, or contract, of the business. Before the Cost Accounts can be unconditionally accepted as accurate it is, of course, necessary that they should be satisfactorily reconciled with the results shown by the financial books; but no Cost Accounts will be much use if one has to wait until the end of the financial year—and perhaps a month or two more—before arriving at any figures at all. One of the most obvious advantages of keeping Cost Accounts is that they provide not merely detailed, but also *continuous*, results of the business that is being done; but it would be absolutely impossible for the Cost Accounts to be kept closely up to date, and to be prepared with sufficient accuracy for it to be safe to rely upon them before they had been reconciled at the end of the year, unless the greatest possible care were given to the matter, both in principle and in detail.

Then, again, Cost Accounts can be generally made to constitute one of the most valuable checks available on the accuracy of the payments made from time to time in respect of wages. The difficulty of establishing a satisfactory check over this item is, of course, well known to you, and probably a complete and really effective system of Cost Accounts represents the only practicable solution of the difficulty. The principle to be applied in such cases (which will, of course, vary in detail according to circumstances) must be that nothing in respect of wages must be debited to any Cost Account, save on satisfactory proof of a corresponding amount of work ordered and performed. If the total of such work for a week, or a fortnight, agrees with the actual payments made to workers during the same period, we have a very valuable and entirely independent check upon the accuracy with which the Pay Sheets have been compiled.

Of course, it goes without saying that one of the most important advantages of accurate accounting is that it tends to discourage, and to make increasingly difficult, irregularities and dishonesty on the part of all accounting parties, from the highest to the lowest. It also provides the only available means by which the efficiency of those responsible for the results achieved may be tested by those who are not in daily touch with the business transactions.

Of late years there has been growing a disposition on the part of both practical men of business and of nonpractical investors to appreciate the advantages of accurate accounting; but progress in this direction is slow, and there is still room for considerable improvement in many cases. The number of private firms, and of individual traders and manufacturers, whose accounts are kept upon a system even reasonably adequate, and are periodically audited by professional accountants, is probably still a minority of the whole. In connection with companies, although the accounts are, as a rule, better kept, and are in the great majority of cases regularly and professionally audited; yet even here in most cases the accounts that come under the cognisance of accountants are those which lead up to the Balance Sheet and Profit and Loss Account submitted to the shareholders, rather than to the detailed returns — Cost Accounts and the like—which form the basis upon which the business managers work. If one were to go further in this direction, and consider the present position of accounting in connection with the accounts of charitable institutions, local authorities, and the like, one might easily occupy hours discussing the extent to which these undertakings suffer through a neglect of adequate accounting; but time fails me; and I can therefore only point out to you the duty which devolves upon us all to do our best to educate public opinion in the direction that I have indicated.

The task is by no means an insuperable one, in that there is already a movement on foot in the direction that I have indicated. We have not to overcome the inertia of an absolutely motionless body, but merely to guide its movement, and, if possible, to do something towards hastening it. The esence of the whole thing is that, in connection with every business undertaking of any description whatsoever, the science of accounting—properly applied—is capable of greatly assisting those at the helm of affairs. In past times every business man was apparently assumed to be equipped with a sufficient knowledge of accounting for this purpose. Now it is beginning to dawn upon the commercial community that this is an unreasonable assumption, and that even the most successful business managers may, without loss of self-respect, seek the assistance of experts in connection with questions of account.

At the present time it seems to me that matters have progressed so far that the future of the movement rests very largely with accountants themselves. Hitherto they have perhaps been too much inclined to apply ready-made and "cast-iron" systems to the most diverse kinds of undertakings, without due regard to their applicability to the requirements of their new situation, or to their adequacy, as giving to men of business that information —that "reliable news"—which they require even more than a reliable history of past results. The faults in the past have, I think, been by no means all upon one side; but, as I have said, of late there are signs of a distinct movement in the right direction, and it will now be the fault of accountants if they fail to rise to the occasion, and to supply those precise applications of the science of accounting that will meet each separate case with a minimum of inconvenience, or dislocation of business, and with a maximum of information and efficiency. In these days of competition business moves too quickly for anyone to rest content with a Balance Sheet and Trading and Profit and Loss Accounts once every six or twelve months: he must be placed in possession of all the detailed information which these accounts imply systematically, continuously. That is to say, he has to be educated into the habit of looking to his *accounts* for information, and not to his own scrappy, and often unreliable, memoranda.

If once a successful business man finds that the information he really requires *can* be obtained from accounts, there is nothing in reason that he is not prepared to pay for such accounts as he may require. But accounting, like everything else, must be prepared to rely upon its merits for adequate recognition; and, for the reasons that I have indicated, many forms of accounting at present in use have no very high claims, as judged from this standpoint. It is no doubt true that the business community has shown itself lamentably behind the times in failing to duly appreciate the importance to itself of accounts generally; but a system of accounts which is itself out of date cannot claim any very exalted measure of appreciation. While, therefore, we may reasonably anticipate that the importance of accurate accounting will be more adequately appreciated by the business community in the near future, it may perhaps not be out of place for me to express the hope that the importance of providing not merely accurate, but also adequate, systems of accounts will receive an increasing measure of attention at the hands of the profession generally, and especially at the hands of accountant students.

BUSINESS ORGANISATION, WITH SPECIAL REFERENCE TO FRAUD

Lawrence R. Dicksee

Incorporated Accountants Students' Society of London.

Business Organisation, with Special Reference to Fraud.—I.*

By PROFESSOR LAWRENCE R. DICKSEE, M.Com., F.C.A

A LECTURE delivered at a meeting of the above Society on 11th April 1911.

Preliminary.

The subject which I have selected for my last two lectures to you is one of such enormous scope that you will doubtless feel no surprise if I state at once that I do not hope to be able to deal with it at all exhaustively. At the same time it is one which is, I think, capable of being dealt with in outline more profitably than some; and as, moreover, the question of Business Organisation, with special reference to the prevention and detection of fraud, is one of paramount importance to all members of our profession, I feel that I shall not be wasting your time in inviting your attention to some of the general principles involved, and to a few of the numerous possible applications of those principles to daily affairs.

Organisation Cannot Entirely Prevent Fraud.

Of course, it goes without saying that it is quite hopeless to attempt to devise any system of accounting that will *prevent* fraud. The utmost that can be hoped for in practice is, I think, to provide such a system of record and of check as will discourage fraud, by making it exceedingly unlikely that any fraud that may be perpetrated will remain undetected sufficiently long to make it worth while. It is, I think, quite within the possibilities that a system of accounting, and organisation generally, can always be devised that will in this way render frauds—or, at all events, serious frauds—unlikely, by making them unremunerative; but that, it seems to me, is about as much as one can hope for, for in the nature of things a system of accounting aims at recording what has taken place, rather than at preventing the undesirable from occurring. In some cases it may accomplish a little more than this; but, to be on the safe side, it is desirable not to expect too much—for to expect too much is to court disillusionment.

Frauds do not always involve Theft.

Another point on which I should like to be clear at the outset is that frauds relating to accounts do not by any means necessarily involve the stealing or embezzling of money, nor is it even essential that they should involve

the abstraction of any form of property. Indeed, some of the frauds most difficult of detection, and therefore most likely to remain undetected until they have assumed serious proportions, are frauds involving misrepresentations as to the amount of profits earned, embarked upon primarily to prevent the discontinuance of a business (or of some department of a business), and thus to secure the continuance of the offending party's present employment. Such frauds are often particularly disastrous, in that the actual result to the undertaking, as measured by the depletion of its assets, is by no means limited to the salary or commission that may be paid to the offending parties. In such cases, sometimes the amounts paid away by way of dividends, which are not justified by the facts or lost by unprofitable trading, may exceed the amount actually misappropriated a hundredfold; but the practical consequences to the undertaking are probably almost the same, whether these moneys go into the pockets of shareholders, or into the pockets of fraudulent employees.

The Importance of "Credit."

On the other hand, it is important to recognise that the whole foundation of our modern business institutions is credit; and that this implies a belief that, provided reasonable precautions be taken, we shall find ourselves fairly dealt with by those with whom we come in contact. It would be impossible to conduct business on modern lines without credit; equally impossible would it be to conduct a business on modern lines without trusting employees, and this although it must be evident that frauds involving any breach of trust would be impossible if no trust were given. It would be quite easy to avoid the risk of being robbed by trusting no one; but the practical result of this frame of mind would be that one would find it impossible to conduct any business at all. No business can be conducted—no profit can be earned—without incurring some risks, and the risk of loss by fraud is just as much one of these inevitable risks as is the risk of loss by way of bad debts. It would seem, therefore, that it is not even desirable to attempt to obviate all risks of fraud; even if it were desirable, we may feel sure that it would be impracticable to do so on terms that left it possible to conduct a successful and profitable business.

Professional Audits not All-Sufficing.

It is probable that, even now, the view most frequently entertained by the general public is that a proper professional audit is (or should be) a complete safeguard against loss by fraud. This seems to be evident from the fact that, in practice, frauds upon a large scale seem rarely to occur without there being some outcry to the effect that the professional auditors have been negligent in their duties. It would take too long, and it would be altogether outside the scope of our present subject, to explain why it is that a professional audit cannot always be relied upon to detect frauds, and I must therefore pass that by altogether. It is, however, I think, quite to the point for me to mention that, inasmuch as the ordinary statutory audit is merely a yearly examination of the accounts, it is in the highest degree undesirable to rely upon that alone for the detection of fraud; for the simple reason that, even supposing an audit could be relied upon to detect fraud under all conceivable circumstances (which in my judgment it cannot), it obviously could not be relied upon to detect all frauds at a sufficiently early date to keep them within reasonable bounds. Hence it is imperative that business undertakings should learn not to rely overmuch on the professional audit for their security, but as far as possible to be self-sufficing in this respect; and to make them so self-sufficing is one of the functions, although not, of course, by any means the only function, of an adequate system of business organisation.

The Basis of Organisation.

In considering the framing of a system of business organisation, with a view to discouraging fraud by rendering its early detection practically inevitable, it is, I think, not unimportant to consider the means at one's disposal. Having definitely recognised what I personally consider to be the first essential point—that it is undesirable to rely overmuch on a professional audit, particularly when that audit is only conducted at infrequent intervals—the next step seems to be to consider how we may organise the employees of an undertaking so that we may place some reliance on their work as a deterrent. Under normal circumstances, I think we are fairly entitled to assume that no one, whatever his precise position, will knowingly allow himself to become a party to a fraud by which he does not benefit; hence the sheet-anchor of any system of business organisation designed to render fraud difficult, by rendering its detection easy, must be so to arrange matters that any irregularities that may take place—and particularly any falsifications of account that may be embarked upon with a view to concealing fraud—shall at the earliest possible stage come to the knowledge of some member of the staff who is unlikely to benefit by their continuance. Further, it is not unimportant to recognise that practically all forms of fraud participated in by two or more persons render those persons liable to an indictment for conspiracy, in addition to being charged with other (perhaps minor) offences; with the result that frauds involving conspiracy become in all cases a serious matter, liable to serious punishment, and thus *ipso facto* less likely to be embarked upon unless the advantages to be gained in the limited time during which they may remain undetected seem overpowering.

We have here, then, two definite principles that we may with advantage work upon :—(1) To organise our work so that every fraudulent error in accounting may as soon as possible come to the knowledge of someone not interested in the fraud remaining undetected; (2) to organise our system of check so as to make it practically hopeless for anyone to attempt singlehanded to carry out any fraudulent schemes; while making assurance doubly sure by from time to time rearranging the duties of our staff with a view to breaking up any groups of conspirators that might from time to time be formed to keep us in the dark as to the true facts. The practical advantages of the second of these two principles are, I think, fairly well known; but I am not so sure that the advantages of the first-named are as well recognised—certainly they are not so frequently acted upon in practice.

Importance of First-Entry Records.

From another point of view also, we may divide the scope of our inquiry into two headings :—(1) To make sure that all facts, or transactions, that affect the financial position of the undertaking with which we deal are duly and promptly recorded in its books of first entry; (2) to make sure that all facts, or transactions, recorded in the books of first-entry are afterwards properly dealt with in the Ledgers, so as to ensure that their true effect be made apparent. Here, again, so far as my experience goes, there is not often much to be found fault with in the way that the second of these two principles is dealt with in practice, but there seems often to be considerable scope for improvement with regard to the first-named. However that may be, the point that I would like to impress upon you this evening is that it is little use devising a system of organisation which merely aims at dealing in the right way with those transactions that find their way into the books of account, if no serious attempt is made to ensure that all facts having any bearing on the financial position are recorded in the one or another of the books of first-entry. This evening I propose to invite you to consider how these two matters may best be dealt with in general terms; and in my next, and last, lecture I propose to carry the matter a little further by pointing out to you the advantages which the loose-leaf system possesses, from the point of view of providing possible safeguards against fraud as well as in the speed of handling the various records.

By Whom Made.

To begin at the beginning, and to get to the heart of the business at once, I should like to point out to you that in the majority of cases no sufficient precautions seem to be taken to ensure that the initial records of transactions are correctly and completely made. In the majority of cases, whatever may be the precise nature of the business undertaking, these initial records are made by those who are held accountable for the financial results achieved, or by subordinates under their command, and therefore, at all events, to some extent under their influence. While I fully recognise the importance of our confining ourselves to recommendations that are strictly practical, I should like to take this opportunity of suggesting to you, for your consideration here and hereafter, that one of the most obvious precautions against fraud is to be found in a very considerable enlargement of the functions of what we may call the Accounts Department of any business.

The Usual Basis of Organisation.

I think it will be agreed that the system of organisation that we usually find in force is one that places the general business manager in supreme control of everything; thus making him responsible not only for the financial success of his operations, but also for the accuracy of the accounts which record what these operations have been. In small concerns, where the general business manager is also sole or joint proprietor, it is probable that one cannot very well improve upon this arrangement; but in the case of large concerns, where the general business manager is only an employee or an officer of the company, it is an arrangement which, it seems to me, it is much more difficult to defend. Perhaps the strongest argument in its favour in such circumstances is that it does undoubtedly make for smoothness of working, and it might perhaps be added that, as a rule, it does not seem to produce manifestly bad results; but thoughtful men must, I think, admit that it provides no very adequate safeguard against the unscrupulous or dishonest business manager, and that it must in the nature of things tend seriously to delay the time when such a manager's irregularities would be brought to light, with the result that they may by then have assumed very serious proportions.

Its Drawbacks.

Another drawback of this system, which does not appear to be so generally appreciated as it might be, is that it tends to starve the accounts department, by limiting the chances of promotion for successful service in that department, thus preventing the department from securing (or retaining) the services of a number of desirable men. I think you will agree with me that under the system of organisation that one generally finds in force, it is a common thing to observe that new employees, entering upon their term of service comparatively young, if not fresh from school, are attached first for a term to the accounts department, and afterwards promoted to service in what, for the sake of contrast, I will call "operative" departments, if, and when, they show signs of real aptitude. The result is that the accounts department is often staffed with mere boys of little or no experience, and men who have been passed over for promotion; that, as a rule, the brain capacity of the average member of the accounts

department is not equal to the brain capacity of the average member of the operative departments of an ordinary business undertaking. The idea of anyone attached to an "operative" department being promoted to a more important position in an accounts department is almost unheard of. I do not want to belittle the general intelligence of the accounts departments of ordinary business undertakings, but I venture to think that you will agree with me when I say that such departments do not as a rule offer much scope for advancement to the young man of real ability. There are, of course, senior positions of importance in the accounts department of a large undertaking; but it is weary work waiting for dead men's shoes, with the result that a large number of those who come into the accounts department in the first instance pass out again before they have acquired sufficient experience to be really very useful servants, while those that remain tend—partly by the force of circumstances, partly owing to the nature of their work—to become increasingly mechanical.

An Independent Accounts Department Advocated.

My idea is that all this might be altered, with advantage to every department, by the formulation of a scheme of organisation upon such lines as these :—(1) That the general business manager should be relieved of all responsibility in connection with accounts. (2) That the accounts department should be self-contained and self-sufficing; as far as possible dissassociated from every operative department, but, on the other hand, in close touch with—and with direct access to—the supreme head of the business. Such an arrangement would, I think, be of the greatest possible advantage all round. It would be of advantage to the "operative" departments, in that it would enable their respective managers to concentrate attention upon the work for which they are best fitted. It would be of advantage to the accounts department, because an accounts department so organised—so "ennobled," if I may use the term—would be in a position to offer quite satisfactory prospects of promotion to all those employees who showed evidence of real ability in this particular direction. Moreover, it would place the head of the accounts department in close touch with its junior members, temporarily attached to the operative departments for the purpose of recording transactions as and when they occur, with the result that these juniors would be working under a man competent to appreciate the manner in which their duties were performed—an arrangement that would give them every incentive to put forward their best efforts; whereas it is notorious that the heads of operative departments are, as a rule, no great hands at accounts, and therefore not likely to instil juniors with any great enthusiasm for elementary work connected with that department. But behind all this the paramount advantage of emancipating the accounts department from the control of the general managers of operative departments would be that we should secure a really independent record of transactions, which is not secured by any of the more usual schemes of organisation, and is in practice not often even attempted. Working upon these lines, the accounts department would make its own first records of transactions from information derived at first hand by actual contact with the operative department; an arrangement which, as I have stated before, would increase the efficiency of the latter by relieving their respective heads from responsibilities, which they are often by no means best fitted to undertake, while possessing the further, and far greater, advantage of making the initial accounting record not so much a record of the operative departments concerning their own acts, as an independent statement of facts by the accounts department, designed, at least partly, with the object of enabling the supreme heads of the undertaking to judge whether the operative departments are being worked well or ill.

Its Relation to First-Entry Records.

My suggestion, then, is that all initial records should be made, not by employees attached to the operative departments, but by employees attached to the accounts department, under the direct control of the chief accountant, who are temporarily lent to the various operating departments for the purpose of being on the various spots where transactions take place, so that they may observe their transactions and record them promptly and faithfully. Possibly you will say that this would be no improvement, in that the members of the accounts department told off for this purpose would naturally for the most part be juniors, who could easily be influenced by those immediately around them, assuming that anyone desired to influence them to betray their trust. There might, no doubt, be something in this view, if the whole of the staff of an undertaking were to be divided into merely two classes—those attached to the operative departments and those attached to the accounts department; but, wherever it seems necessary, it is quite easy to carry the idea a little further. Thus, in an ordinary commercial concern, the great bulk of the transactions centre round two classes of records—movements of cash and movements of goods. It is quite easy—and, indeed, at the present time it is usual—for movements of cash to be dealt with by a special staff of cashiers, organised under a chief cashier at the head of that department; similarly, in a large merchant's business (and, with variations that are not really material for my present purpose, in a large shopkeeper's business), the actual handling of goods is principally, and sometimes wholly, in the hands of a packing (or transport) department, usually subdivided so that goods inwards and goods outwards are dealt with by distinct staffs. For purposes

of organisation, however, it would not be difficult to work something upon the lines that the accounts department is advised of all movements of goods by the transport department, and of all movements of money by the cashier's department; and in this way, unless there were collusion between members of one department and members of another department, it would be exceedingly difficult for those interested in the success of an operative department to arrange that false information as to the facts should be given to the accounts department. Whatever little risk there might be under this heading can be reduced to "vanishing point," in the case, at all events, of large concerns, by a system of organisation which involves a rearrangement of the duties of individual members of the various staffs from time to time, thereby making it impossible for anyone to rely upon it that those with whom he has been working in collusion in the past will be available for that purpose in the future.

Precautions Against Collusion.

This rearrangement, or shifting, of duties is, I think, a very important part of any system of effective organisation, no matter what its precise details may be. It is undoubtedly the most effective—and, indeed, the only effective—safeguard against collusion. It is thoroughly effective, in that it is manifestly not worth the while of any fraudulently disposed individual to run the risks of securing the co-operation of a confederate (including the risk of being "given away"), when there is no assurance that, assuming the process of demoralisation has proved successful and a suitable confederate has been secured, he will be available for the desired purposes, even on the day following. It is not, of course, convenient that these changes of duties should be made at very frequent intervals, for that would certainly not add to the smoothness of the working of the machine as a whole; but in a large concern there is certainly no difficulty in making some few changes every week, and so long as changes are made irregularly, and without prior notice, they have a deterrent effect which it is impossible to exaggerate.

Unauthorised Entries in Accounts.

Another important safeguard, designed to ensure the detection of fraud at the earliest possible moment after its commission, is to impose a very definite limit to the duties to be performed by each member of the staff within a given period of time; in particular it is, I think, imperative to lay down definite rules as to who, from time to time, is authorised to make entries in each of the various books that may be in use. In the absence of such a rule, obviously it is open to anyone who can secure access to a book to make an erroneous, or fictitious, entry therein, with the express object of concealing fraud; and a really clever man might sometimes by this means be able to cover up his tracks after he has been removed from one sphere of duties to another, when, but for this, a new man taking over his duties must at once have discovered the irregularities. For this reason, if for no other, there is much to be said in favour of the annual holiday, which (while it lasts) does at least ensure that the absent party can make no entries in any books whatever. Doubtless most persons will recognise the force of this argument when it is presented to them; but in times of pressure it is often felt that the immediate need is paramount, and that, in face of the present emergency, rules must sometimes be over ridden. There is much to be said in favour of this view; and because there is so much obviously to be said in its favour, I should like specially to caution you against what, it seems to me, is a thoroughly undesirable practice, that is very frequently adopted by business houses in times of pressure—namely, the practice of instructing the most rapid workers, when they have finished their allocated tasks for the day, to help the slower workers who are behindhand, in order that the day's work may be finished as soon as possible and no one work more overtime than is really needful. The advantages of this arrangement are obvious; the disadvantages are, it seems to me, less apparent, and therefore worth considering. In the first place, unless the period of pressure be extremely short-lived, such an arrangement is almost certain to prove wholly useless. If, in busy times, a man finds he gets away no earlier because he has worked rapidly throughout the day, because he is then told off to assist another who has been taking things very much more easily, it is only reasonable to suppose that he will very soon learn that he gains nothing by working rapidly; thus the whole staff will soon be in competition, not each to perform their allotted task as soon as possible, but each not to be found at the end of his allotted task before the others, with the result that a general " speeding down " process is set going. That is one obvious objection to this plan from the point of view of practical office management; but another, to which I would like especially to direct your attention this evening, is that such an arrangement gives the rapid worker the opportunity of working on books which (theoretically) are not then under his control. In all probability they are under the control of one less competent, or less energetic, than himself, and therefore of one who is not likely to raise any great objection to the precise form of entries that he makes, so long as the desired result is achieved—which, in his case, is that the day's work is finished at the earliest possible moment. Further, I would like to point out to you that the class of man who deliberately embarks upon a system of fraud and falsification of accounts that stands the least chance of success, must be one possessed of more than average ability; therefore, if there be such an one in the employ ment of the undertaking, it is he who will be allowed this

licence to assist others, and by that means to secure opportunities of making entries in their books of account, which may suit his purpose by enabling him to postpone the detection of his own frauds. I do not say that under no possible circumstances is it safe to allow one bookkeeper to assist another temporarily in his work; but I do want very strongly to point out to you that, unless this is authorised with a full appreciation of the dangers involved, the results may easily prove disastrous. In any event I doubt the expediency of the arrangement, as a question of ordinary office management.

Successful Falsification must be by Double-Entry.

Assuming that we have been able so to organise our accounts department that it is able to secure a reliable first-entry record of all transactions that take place, the next point to which I would like to draw your attention is that, assuming the accounts are kept by double-entry, no falsifications of accounts can remain undetected beyond the date of the usual (interim) Trial Balance, unless they—like everything else—are recorded by double-entry. If those interested in the falsification have no access to the first-entry records, and no means of tampering with them, this means that they must make two distinct false entries (either of omission or commission, or one of each) in order to prevent the fraud becoming apparent by the non-agreement of the Trial Balance. The larger the undertaking and the more numerous its staff, the more difficult does this process of fraud by double-entry become; for it means, as a rule, that any two accounts that would be likely to be affected by any legitimate transaction will be in distinct Ledgers, and therefore under the control of distinct Ledger-keepers. The falsifier is thus perforce driven in such cases to manipulate the records in two distinct Ledgers, which with the proper system of organisation will be impossible; or else he must make his double-entry falsification by two disjointed halves, thus doubling the risk of detection.

Sectional Balancing.

The employment of sectional balancing, if thoroughly carried out with the raising of the suitable Adjustment (or Control) Accounts in the Departmental Ledger, and also in the Chief (or General) Ledger, places further difficulties in the way of any system of fraud, because the Control Accounts in the General Ledger are, of course, beyond the control of any subordinate. And similarly, if it be the chief accountant who is interested in the fraud, the manipulation of the Adjustment (or Control) Accounts in the departmental Ledgers is dangerous in the extreme, on account of the suspicion it must give rise to in the minds of the subordinate Ledger-keepers. As I shall explain to you hereafter, the loose-leaf system of first-entry possesses a very valuable advantage here, in that, by the aid of carbon sheets, it multiplies the original record, supplying a copy to each of the various Ledger departments. Each Ledger department therefore arrives at its totals independently from its own set of copies; it would be useless for one Ledger Department to manipulate the sheets under its control in order to arrive at a false total; for, were it to do so, the immediate result would be that its figures would not agree with those arrived at by the other departments, and an independent inquiry into the source of the difference would at once disclose what had been done.

Independence of Accounts Department Essential.

In the absence of collusion, however—and, as I have already said, collusion may easily be made unlikely, because unprofitable, by an occasional shifting of the respective duties of the different employees—there is really no inducement for a Ledger-keeper to attempt to falsify his accounts, unless he is entrusted with duties that ought properly to be undertaken by someone not attached to the accounts department. If the man in charge of a Debtors' Ledger is also entrusted with the collection of accounts (and thus combines the functions of a cashier) there is, of course, every inducement to falsification, should he desire to misappropriate some of his collections. Similarly, if a man in charge of a Creditors' Ledger is also entrusted with the payment of accounts, he may sometimes be tempted to falsify his record with the object of securing the handling of a cheque drawn in payment of an account that is not actually due, and may therefore be misappropriated without any subsequent inquiry being raised. Similarly, if a man in charge (say) of a Stores Ledger be also the store-keeper, there will be every inducement for him to manipulate his record to conceal a deficiency of stores, or perhaps even to conceal a surplus of stores caused by careless or wasteful handling. It is for these reasons that I emphasised, in the earlier part of this paper, the importance of entirely disassociating those attached to the accounts department from any responsibility for the desirability or the undesirability of the position of affairs that their respective records might disclose. As a rule, the importance of this view seems to be fairly well recognised; but what is, perhaps, not sufficiently appreciated is that an occasional departure from the usual, and desirable, practice may have all the undesirable and unfortunate consequences of the deliberate and permanent adoption of a bad system. From some points of view the appearance of a rare opportunity may be even more undesirable than its perpetual presence, as adding to other things the extra force of a sudden temptation.

The Beginnings of Fraud.

It ought, I think, not to be overlooked that in the majority of cases those who have been detected of fraud in connection with accounts did not enter into their employment with the express intention of committing such fraud. In some few isolated cases there may have been this deliberate intention from the outset, but they are certainly the minority. As a rule frauds are the result of a sudden temptation (that is to say, of a fresh opportunity, or of an opportunity newly appreciated), combined with some outside pressure, such as the urgent demands of an importunate creditor (often brought about by intemperance), or the hope of easily acquired gain as the result of some lucky bet on some particular race or match. In most cases the first fraud is comparatively small in extent, and was never intended to be more than a temporary abstraction of employer's moneys—euphoniously regarded as a loan. It is safe to say that the majority of such beginnings would never have occurred at all had the system of organisation in existence been sufficiently thorough to make the risk of detection before the supposed loan could be repaid a really serious one. But a fraud of this kind once committed, if not discovered, constitutes very naturally a standing temptation to repeat the offence whenever the same need (or supposed need) for temporary assistance recurs; and with each repetition the fear of detection is blunted by immunity, while the desire for money grows apace with what it feeds upon. Thus, practically all large frauds have their origin in a series of petty frauds which bad organisation has failed to detect.

And their Continuation.

It is important to bear in mind that, where the amount originally stolen has not been refunded, but merely made good out of moneys subsequently abstracted, the amount so taken each time has to exceed the aggregate amount stolen on all previous occasions. Thus petty frauds, often repeated, accumulate to appreciable sums at a very rapid rate. Similarly, with regard to those frauds which are the result of a desire to exaggerate profits or to conceal losses, usually by an exaggeration of the value of stock-in-hand, it is important to bear in mind that, supposing an over-valuation of £500 would achieve the desired result in the first year, in the second year an over-valuation of £500 will do nothing more than cover the previous year's falsification. If it is desired to exaggerate the profits for the second year, the stock must be over-valued by more than £500; and so here, again, if the frauds remain undetected for any appreciable period, they may easily accumulate to a surprisingly large total.

The Duty of Employers, and Conclusion.

I would put it you that, apart from the duty that the directors of a company owe to shareholders, and that the proprietors of a proprietary business owe to themselves, there is a further duty that they owe to their employees—not, through their own slackness, to place unnecessary temptations in the way of others. It is not sufficient for employers to employ professional auditors, and therefore to assume that they have done the whole of their duty in this matter, unless they make special arrangements with such auditors to perform such an investigation as will be really effective for this purpose, which the ordinary statutory company audit certainly is not. With comparatively small concerns, the professional audit conducted at frequent intervals is probably upon the whole the best safeguard against fraud, because with these concerns the staff is not sufficiently numerous to admit of its being organised upon a really effective system of internal check; but, with really large concerns, a proper arrangement of the respective duties of the staff should be sufficient to provide for the early detection of any frauds (other, perhaps, than those that might be committed by heads of departments), and upon the whole in such cases this perfection of internal organisation is, I think, to be preferred to reliance upon outside help. In the case of undertakings of sufficient importance to command their own staff auditors, the problem presents but little difficulty in practice, because in that way the desired independence on the part of those charged with the checking of the detailed work may readily be secured. But, even in the case of undertakings not sufficiently large to make the employment of staff auditors desirable (and these must always be in the majority), there will, I think, be found little difficulty in organising an efficient system of internal check, provided the importance of so doing be duly recognised, and provided the system is given a reasonable chance of success by arranging that the accounts department shall be really independent of operating results, and therefore in a position to do its work unhesitatingly and without fear of consequences.

BUSINESS ORGANISATION,
WITH SPECIAL REFERENCE TO FRAUD

Lawrence R. Dicksee

Incorporated Accountants Students' Society of London.

Business Organisation, with Special Reference to Fraud.—II.*

By Professor Lawrence R. Dicksee, M.Com., F.C.A.

A LECTURE delivered at a meeting of the above Society on 26th April 1911.

Preliminary.

I propose to conclude my remarks to you on the subject of Business Organisation, with special reference to Fraud, this evening with some observations on modern business methods of first-entry record; but before doing so, in order to make my meaning clearer, it is, I think, desirable that I should supplement what I have already said by some short explanation of the Card Ledger.

Card Ledgers.

The Card Ledger differs somewhat materially from the Loose-leaf Ledger, in that the various sheets of which it is composed, instead of being the thickness of ordinary Ledger paper, are sufficiently stiff and substantial to enable them to be handled without the protection of any binding; and instead of being immovably fixed together by a locking attachment while actually in use by the book-keeper, they are stored away vertically in drawers, or compartments, between other cards—called "guide cards"—which, being somewhat higher, project above them, thus enabling letters (or numbers) to be written (or printed) thereon which facilitate a ready reference. It will be obvious that many of the arguments that I have put forward in favour of the Loose-leaf Ledger cannot in fairness be claimed for the Card Ledger, because it is at all times "loose," instead of being firmly bound while in use. At the same time, the Card Ledger possesses most of the distinctive advantages of the Loose-leaf Ledger, in that it permits of the accounts always remaining in a constant order; allows of their indefinite expansion from time to time; and (like the Loose-leaf Ledger) is "perpetual," in the sense that the time never arrives when all the accounts have to be started afresh at the same moment.

Alphabetical and Numerical Arrangements Contrasted.

Two arrangements of the Card Ledger are possible—alphabetical and numerical. With the first (as the name implies) the cards are kept strictly in alphabetical order, and accordingly no index is required; but this, as it seems to me, is the sole advantage of this particular arrangement, and against it there is the powerful disadvantage that much inconvenience will arise if a card be accidentally misplaced or fraudulently destroyed. This disadvantage, however, is entirely obviated by the employment of the numerical system and a suitable form of card. With the numerical system there must, of course, be a separate index, which may also be in card form. When a number has been allocated to an account, that number remains constant; but when an account becomes absolutely dead the next new account that is opened is given the number of that dead account, so as to avoid an accumulation of dead numbers. The cards are arranged in the drawers behind guide cards which separate the hundreds, and other guide cards which separate the tens, the unit number is further indicated by a circular projection from the top of the card; but, instead of the cards all being cut with the same outline, they are cut in a series of tens, the projection on the cards with the unit number " 0 " appearing on the extreme left, while the projection on those with the unit number " 9 " appears on the extreme right, the other unit numbers projecting in order in between. With this arrangement the unit number attached to every card is always in sight, and the projections catch the eye at a glance, so that a missing card can be detected at once by the absence of the corresponding projection. If a card has been misplaced that projection cannot, of course, shift from right to left, it can only shift up or down the drawer. If this type of card be employed, and it be the regular rule for the head of the department to inspect the drawers containing the cards night and morning, it is a very simple matter for him to satisfy himself that all the cards are in order, or to ascertain within a minute or so that a card is absent, or out of place. To avoid blank spaces, which would attract attention unnecessarily, dead cards are retained in the current drawer until their places can be taken by new cards to which the same number has been allocated. As a card is used up the balance is taken forward to a new card cut with the same unit number, to which is allocated the same account number as the old card, but

a new serial card number (or letter), so that the first card of an account might be (say) 49, the second 49*a*, and so on. As the cards are withdrawn from the current drawer they are put away in "closed accounts" drawers, so that all the cards relating to one account are together. This means that the same system of supervision at a glance cannot be exercised with regard to the closed accounts; but as no cards would be removed to the "closed account" drawers until they had been passed by the auditors, this absence of a readily applied check here does not seem to be a serious disadvantage.

As Compared with Loose-leaf Ledgers.

So far as my inquiries have gone the number of business houses employing Card Ledgers seems to be distinctly less than the number employing Loose-leaf Ledgers, but it is sufficiently great to show that in the opinion of many competent business men this type of Ledger has its distinctive advantages. Probably one reason for its being less used is that the handling of such Ledgers is necessarily quite different from the handling of ordinary Book Ledgers, whereas a clerk accustomed to the use of bound books naturally finds no difficulty whatever in handling Loose-leaf Ledgers with rapidity. Another disadvantage of Card Ledgers is that, for facility of handling, the cards must be comparatively small, and are therefore not very suitable for the record of entries relating to very active accounts. For that same reason, however, they are particularly suitable for accounts on which comparatively few entries per month have to be recorded.

You will observe that Card Ledgers differ from Loose-leaf Ledgers in the somewhat important respect that while they are actually in use by the bookkeepers they may fairly be described as being in a loose condition; whereas, the so-called Loose-leaf Ledger while in use is not loose at all, but is just as firmly and immovably bound as any ordinary form of book. Modern methods of first-entry are similarly divisible into two main classes: (1) That which follows the loose-leaf idea as applied to books of first entry, keeping the leaves in use firmly bound together while in use, while retaining the advantage of elasticity and minimum bulk of leaves in actual use at one time by the aid of the loose-leaf binding; and (2) that which frankly discards the idea of the close binding together, and—by making each separate entry on a distinct sheet—secures the utmost degree of flexibility for the record, relying for security against fraud on manifold copies of the original entry obtained by the aid of carbon sheets, and distributing the copies in series to the various departments, so that each series may serve as a check against any suppression, or falsification, of the series preserved in some other department. For the sake of distinction, we will call this latter the Slip System.

Records of Correspondence.

What I shall have to say to you this evening under this heading may be regarded by some of you as so revolutionary that, in order to combat at the earliest possible moment what I cannot help thinking must be regarded as a by no means unnatural prejudice in favour of bound books, I will ask you to review with me the history of office records concerning correspondence. It is not necessary, for our present purposes, to go back into the "dark ages." Even in the days when I was learning bookkeeping at school, the text-book that we used dealt with this subject of commercial correspondence records by stating that it was the practice for merchants to keep two distinct books, viz., Letters Outwards and Letters Inwards. In the first-named book were transcribed by hand copies of all letters issued by the business house; in the second-named the originals of the letters received by the business house were pasted in order of date, the book being in the nature of a scrap book, or Guard Book. I believe that some examples of the Guard Book still survive for the preservation of invoices of goods inwards, but I must confess that I have not seen one lately.

Press-Copies.

I imagine that there can be few of you who would regard this as a really satisfactory method for the record of the correspondence of a modern business house. If I am right in this assumption, I have paved the way towards enlisting your sympathy in our inquiry as to what improvements more modern methods can effect. As regards correspondence outwards, the Letter Book in which press-copies of the original letters issued were retained was clearly an enormous improvement, in that it secured the necessary copies at a very much smaller expenditure of time, while at the same time providing a far more perfect safeguard than before in that they were really exact copies of the original letters sent. In all but the smallest concerns, however, the copying of correspondence outwards in ordinary bound books presents the disadvantage that it involves a copious system of indexing, which renders reference to any series of letters a somewhat laborious process; while at the same time, it is difficult to subdivide the correspondence into departments unless the actual letters are written by clerks attached to different departments, because of the risk—which must always remain a very appreciable one—that, if an attempt be made to divide the correspondence departmentally by providing separate press-copy books for each department, there is always a liability to this kind of division being defeated by certain letters being copied in the wrong books.

Rotary Copiers.

To get over this difficulty it has latterly become the practice of many business houses to copy their correspondence on loose sheets; and, to enable this to be done rapidly, various types of rotary copiers have been invented which copy the letters on to a roll of paper, afterwards cutting the roll into sheets of uniform size. Apart from the fact that rotary copying is more speedy than the older practice, the advent of loose sheets marks an important departure, in that it makes it a comparatively easy matter to file the records away in any desired series; with the further important proviso that, as and when circumstances seem to render such a course desirable, the series may be further split up or modified in any manner desirable, with but little additional trouble.

Carbon Copies.

But all forms of press-copying—rotary or otherwise—are open to the disadvantage that they do not always produce perfectly legible copies; hence an increasing number of business houses at the present time are abandoning the use of press-copies altogether, and are substituting therefor what are called "carbon copies." The point that I would like to impress upon you here is that the development of business organisation in the matter of correspondence has been very materially on the side of improvement on pre-existing methods; the substitution of mechanically prepared copies for hand copies not merely saves a considerable amount of time, it further insures absolute accuracy; while it is found in practice that the abandonment of the bound books, and the substitution therefor of loose sheets, or slips, does not cause those inconveniences that might perhaps at one time have been expected to result.

"Flat" Filing.

I will not waste your time by following, in the same way, the history of the evolution of business organisation with regard to correspondence inwards. By this time everybody is, I think, agreed that it would be a pure waste of time to attempt to apply to such records the imagined security of the bound book. For a very great number of years past everybody has been content to deal with correspondence inwards as a record on loose-leaves, or slips; and, so far as I am aware, no one has seriously thought of reverting to the older practice on account of the increased security which it would undoubtedly provide here, if in point of fact it did provide increased security anywhere at all. I might point out to you, however, that while the intermediate idea was to fold letters inwards up, and laboriously inscribe a summary of their contents outside in the form of an endorsement, the modern idea (which is, in my opinion, immeasurably superior) is to keep the letters flat, so that the actual contents may be available at first-hand to catch the eye of the inquirer.

First-Entry Records on Carbon Basis.

Now having, I hope, to some extent prepared you for what I am about to say, by reminding you of the various

stages of evolution with regard to business correspondence, the next point to which I wish to draw your
attention is that this same idea of producing any desired
number of copies of an original record by the aid of
carbon sheets or leaves, or slips—each relating only to
one transaction—is, to say the least of it, equally suitable
for the record of every conceivable kind of business transaction ordinarily recorded in so-called books of first entry;
and that, so far from introducing a new element of danger
into our system of accounting, under normal circumstances
it provides an additional safeguard for the accuracy of
the original entry precisely at the point where that safeguard is most needed for practical purposes, for the
reasons which I mentioned to you in my last lecture.
In the time now at my disposal I cannot hope to explain
to you all the possible ramifications of this idea; but I will
mention the more important, and some of the various ways
in which the idea may be applied to each.

Sales.

In an ordinary trading concern the record of sales is
undoubtedly the most voluminous of all, and therefore the
one most likely to benefit by the application of modern
labour-saving devices. The old plan, you may remember,
was for the man actually putting the goods together ready
for packing to call out the quantities, descriptions, and
prices to a junior—called an entering clerk—who inscribed
them in a Sales Day Book. In the intervals when he was
not so engaged, the entering clerk extended the prices into
the money column, and wrote out from his Day Book
entries the invoices which were to accompany the goods
despatched to the customers. The whole operation was
performed by hand, and although entering clerks being
confined to one class of duties often attained a remarkable
degree of speed and efficiency, it is clear that the system
provided no assurance whatever against some occasional
discrepancy between the Day Book entries and the
invoices despatched.   Experience shows that such discrepancies occurred at least sufficiently often to point to
the desirability of some improved method, if possible.

One step forwards was to have headed invoice forms
bound up in books, like cheque books, but with blank
pages behind the various headed forms, three or four of
which appeared on a page. With this form of Invoice
Book it was possible by the same operation to write the
invoice to be despatched to the customer, and to obtain on
the blank pages a facsimile carbon copy thereof, to be
retained in the book as the Day Book entry; or sometimes
the process was reversed, the original entry being written
in the book and the carbon copy forwarded to the customer.
In a merchant's business, where the original invoice often
has to be forwarded in duplicate, or triplicate, this
arrangement naturally effected an even greater economy

of time, while still preserving the absolute assurance that
all the copies of the record must agree, unless one or
another of them had been deliberately altered.

With the advent of the typewriter, however, the employment of immovable bound books naturally became increasingly inconvenient, although by no means necessarily
impossible; still it did undoubtedly hasten the movement
in favour of abandoning the employment of bound books
for the record of sales, substituting therefor entries on loose
leaves or sheets made up in series distinctively coloured so
that there might be no confusion as to which copy was to
be regarded as the original invoice, and which the record
or records for office purposes.   The advent of the loose-
sheet copying of the original invoice marks a very
important departure in connection with large business
concerns, for inasmuch as there is no limit (in reason) to
the number of manifold copies that can be obtained by
the same operation, it is quite simple to arrange that one
set of copies shall be forwarded to the Ledger department
for posting to the debit of the customers, and another set
to the dissecting clerk, who analyses the sales departmentally, thus producing the credit totals for the corresponding nominal accounts in the General Ledger.   In a
large business both Sold Ledger Department and Dissecting Department may, with advantage, save time by the
employment of mechanical adding machines to summarise
these sheets. Among other advantages of this arrangement, I would point out to you (1) that it enables the
Ledger clerks to be advised of all transactions actually
taking place much more rapidly than would be practicable
if the entries were made in bound books; (2) that any
manipulation of the sheets that may be made either by
Ledger clerk or dissecting clerk must become immediately
apparent by the non-agreement of their respective daily
totals. As you are no doubt aware, the employment of
bound books for first-entry records usually means that
these bound books have to be duplicated, so that each set
may be in use on alternate days, when the other set is
being posted up by the Ledger clerks; this multiplication
of books can, of course, be avoided entirely by the employment of loose-sheets. Moreover, in many cases the use of
bound Day Books presents an insuperable barrier to
sectional balancing with any pretence to minuteness, for
it is rarely practicable to have a separate Day Book (in
duplicate) for each separate Sold Ledger. It is here,
perhaps more than anywhere else, that the advantage of
the slip system comes in; for sectional balancing, all that
is necessary is to sort out the sheets into separate heaps, as
required by each Ledger clerk, and the total of each Ledger
clerk's heap (mechanically arrived at) represents the total
that he requires for purposes of sectional balancing; while
the daily totals of all the Sold Ledger clerks' postings

should, of course, agree with the daily total of the dissecting clerk's summary of the day's sales.

Where Card Ledgers are in use, Sales Sheets are particularly convenient as a means of economising the time of skilled bookkeepers. Boys (or juniors in training for more important positions) may be employed to sort out the sheets according to the accounts affected, placing them in heaps either above or below the actual Ledger cards on which the postings have to be made; the Ledger clerks then come to their work finding it already half done.

A modification of the same arrangement of what I may call loose-leaf ideas is very suitable to concerns not quite so large, which yet appreciate the advantage of having their Sold Ledger postings absolutely up to date. This is nothing more nor less than a loose-leaf Day Book, written up in what I may call the old-fashioned way, but, of course, with any form of ruling that may be found convenient. The sheets, during entry, will be retained in some form of binder; but, unlike the bound Day Book, as each sheet is filled up, and has therefore been finished with by the entering clerk, it is handed over to the Ledger-keeper for instant posting. There is no practical difficulty in the way of having the sheets of the Loose-leaf Day Book consecutively numbered, which, of course, provides an absolute safeguard against any of them going astray; but in practice the danger of sheets going astray is reduced to vanishing point, if copies in series be forwarded at frequent intervals to two (or more) distinct departments.

Purchases.

You will readily understand that purchases can be dealt with in precisely the same manner, with equal facility; but, inasmuch as the actual volume of purchases is rarely more than ten per cent. of the volume of sales, it is not so often that there is any pressing need for a form of slip Purchase Book. In any event, of course, one can work from the original invoices actually received with the goods. These must be entered in a register, and a carbon copy of the register entries may be used as the basis for what follows. Usually, however, a register on what I have described as the loose-leaf system is sufficiently elastic for practical purposes; particularly if the sheets are printed with analysis columns, to enable the purchases to be dissected departmentally.

Returns.

The same remark applies, of course, to sales returns and purchases returns, neither of these is likely to assume large proportions; but on the whole it is probably convenient that whatever method be adopted for the record of sales should also be adopted for the record of sales returns, so that the Sold Ledger clerks' work may be similar in both cases.

Cash Records.

With regard to cash records, it is equally practicable to adopt either the slip system or the loose-leaf system. If the slip system be preferred, we must work as regards receipts from carbon copies of the actual form of acknowledgment forwarded to the customer as a receipt for his payment. So long as these slips are numbered consecutively, and care be taken to see that all numbers are accounted for, the system is, to my mind, distinctly preferable to the more usual form of counterfoil receipt book. There may quite conceivably be a discrepancy between the counterfoil of a receipt book and the actual receipt itself, due to mere inadvertence; at all events it would be difficult in the extreme to prove that such a discrepancy was fraudulently intended. On the other hand, when carbon copies are employed, no such discrepancy could possibly arise inadvertently; and, indeed, it would be difficult for it to occur at all under normal conditions without attracting the suspicion of some onlookers. As regards payments, slips may similarly be based upon manifold copies of the actual cheques.

There is, I know, still in some quarters a prejudice against typewritten cheques, on the ground that typewriting ink is not indelible. In these days, however, it is a perfectly simple matter to obtain indelible typewriting ink, and then, of course, the difficulty becomes purely imaginary. Those who prefer hand-written cheques may still employ the slip system. It is quite practicable to obtain a carbon copy from an original written by hand. Or, if it be preferred, the counterfoils, written in by hand, may also be perforated so as to become detachable for use as slips: but in the latter event they should, for convenience sake, be decidedly larger than they customarily are.

If it were thought worth while, either receipt books or cheque books might be prepared in loose-leaf form, so that the counterfoils (or duplicates) may speedily be passed on to the appropriate Ledger departments, in cases where it was thought not desirable to adopt the slip system in its entirety; but I do not know that there is any special advantage to be gained here. If the idea is merely that it is desirable to retain the original record relating to such important matters in book form, it is quite a simple matter to arrange for an extra carbon copy to be taken, and for that copy to remain in the original book permanently; and it would be quite possible to do this, even if typewriters were used.

Bills of Exchange.

You will no doubt readily understand that the same idea could be applied with equal facility to the record of Bills Receivable, and even to Bills Payable, although here a little modification would be required, as the basis of the entry would there have to be a typed copy of the bill, which should be initialled by the party actually accepting the original.

Other Applications.

The plan is equally suitable to all sorts of occupations, where the entries are sufficiently numerous to make it worth while; and, indeed, in spite of the fact that solicitors are perhaps among the most conservative of men, it is not without interest to note that for a great number of years past many firms of solicitors have built up their draft bills of costs on some rudimentary application of the slip system, each entry being on a different slip of uniform size, the slips aferwards being sorted out and filed away under the headings of the various matters concerned.

Stores Records.

The idea is also particularly suitable for records of stores issued. The actual demand note (or warrant), which represents the storekeeper's voucher for parting with stores, may be manifolded so that the copy finds its way without loss of time to the man in charge of the Stores Ledger, who accordingly forthwith credits the appropriate Ledger account therein; while another copy goes to the costs department, enabling the value of the stores issued to be debited to the appropriate process, or contract.

Summary of Advantages.

The essential advantages, you will see, are : (1) That time is not wasted on the unnecessary multiplication of hand copies of the same record; (2) the risk of copying errors, which frequently cause endless trouble, is entirely eliminated; (3) that there is no temptation for anyone to attempt to falsify one copy of the record, for so to do would help not at all to conceal fraud; (4) that each separate department gets to work practically simultaneously, with the result that the bookkeeping is far more closely up to date; (5) that the system lends itself to a proper organisation of the staff, as providing a considerable amount of work that may quite easily be performed by juniors. Finally, I would like to add that the sole apparent disadvantage of the system—that all traces of a record might be lost—does not seem to arise in practice; and when I say that it does not seem to arise in practice, I may, perhaps, be allowed to add that my experience in matters of accounts is not entirely theoretical, seeing that I have myself been in practice for some 24 years.

Suggestions as to Instalment of Modern Methods.

By way of conclusion, I should like to add a few hints as to how modern methods of business organisation may, in my judgment, best be installed, for the benefit of those of you whom I may have succeeded in converting to a more lively appreciation of its advantages. The first thing, it seems to me, is to bear in mind the all-important necessity of overcoming every prejudice against the proposed change. It is practically hopeless to expect to

achieve success if the bookkeeping staff be not enthusiastically in favour of the alterations contemplated—no matter what may be the respective merits of the two systems. The first point, therefore, is to educate the staff up to an appreciation of the advantages of the newer methods. When one is dealing with men of sufficient age to have firmly set ideas, I find that it is far easier to persuade them as to the advantages of the loose-leaf system than those of the card (or slip) system; and this, of course, is quite natural, for while in use a loose-leaf system is handled in precisely the same manner as the bound book system, with the result that the bookkeepers have nothing fresh to learn as to its use. Young men, however, have not, as a rule, the same prejudice against card (or slip) systems; and in a comparatively few years, I imagine, there will be nothing to choose between the two from this particular point of view. Another somewhat important matter to be borne in mind, however, is that so much has been said from time to time as to the economic advantages of modern methods that this has not unnaturally induced a fear of unemployment on the part of some bookkeepers. It is as well to recognise this, for it is undoubtedly the fact that a bookkeeper employing modern methods can accomplish at least 50 per cent. more work than one rigidly adhering to the use of bound books. To combat opposition based on this standpoint it is important to suggest in the first instance that, if a reduction of the bookkeeping staff were in contemplation, it would certainly not be the most experienced and most valuable bookkeepers that would be dispensed with. It is always the indifferent workman who has the most to fear from unemployment; in this way one may avoid estranging the sympathies of at all events the better class of bookkeeper. But I would point out that the clerical staff of practically every business concern is inadequate; almost everywhere one finds the same view expressed—that accounting, being a non-productive department, its expenses must be kept down to the lowest possible level; and, as a rule, they are kept down to level considerably below that of real efficiency. An economy in the recording departments of the financial side of a business house would enable greater expenditure to be incurred in other directions, notably in connection with the cost department, and on financial and statistical records generally; while there can be no question in my mind that these newer varieties of activity would be far the most interesting to the man of real ability. If these facts be pointed out, it is not, as a rule, difficult to get the staff on one's side; to get them really interested in the work, and eager to prove its success. The next step, I think, is to guard against extremes; to introduce whatever reforms are deemed desirable as gradually as possible. With first-entry records this is not always easy; but even here something may be done, by installing the system first (say) with regard to purchases, then to sales, and afterwards to cash; opening out new fields in connection with additional costing records, and statistics generally, as opportunities arise.   With regard to Ledgers, however, it is quite a simple matter to proceed by instalments.   There, I would say, always begin from choice with the most proficient Ledger-keeper; instal him with the new system first, and use your best influence to ensure that when he has done his work he is not called upon to help others with theirs.   It will then be but a very short time before the remainder of the Ledger-keepers notice that the new system lightens the work of the Ledger-keeper; and when that fact has been appreciated all opposition is likely to be at an end, and—so far from there being any further reluctance to accept the reforms—each Ledger-keeper will then be eager to be the next to have his books converted.

Conclusion.

I need hardly add that I am fully conscious that these few remarks that I have the opportunity of presenting to you on the subject of Business Organisation with relation to modern methods, and with special reference to Fraud, have been anything but exhaustive; but if I should have succeeded in arousing your interest in the matter, in suggesting to you that there are possibilities in these new methods which seem to promise a far more efficient and all-round serviceable system of accounting than is ordinarily practicable where the employment of bound books of account is adhered to, I feel that I shall not have been altogether wasting your time; and that, in proportion as you act upon, and profit by, my suggestions, so you will be able increasingly to advance the interests of your clients, and also the progress of the science of accounting which we all have at heart.

SOME SUGGESTIONS ON STOCK ACCOUNTS AND STOCKTAKING

Lawrence R. Dicksee

The Chartered Accountant Students Society of London.

Some Suggestions on Stock Accounts and Stocktaking.

By Professor LAWRENCE R. DICKSEE, M.Com., F.C.A.

A PAPER read at a meeting of the above Society, held on Wednesday, 9th April 1913, at 6 p.m.

In choosing as the subject of my paper to you this evening, "Some Suggestions on Stock Accounts and Stocktaking," I have to a large extent been influenced by the hope that, the subject being one to which but little attention has hitherto been directed, at all events by lecturers, I may, by its mere novelty, arouse your interest, and thus encourage a discussion which may be useful to us all, as bringing about an exchange of views and of experiences.

You may perhaps remember that, a year or so ago, on one of those occasions when the lay press was devoting space to the consideration of "the value of an audit" in the fitful intervals available between the discussion of more exciting and more popular subjects, the question was raised—by no means for the first time—as to how far it was reasonable to expect a company auditor to make himself responsible for the valuation placed by the directors, or their manager, on the amount of Stock-in-Trade on hand. It seemed to me at the time, and it seems so still, that the primary duty of a company auditor is to audit the accounts of a company, and to give his opinion as to whether or not they represent a true and correct view of that company's position, so far as he is able to gauge from the material that is placed before him. But at the same time it has occurred to me, and doubtless it must have occurred to many of you, that the weak part about the audit of the accounts of any ordinary trading concern is the stocktaking valuation—a valuation which is not based on any continuous record of the movements of goods, but solely on an inventory taken on a particular date.

In the ordinary course of events, so far as my experience goes (and if any of you have a different experience, I hope you will let us have the benefit of it later on), Stock Accounts are for all practical purposes non-existent in connection with the ordinary trading company, and accordingly cannot be audited in the sense that the accounts themselves are audited. We know, of course, that there are exceptions : thus it is now the rule, rather than the exception, for a manufacturing concern to keep more or less reliable records of the receipts and issues of its stores of raw materials. Similarly, it is customary for hotels, and wine merchants, to keep fairly reliable Stock Accounts; and jewellers, as a rule, keep Stock Accounts which certainly do not err on the side of simplicity. In the great majority of cases, however, if any record at all is kept of the daily movements of the actual goods that are dealt in (the goods from the sale of which the undertaking derives its chief profits), those records are not organised by the Accounts Department; but are mere memoranda, more or less imperfect and unreliable, kept by (or under the supervision of) the departmental managers, and as such in no way link up with the system of accounts as a whole, nor do they form any part of the record that comes within the cognisance of the auditor in the ordinary course of events.

We are, I take it, all agreed as to the great superiority of the ordinary commercial system of accounts over the system now employed only by Government Departments and certain charitable and kindred institutions, under which only transactions involving the actual receipt or payment of money are recognised and recorded; but, in the complacency bred of the admitted superiority of the commercial system, we are, perhaps, a little apt to overlook the fact that it, in its turn, is singularly incomplete —perhaps more incomplete as a system of recording business transactions than the so-called "cash system" is as a system of recording the transactions of a Government Department or of a charitable institution. It is doubtless a distinct step forward to recognise that something of sufficient importance to be worth recording has occurred when a business man has entered into an obligation which, sooner or later, will mature into a liability on the part of someone to pay somebody else an agreed sum of money, instead of waiting until the actual payment takes place before making any record whatever of what has occurred; but it is, I think, shutting one's eyes to the conditions under which business is transacted, to assume (as the ordinary commercial system of accounting apparently does) that business is exclusively made up of the incurring of liabilities to make payments at future dates, and their subsequent discharge. Under that system, with great elaboration of detail, we keep our Bought and Sold Ledgers on a very complete system of double-entry, so that if we want to see the state of any particular account at any given moment of time, we may not only see how the account stands at that particular moment, but exactly why it so stands and what are the various items (or transactions) that have brought about the stated result; but, in spite of the fact that the real basis of both Bought and Sold Ledgers is, to a very large extent, made up of the movements of goods inwards and outwards, we make no similar attempt to keep any account (or series of accounts) that will give us a continuous record of the movements of our goods, such as would enable us to keep an effective supervision over those responsible for the safe custody of these goods, or an independent check upon those responsible for the periodical valuation of the stocktaking. On the contrary, the Goods Account of itself for all practical purposes shows nothing at all. Before any meaning whatsoever can be attached to it, it has to be supplemented by the periodical stocktaking valuation; and it is not until that valuation has been compiled that one is able to prepare the Trading Account, which, in the nature of things, is the very foundation of the whole system of accounts in connection with every trading business.

But, even with the aid of the Trading Account, we may well ask ourselves what it is that we have achieved? Granted the correctness of all the other figures, the Trading Account, as ordinarily complied, provides us with a figure of Gross Profit; and if the figure so arrived at is one that commends itself to our credulity, as being probable under the circumstances, it is very apt to be accepted off-hand—or, if not precisely off-hand, at all events without any very serious attempt to inquire precisely how that aggregate total of Gross Profits has been built up. Indeed, a Scottish Chartered Accountant of considerable experience once expressed the view that a figure of Gross Profit, so compiled, was really nothing more than "an unreconciled difference in books"; and although this may be a somewhat exaggerated view of the position, the customary method of arriving at Gross Profits is very similar to—and has most of the defects of—the manner of arriving at Net Profits by single-entry that was at one time almost universal. Whatever may be its conveniences, it presents the serious defect that at this particular point our double-entry system is powerless to detect clerical errors, or fraudulent manipulations. Whatever may be the explanation, and whatever may have been the motive,

if the Stock has been over-valued, the Gross Profit (and for that reason also the Net Profit) will have been over-valued to precisely the same extent; if the Stock has been undervalued, both the Gross Profit and the Net Profit will be undervalued to the same extent.

In this connection it is, I think, not without interest to consider the normal proportions of Stock towards Net Profit. If we find that, in the majority of cases, the total value of the unsold Stock was very considerably less than the annual Net Profit, the risk of any error in the stock-taking valuation might be regarded as comparatively unimportant; but, looking through the published accounts of a dozen large trading concerns taken at random, I find that in only one case is the Net Profit larger than the stocktaking valuation; that on the average the Stock is nearly three times as large as the annual Net Profit; thus an error of (say) 5 per cent. only in the valuation of the Stock would cause an error of nearly 15 per cent. in the statement of the annual Net Profit. It will thus be seen that the matter is one that may very easily assume quite serious proportions, even when the extent of the actual error is not particularly alarming in itself; but, of course, the risk of inconvenient consequences, arising from errors in the stocktaking valuation, does not stop here. In the majority of cases selling prices are governed almost entirely by considerations of profit. If one forms the erroneous conclusion that one's profits are larger than they really are, there is a strong likelihood that future selling prices will be reduced, with the result that future profits will be appreciably curtailed until the extent of the error has been comprehended. Conversely, if Stock has been undervalued, there is a likelihood that selling prices will be put up, which, in these days of competition, is likely to mean that much business will be lost altogether which might have been transacted at a reasonable profit. The question which I invite you to consider with me this evening is as to whether it is desirable that traders should continue to keep their accounts on a system which thus fails to give them any assistance whatever on one of the most vital matters in connection with the conduct of their business; and then, if you agree with me that such a state of affairs is undesirable, we may pass on (as time permits) to an inquiry as to whether it is practicable to suggest any amended system that will remedy these defects, without imposing any prohibitive charge upon profits, or involving so much "red tape" as to make the ordinary conduct of business practically impossible.

First of all, as to whether any alteration is desirable: I do not propose to overload this part of my paper by elaborating all possible arguments that might be raised. I have already drawn attention to the necessarily unsatisfactory features of accounts which provide the trader with no explanation whatever as to how his Gross Profit has been arrived at, save perhaps on the assumption that all the sales he has effected in any one department have been effected at a uniform rate of profit. After all, if I can establish one really convincing reason in favour of a change, I should have carried my point quite sufficiently to justify proceeding to my inquiry as to how a better state of affairs can be brought about without incurring a prohibitive increase in standing expenses; and since I am addressing an audience of professional accountants and accountant students, I naturally prefer to select as my argument the greatly increased facility for audit.

In the nature of things, where there is no record there can be no audit. On the other hand, it is a perfectly simple matter to audit any transactions, no matter how voluminous or how complicated, if they have all been duly recorded. Some of us doubtless have had experience, at one time or another, of errors in stocktaking valuations, fraudulent and otherwise. Those of us who have had no such experience must at least have heard of such cases, of which perhaps the best known are the misfeasance summons brought against the auditors of *The Kingston Cotton Mills, Lim.*, the case of alleged negligence (heard comparatively recently by the Lord Chief Justice) in the combined actions of *Mead v. Ball, Baker & Co.*, and *Henry Squire (Cash Chemists), Lim. v. Ball, Baker & Co.*, and the criminal proceedings arising out of the winding up of *Measures Brothers, Lim.* In each of these cases it was evident that there had been persistent and deliberate over-valuation of Stock extending over several years; but the auditors were held not to be responsible in the two first-named cases, and in the third case the question of their responsibility never came before the Court at all. I need perhaps hardly remind you that in every case where a fraudulent falsification of accounts is possible without detection, it is (to say the least of it) quite conceivable that a wholly innocent mistake might have passed undetected with equal facility. The auditor, as we know, is not responsible in law for the stocktaking valuation. He usually does not begin his audit until after the Stock has been " taken," when, of course, it would be too late for him to verify items, even supposing he possessed the necessary technical skill to enable him to distinguish between one kind of goods and another— which, after all, would be a quite unreasonable assumption to make in all cases, however true it may be in some. The auditor's duty in connection with the stocktaking under present conditions appears to be of a very limited description. If the amount of the stocktaking valuation be such that its incorporation in the accounts will produce incredible results, then certainly the auditor will be negligent, if, without further inquiry, he believes the results which the accounts show; but this is about as far

as the auditor's legal liability takes him, provided the correctness of the valuation has been certified by some responsible officer of the company. Indeed, although it is, I believe, the invariable practice of auditors to verify the clerical accuracy of stocktaking valuations, it is quite doubtful whether even this is required of them. On the principle that it is useless to strain at the gnat, if one must perforce swallow the camel, it is at least open to question whether the auditor is not just as entitled to accept the certificates of the clerical staff that the clerical work has been accurately performed, as he is to accept the certificate of (say) the general manager that the valuation of the various items has been conducted on proper principles. However that may be, the amount of work that the auditor is able to put into the verification of a stocktaking valuation is necessarily of a very limited character; so limited that he cannot in reason be expected to be responsible for the ultimate figure, as actually incorporated in the accounts themselves; and, bearing in mind that there is under ordinary circumstances absolutely nothing to check this figure, except (as I have said) the reasonable probability of the results shown by the accounts incorporating it, if we are going to look the facts in the face, we must admit that for all practical purposes there is no effective audit so far as this part of a company's accounts is concerned—for the all-sufficient reason that there is no record of day to day transactions capable of being audited, or capable of being used in any way as a check on the stocktaking inventory.

If there were such a record, the whole position would be different, and in every way more satisfactory. If traders kept Stock Accounts, showing their purchases and sales under suitable headings, thus raising accounts which would show from day to day the balance of Stock on hand under each such heading, these accounts would be available as a verification of the quantities of goods included in the stocktaking inventory; and they would make the verification of prices a comparatively simple matter, even to one unversed in the intricacies of the particular industry concerned. I do not say that, under such circumstances, it would be impossible for a fraudulent managing director, or a fraudulent stock-keeper, to hoodwink the professional auditor, who is naturally an expert in accounts rather than in commodities; but I do say (and I think you will all agree with me) that if any reasonably accurate system of Stock Accounts could be installed, kept by those attached to the Accounts Department rather than by those attached to the various trading (or operating) departments, such frauds would be rendered far more difficult and more dangerous, and for those reasons would be far less likely to occur.

Another argument in favour of such Stock Accounts, which is perhaps more likely to appeal to the average ccmpany director than mere facility for audit, is the greatly improved position of the company in the event of its having to claim to be indemnified against loss under a policy of fire insurance. It is true that fire insurance companies are in general not over-strict in the matter of insisting upon absolute proof of loss. If they were, I really do not know what would be the use of a fire insurance policy to the average trader. But, for all that, it would be much more satisfactory all round, and would, I am satisfied, produce better results to the honest claimant if he could produce records showing the exact (or even the approximate) quantities of the different kinds of goods that he had in hand at the time when the fire took place.

Much more might be said under this heading, as to the advantages to every trader of reliable Stock Accounts, if, indeed, there were any real need to labour the point; but, as time presses, I will proceed without more ado to the inquiry as to what is possible in the direction of Stock Accounts, having regard to practical considerations, and especially to the necessity of avoiding any over-elaborate system which would interfere with the despatch of business and materially increase the costs of working.

To deal at all adequately with this part of my subject, it would be necessary to devote an entire paper to the problem as applied to a single industry—or at least to a single class of industry. Accordingly, I can only hope to put my suggestions to you in quite general terms. I trust, however, that what I may have to say will arouse your interest in the subject, and induce you to inquire for yourselves what might be done in connection with some one, or more, of the audits with which you come in daily contact.

The first point that suggests itself as an insuperable, or almost insuperable, difficulty is the fact that (so far at all events as retailers are concerned) goods are continually being handled in quite small quantities, with the result that the record, if it is to be a detailed record of trans-actions, must necessarily be a very voluminous record of transactions often quite small in themselves. I admit the difficulty; but if we are never to make a move in the direction of progress until we are certain that we are in a position to achieve perfection, I am afraid that progress will always be slow. To take the case of the ordinary retail establishment—the case which seems to present the maximum amount of difficulty—What do we find? In the vast majority of cases, nothing like the whole of the retailer's stock is in his shop windows, or even on the shelves behind the counters. The bulk of his stock is, as a rule, stored elsewhere, "in reserve"; and the depart-mental manager always keeps some sort of Stock Accounts in connection with this reserve stock. My point is that, in so far as he thus attempts to keep his own Stock Accounts, he is wasting his time and the time of his employers, who probably employ dozens of young men far more competent to keep such accounts than he is, at perhaps one-tenth of the salary that they pay him. A very little additional expenditure (if, indeed, there need be any additional expenditure at all) in the way of supplying assistants from the Accounts Department to keep the records of movements of Reserve Stock in a systematic and reliable way would regularise these accounts, and make them suitable for our present pur-poses; at the same time, they would be at least as useful to the departmental manager as the sort of record that he now keeps, while leaving him free to devote the whole of his energies to work which (presumably) he is much better fitted to accomplish satisfactorily.

The introduction of organisation into this part of the work would undoubtedly lead to good results all round. It would lead to a definite location for each kind of goods. It would probably lead to each kind of goods being formally identified with a distinctive number, so that thereafter no special technical knowledge would be neces-sary on the part of those called upon to handle the goods, or to prepare the stocktaking inventory. The tedious business of stocktaking would thus be made propor-tionately easier, while the responsibility of advising departmental managers when stocks get short might be thrown upon the Accounts Department; in many cases this last would be a distinct advantage, as the movements of the Accounts Department (if it be worthy of its name) should at all times be methodical, whereas those of departmental managers are sometimes very much less so.

Even if the idea which I am putting before you could be carried no further in practice than the systematising of records of movements of goods into, and out of, Reserve Stock, we should have made a distinct step forward; but there remains to be considered the question as to how far it would be practicable to go in connection with records of the movements of goods behind the counter, and in the shop winodws. Here, speaking (as we are speaking) in general terms, I can only offer a few general suggestions. It is possible they may seem to you to be impracticable; but the question as to whether or not any particular innovation in the matter of improved organisation is feasible depends, I have always found, chiefly on the views of those who have got to carry it out. Within limits, any reasonable system can be carried out successfully in practice, if those upon whom the actual work devolves can be convinced that it is really worth while. Doubtless, from time to time, we have all of us come across systems, which, because of some defect in fundamental design, represent so much wasted effort. Practically anything can be accomplished, if it is thought worth while; and so long as the details are well thought out it is usually quite possible to get what one wants, without increasing the work that any individual (or any class of individuals) have got to perform from day to day. I will make, then, just one or two general suggestions under this heading, leaving you to elaborate details to suit individual purposes.

First of all, I need perhaps hardly remind you that in every retail concern, where goods are sold by numerous assistants, there must of necessity exist a system of marking all goods in such a way as to indicate their respective selling prices. Sometimes goods are sold in fixed units, or quantities; at other times lengths may be cut off rolls of goods (as in the case of textile fabrics), or the required quantities may be sold by weight from bulk. The suggestion which I have to put forward—which I put forward in quite a tentative way, not as essential to my scheme, but as being merely one possible way of carrying it out in practice—is that where articles are sold in definite units, there should be attached to the marking ticket a detachable stock ticket (or slip) sufficiently identifying the nature of the article for stock-keeping purposes, which slip should be detached by the salesman when he sells the goods, and placed by him in some lock-up receptacle. Similarly in the case of goods which are sold in smaller quantities from bulk, there should be attached to the marking ticket a corresponding number of perforated stock slips, each representing a definite unit of quantity—or (if necessary) slips of different colours, representing different units of quantity. By this means it would always be possible, by inspecting the marking ticket and the stock slips attached, to ascertain the actual quantity of each kind of goods that should be in stock. The stock slips detached by the various salesmen, and deposited by them in their respective lock-up receptacles, should from time to time be transmitted to the Accounts Department, where they would be sorted out according to the kinds of goods they represented, a process which would be rendered easy by the identification numbers. Having sorted them out into heaps, it would be a simple matter to arrive at daily totals of sales under different headings by means of a mechanical adder; and these daily totals might be entered up on cards representing Stock Accounts for the different kinds of goods. At frequent intervals the Stock Ledger clerk should compare his Ledger balances with the tally of slips unsold attached to the marking tickets of the various kinds of goods; in that way all clerical errors would be discovered, and when discovered could be easily adjusted, while early attention would be drawn to any irregularities.

The system is one by which a very effective and detailed record of stock movements could be maintained, even in connection with a retail business, at a cost which would be negligible, expressed as a percentage on the Sales or on the Gross Profit. But, of course, I am only giving it to you in outline; the details would have to be elaborated to suit each particular case.

Some may object that any such system would be impracticable on account of the time that would be occupied in adjusting the discrepancies that would inevitably be discovered. One might as well argue that double-entry is undesirable, because of the time occasionally occupied in detecting errors causing differences in balancing which, under a single-entry system, would never have been brought to light at all. Surely it is only reasonable to assume that, in the ordinary course of events, all kinds of errors that any system of accounting may bring to light are productive of loss, but that the tendency is to reduce the number of errors the more strictly they are inquired into; thus here, as elsewhere, careful attention to detail, combined with a proper system of organisation, pays, although exactly how and why it pays may not be at once apparent to the superficial inquirer.

In judging these suggestions, I would ask you particularly not to condemn them off-hand on account of the amount of clerical work that they would involve. Although I have been dealing with the subject only in general terms, I have been taking the case of the ordinary shopkeeper, which is the one that probably presents the greatest difficulties in the matter of mere bulk of record. There must be many cases in which detailed Stock Accounts could be kept which would involve very much less clerical work; but, even in the case of the shopkeeper, I very much doubt whether the addition to the existing clerical staff need be very great. I think it would be very much more a question of systematising and regularising a great deal of work that at present goes to waste. In most shops special commissions are allowed to the salesmen on certain "lines" of goods. How do you suppose it is possible for the accounts, showing the commission that each salesman is entitled to, to be prepared, and to be checked, without performing work which, if properly directed, would go a long way towards building up reliable Stock Accounts all round? There was a time—not so very long ago, either—when most manufacturers considered it impracticable to keep really detailed accounts of their stores of raw materials. Thanks to the great facilities provided by card and loose-leaf systems, the number of manufacturers holding those views is rapidly diminishing; and, as instancing what may be accomplished by good organisation, I might mention the case of one manufacturing business with a subscribed capital of about a million sterling, which has its Stores of raw materials divided into 1,200 Ledger Accounts, which are accurately kept, and made to balance, at a cost in clerical salaries of less than £3 a week.

So long as one does not want to do a thing, it is always easy to find many excellent reasons why it is impossible; but directly the advantages of reliable Stock Accounts are appreciated, the difficulties in the way of keeping them will, I am convinced, be found by no means insuperable, and I have little hesitation in saying that in every case the cost is likely to be more than recouped out of the resultant economies. So long as the present practice continues there will always be a weak point in the audit of the accounts of concerns where the normal value of the Stock-in-trade largely exceeds the average annual Profits, because there will be no satisfactory means open to the auditor of verifying the stocktaking valuation. It is manifestly unreasonable to blame company auditors for the present position of affairs; but it is, I think, for us, as accountants, to be continually on the look out for new ideas— ideas that, if developed, will tend to increase the value of our work, and to add to the efficiency of the business concerns with which we are connected. So long as we remained wedded to the old "Italian" system, and regarded entries in bound books as the only reliable mode of record for accounting transactions, so long was any detailed record of Stock movements impossible to the great majority of business houses; but, now that we have definitely discarded this old-fashioned notion as to the sanctity of bound books, and have recognised that other methods of accounting may be devised, equally safe, and far more efficient, it is time, I think, that we should seriously direct our attention to the question whether these new methods cannot with advantage be extended to the systematic record of movements of goods as well as of money and monetary liabilities, thus making the accounting system of an ordinary trading concern a complete system of accounting in every respect, and accordingly one capable of being audited with a degree of completeness which in the nature of things has hitherto been impossible.

MODERN ACCOUNTANCY METHODS
IN RELATION TO BUSINESS EFFICIENCY

Lawrence R. Dicksee

Modern Accountancy Methods in Relation to Business Efficiency.

By L. R. Dicksee, M.Com., F.C.A.

A Lecture delivered at the Hall of the London School of Economics and Political Science (University of London), Clare Market, Kingsway, W.C., on 13th October 1914, Sir William Plender, F.C.A., in the chair.

I need perhaps hardly say that, in the limited time available to me this evening, I have no intention of attempting to give you anything like a complete survey of the whole subject of accounting, and the various methods employed under modern conditions to achieve its purposes. Such a task would be altogether impossible, and would perhaps (even if it were possible) not be altogether appropriate to the present occasion, when there are doubtless many among my audience who have not hitherto made any serious study of the subject. My aim accordingly will be not so much to impart information this evening as it will be to arouse your interest in the science of Accounting by some suggestions as to the uses to which it has been put in the past, and still more as to the further uses to which it might be put in the future with great advantage to all concerned ; and, in proceeding upon these lines, it will be my aim (as far as possible) to avoid technicalities.

To many persons the study of Accounting seems altogether uninteresting, because, to their minds, it is inseparably connected with the handling of huge masses of figures. While I certainly would not go so far as to assert that useful accounts can be designed, or even kept, by those who have " no head for figures," it is, I think, important that it should be quite clearly understood at the outset that Accounting is not primarily a question of handling figures at all ; that it is indeed essentially a question of recording events, and that the use of figures in connection with this record is merely a means to enable the events so recorded to be readily marshalled in such a form as will enable one, not merely to grasp the significance of each separate event, but also the combined effect of any desired series of events. Accordingly it is quite wrong to suppose that the study of Accounting must necessarily be dry and uninteresting, merely because one finds oneself unable to take any great interest in mathematical problems.

The word " Account," as you all know, by no means necessarily means a statement, or a bill, showing the monetary indebtedness of one party to another. One can with equal propriety speak of the " account " of a battle, a railway accident, or any other event ; and that, indeed, more nearly represents the real significance of the word. Quite possibly any very clear description of a battle would involve some mention of figures, some comparison of figures and some general deductions drawn from marshalling those figures together ; but it would be impossible to convey any intelligent description of a battle or a railway accident by the use of figures only, and it would be equally impossible by the use of figures only to convey any very complete impression of the practical effect of business transactions. But, because business transactions tend as a rule to run on certain fairly well-defined lines—tend in fact, to run " in grooves "—it is practicable, in connection with business accounting, to adopt methods that enable the purely verbal description of the facts to be reduced to a minimum ; and that, of course, is an arrangement that makes for convenience, in that by reducing the mass of words that have to be read before the account can be interpreted, one is able to save a corresponding amount of time without introducing any corresponding element of uncertainty.

Clearly, however, it is only in so far as it may be possible to save time without any uncertainty resulting that the device is one to be encouraged, and it is, of course, important to bear in mind that those who seek to understand accounts must be familiar with the conventional methods employed ; in just the same way, anyone wishing to de-code a telegram sent in cipher must first make himself familiar with the cipher employed. Following this analogy a little further, the man who only has occasion to de-code cipher telegrams very occasionally need not, of course, memorise the code (or cipher) employed ; but one who is continually employed on such work must necessarily have the code at his fingers' ends. For instance, it would be hopeless to expect anyone unfamiliar with the Morse code to be a successful wireless operator, although perhaps at first glance one might be inclined to think that anyone could note down " dots and dashes," and afterwards translate them from the book. It is, I think, a quite safe generalisation, that a certain amount of knowledge, sufficiently deeply rooted to be worthy of the name " knowledge," is necessary for the successful pursuit of any study ; and in connection with Accounting, no one is likely to get very far until he is thoroughly familiar with the ordinary conventions of Accounting, which constitute the technique of that science. But, for our purposes this evening, we can, I think, quite safely put all these upon one side, and proceed to consider the question. Granted that there is a workable technique of Accounting, of what practical use is Accounting to the business man ?

We know, of course, that, even to-day, all business men do not keep proper accounts. Were this not the case it would clearly have been quite unnecessary for Parliament to pass an Act, which only came into force six months ago, making it a criminal offence for a bankrupt, who had failed on a previous occasion, to be unable to produce accounts reasonably disclosing the nature of his business transactions. We also know (or, if you do not happen to know it, you may, I think, safely take it as a fact from me) that in over 70 per cent. of the bankruptcies that have occurred in this country during the last thirty years no proper accounts have been kept by the debtor. It is not perhaps always easy to distinguish between cause and effect. Doubtless some traders in financial difficulties give up keeping any systematic record of their transactions simply because they have no heart to go on recording events that are uniformly depressing. Others may give up keeping accounts, or abstain from starting the keeping of accounts, because from the outset they intend to be dishonest whenever the opportunity arises; in such circumstances, a truthful record of their achievements would be most incriminating. But, making all due allowance for those cases in which the fear of impending bankruptcy, or the desire to be dishonest, is the reason for not keeping proper accounts, there can, I think, be little doubt that, in a far greater number of cases, it is the failure to keep proper accounts that brings about the bankruptcy; because, in the absence of such accounts, the trader has nothing but his memory to rely upon as to where he is and what he has been doing.

We have doubtless all heard of remarkable men in the past who achieved large fortunes—or at least became well-to-do from very small beginnings—and yet have kept no accounts, and were perhaps not even able to read or write. There are doubtless well authenticated cases of such successes in the past, and it is perhaps conceivable that similar successes may yet be achieved in the future, although the trend of modern business has certainly altered in the direction of making that less and less likely. But, however that may be, I do not think that anyone would be likely so far to confuse cause and effect as to suggest that anyone in the past achieved success in business *because* he was unable to read or write; nor, after a little reflection, do I think anyone would contend that neglect to keep proper accounts would be likely to increase a business man's chances of success.

This, after all, is a matter which (within limits) each one of you can readily test for himself or herself, even although you may have no direct connection with business. In one sense we all have business affairs, for we all have our own personal expenses, and we have to obtain from some source or other the means of meeting those expenses—quite commonly it is the last-named that presents the greater difficulty. Some of you perhaps keep a systematic account of your personal receipts and payments; others may never have attempted anything of the kind. Others, again, may have attempted it in the past, and given it up, because you were never able to make your accounts come right—because, in some extraordinary way, you never had in hand the money which your record showed that you ought to have in hand. Were it possible to make any systematic comparison, there can, I think, be little doubt that it would be found that those of you who have succeeded in keeping a correct and systematic record of your receipts and payments have also succeeded in getting very much better value for those payments than those of you who keep no such accounts. A contemplation of expenditure incurred sometimes gives rise to feelings of depression that one should have wasted so much money; but, at all events on the majority of characters, it will in the long run tend to avoid similar waste in the future. If it did not, the value of the record would, of course, be very slight indeed, but at all events the vast majority of persons are capable of learning something by experience. But no one can learn anything from events, the significance of which they do not appreciate. The importance of the record here is not that it enables one to consider in a hazy sort of way (which may be quite misleading) events which one believes to have occurred, but rather that it provides us with definite and reliable information as to what actually has happened, so that, having the facts clearly before us, we may benefit by the experience, if we are not wholly unteachable.

In the nature of things there can be no miraculous property in accounts which enables them of themselves to achieve any useful purpose whatever. One might just as well have no accounts at all, as have accounts that are never looked at at all. This perhaps sounds very obvious when stated in this form, but I venture to think you would be surprised if you knew what a large proportion of so-called business men do in fact never look at their accounts from year's end to year's end.

But if the average business man is not so wide-awake as he should be to the importance of profiting by his experience through an intelligent survey of his accounts, there is at least one function of accounts that he does usually understand quite well; indeed, sometimes he understands it so well that he thinks it is the only use to which accounts can be put. And that is as a record of transactions between himself on the one side, and his customers or supplying houses (as the case may be) on the other side. Accounts, properly kept, will disclose everything that has happened in whatever form may be most convenient for subsequent reference. Among other things, they will collect together under one heading the transactions of a business house with each one of its customers, so that an inspection of this account, or heading, will show at a glance the indebtedness incurred by that customer from time to time, how and when he discharged that indebtedness, and what (if any) balance remains undischarged. A separate account on these lines dealing with the transactions of each separate customer enables us to see, not merely that we are getting in all the debts that are due to us as and when they should be received ; it also enables us, if we have eyes to see, to find out which accounts are growing, and which accounts are dwindling or even dead ; and incidentally it will also show us which (if any) accounts are growing bigger than we like to see them. If necessary, these accounts can with a very little ingenuity be developed so as to enable us to see which kind of goods that we trade in is mostly in demand with each separate customer ; indeed there is no limit to the way in which our transactions with customers may be split up, or classified, from different points of view, or aggregated to enable us to arrive at general impressions along particular lines. What I have said with regard to customers' accounts applies equally to the accounts of supplying houses—those from whom we purchase supplies of manufactured goods or raw materials, as the case may be.

As I said just now, even the most unbusinesslike man appreciates the value of accurate accounts with his debtors and with his creditors, but that does not mean at all that he necessarily appreciates all the various ways in which such accounts may be regarded, a few of which I have just mentioned. What it does mean is that he recognises the importance of knowing what is owing to him, and knowing what he owes ; and so often is it the case that he is unable to appreciate the value of anything more than this, that accounts giving this very incomplete information have for very many years past been dignified with the name of a " system." " Single-entry," as this so-called system is called, is a thoroughly incomplete system of accounting, in that it only shows one of the very many things that the intelligent trader, or manufacturer, would require to know ; but in spite of its incompleteness it is quite inaccurate to describe it as " single-entry," in that the term so used is naturally used in contrast with the term " double-entry." The employment of the word " single " in opposition to the word " double " clearly suggests (if it means anything at all) that the former system involves only half the labour required to complete the record upon the latter, or " double-entry," system. This is a most misleading view of the position. It would involve too many technicalities for me to explain to you this evening the real difference between single-entry and double-entry, but you may take it from me that, so far from double-entry involving twice the work of single-entry, it need not at the very outside involve more than 20 per cent. additional labour ; indeed, an up-to-date double-entry system often involves considerably less time in the keeping than the old-fashioned single-entry system.

But even if the double-entry system did involve twice as much work as the single-entry it would be well worth the extra time, trouble, and expense involved, as it provides very much more than twice the amount of useful information, and furthermore provides an automatic check upon its accuracy, which, if not absolutely unfailing, is a very good check for practical purposes so far as it goes. Probably the origin of the idea that single-entry involves much less clerical work than double-entry is that the automatic check provided by the latter draws attention to clerical errors, and accordingly demands that these errors shall be searched for and discovered—a process that naturally takes time, particularly if no modern labour-saving devices be employed, and the bookkeeping staff be inexpert. It is obvious, however, that if the staff make mistakes under the double-entry system, they are at least equally likely to make mistakes with single-entry. The fact that single-entry provides no means of ascertaining whether mistakes have been made or not naturally prevents time being occupied in the searching out for those mistakes and correcting them ; but this saving clearly cannot in fairness be regarded as an advantage of single-entry. If one were content with incorrect records, one could save the time that has to be occupied in looking for mistakes, even under double-entry. But manifestly the proper course is not to pretend that no mistakes exist, and abstain from adopting checking devices, for fear mistakes should be discovered ; but rather to devise methods which in the first instance will make mistakes unlikely, and in the second instance enable them to be detected rapidly when they do occur, by means of one of the somewhat numerous modern devices for sectional balancing now in general use.

Whatever may be the nature of the business concern whose accounts are being recorded, the events that are incorporated in its accounting records are usually described as " transactions." The word " transaction " is so generally employed in this connection that its true meaning is very much in danger of being lost sight of. If (discarding all technicalities) we were to regard the accounting system of a business as a diary, or daily record of events, we should doubtless realise that no diary kept by human hands could possibly be absolutely exhaustive ;

also that in so far as it fell short of being exhaustive it would be incomplete, with the result that, no matter how ingeniously we might marshal and recapitulate the recorded matter, it would still remain not a complete record of everything that had happened, but merely a record of such events as we had thought to be of sufficient importance to merit a record in our diary. The moral of this is, of course, that in this imperfect world we must never expect a statement of accounts to be otherwise than incomplete in the sum of its aspects; also that we must ever be on the alert to realise that omissions that are unimportant from some points of view may be important from other points of view; and in particular that, if for any reason we wish to review past records from an entirely novel standpoint, we may find that we have not got available all the necessary material for this new review of past records.

I said just now that the word "transactions" had been adopted as a sort of technical term in connection with accounting records. The term itself, of course, means precisely the same thing as "cross-dealings" or "transfers," and in one sense it aptly states the somewhat obvious fact that practically every conceivable form of business activity involves the passing of some form of wealth from one party to another. Someone receives the benefit of every such transaction at the hands of somebody else, who has imparted that benefit. One might express this by saying that there can be no receipt without a corresponding payment, were it not for this fact that the term "payment" (as ordinarily used) is limited to monetary payments, whereas here, of course, we are thinking of the disbursement not merely of moneys, but also of commodities of different kinds, or services of different kinds, all of which either have an agreed—or at all events an ascertainable—money value, and are therefore capable of being expressed in terms of money, subject to the proviso (and this, of course, is important) that the money value attached to them may require to be reconsidered later on, because it may be subject to alteration.

The idea of every transaction representing a flow of wealth from one party to another is exceedingly convenient because it lends itself very well to the double-entry idea, the essence of which is that there must be two parties affected by every transaction, and that if you record each transaction from the point of view of both of those parties you have recorded it completely. I have no desire to belittle the double-entry system of accounting. The mere fact that it has survived for more than 400 years as being *par excellence* THE system of recording business transactions shows, at least to my mind,

that it must be a system possessing very considerable practical merits or it would not for so long have stood the test of time. The time test is not, of course, conclusive in itself; but when we reflect upon the enormous differences between the handling of business affairs to-day and during the latter half of the fifteenth century, we must see, I think, that a system that was able to adapt itself to such a very remarkable development of business affairs must be one that has stood the test of time and firmly established its rights to be considered as embodying at all events some permanent principles. At the same time I should like to draw your attention to the fact that nothing ever tends to delay real progress more than the fixed idea that perfection has already been achieved. In a general way, of course, we all know, and admit, that absolute perfection is unattainable by human beings; but a very superficial study of history is sufficient to show that the impression that perfection had been achieved (if only by a single individual) has often been responsible for the stagnation of some art or science for a generation or more.

The fallacy of the supposed perfection of the double-entry system, as handed down to us by the Lombardy merchants of the fifteenth century, is that, so to speak, it views everything in one plane. It is about as true to nature as a system of geometry which regards plane geometry as the only kind in existence, and ignores the fact that there is such a thing as solid geometry. One might even go further, and suggest that in recording the mutual transactions of human beings one ought really to take some account of the fourth dimension; but I purposely avoid pressing this illustration, not because I think it without importance, but because it is unnecessary for my present purpose and because I do not wish to estrange your sympathies by appearing to be unduly fantastic.

To come back to business transactions—that is to say, the actions and reactions of human beings upon each other, which it is desirable to record systematically in order to obtain a correct presentment of their combined effect to date, and in order to gather therefrom experience that will guide us in the conduct of further transactions in the future, to our own better advantage. Regarded from this point of view, what more simple human action can one think of than that of throwing a stone into a pond? Yet, directly we begin to think how such a transaction might—and indeed, should—be recorded, how infinite are its effects! The obvious result is, of course, that the stone sinks. Scientists are able to tell us to a nicety the rate at which it sinks, and demonstrate that that rate depends hardly at all upon the weight of the stone, but solely upon the distance from which it falls, the curve at which it strikes the water, and the density of the water itself. If the pond has a rocky bottom, the stone, having once rested there, will probably remain immovable, or practically immovable, unless disturbed by some external force; but if the bottom of the pond be soft, the stone will continue to exercise a penetrative power which, disregarding external circumstances (and they may easily be important) could no doubt be calculated, if the nature of the bed were known and it were uniformly consistent. The energy that cast the stone into the pond might perhaps be said to lose its force when the bottom is reached, but the energy represented by the dead weight of the stone itself would represent a continuing force, which under favourable conditions would make for further continuous movement. All this represents only one aspect of what has happened, although, of course, even that aspect is capable of being expressed from two points of view, inasmuch as every movement of the stone naturally represents a corresponding movement of the substances through which it passes, and this, following the analogy of ordinary commercial accounting, may be regarded as embodying the principles of double-entry; but to say that it represents a complete statement of the phenomena produced by throwing the stone into the water is to show ourselves very deficient in observational powers.

Apart altogether from the vertical movement of the stone sinking through the water, there will be a re-action caused by its passage, which is evident even to the most casual observer in the circles, or ripples, on the surface. Very little observation will show that the number of such ripples is determined broadly by the velocity of the stone; but, if the pond were sufficiently large, those ripples would seem to lose themselves in the level surface after a time. Yet a little thought certainly seems to suggest the idea that while the disturbance is greatest in the centre, and somewhat rapidly diminishes with each successive circle of ripples of gradually increasing size, there must be some law determining the diffusion of energy; that, however rapid the decrease of energy to create ripples may be, so that even at a comparatively short distance from the point of contact the energy may be only a minute fraction of the original energy, yet under no circumstances can a reflex action thus produced ever arrive at absolute zero. Whether the ripples be perceptible to the naked eye or not, some reflex of the original force must in all cases reach the boundaries of the pond, no matter how large the pond may be; and even there it cannot be altogether lost, but must be taken up (although no doubt only to a modified extent) by the surrounding land. This also we can all test for ourselves, on a sufficiently small pond with sandy banks, by noticing the cumulative effect of successive ripples on the form that these banks assume. But there is yet another effect of dropping the stone into the pond, to which I should like to draw your attention, and that is its effect upon the air over and surrounding the pond. This in the nature of things is far less obvious; but it must, when you come to think of it, be just as real, even if less easily observable. Every disturbance in the level of the water must create a corresponding disturbance in the atmosphere above it, and, although in a less degree, of course—every subsequent movement of the surrounding land must have some effect (however slight) upon the atmosphere above it. Thus, in this very simple illustration, we see that, apart from the obvious effect of the vertical disturbance caused by the stone falling, there is a resultant horizontal disturbance caused by the ripple, which in its turn causes an atmospheric disturbance, moving partly vertically and partly horizontally.

My object in drawing your attention to this very simple example of natural phenomena is to suggest to you that double-entry (as understood in the middle ages, and as to a large extent still practised under modern conditions) is but an imperfect observation of all the consequences of those events which are conveniently called "business transactions." For some purposes it may be a sufficient record. It may be that the reflex actions caused by business transactions are sometimes so slight as to have little or no perceptible effect upon human happenings; but it is, I think, at least very certain that Accounting records based upon these lines are as incomplete as would be, say, scientific observations of the ripples on a pond that left out of account the depth or diameter of the pond on the one hand, and the atmosphere above it on the other hand. It may well be that, for the great majority of business operations, observations in a single plane are sufficient for practical purposes; but it is, I think, even more certain that, being incomplete, as they necessarily are, observations that seem adequate to one generation may—and indeed will—sooner or later be found seriously inadequate to another generation of business men working under very different conditions.

It is good to know the prices at which we can sell our goods, and what is owing to us for the goods we have sold. It is better to know what it ought to cost us to produce and deliver our goods. It is better still to know exactly what the costs of manufacture and of transport are from time to time, so that we may take advantage of everything that is in our favour, and seek to improve even the unfavourable conditions. But it is best of all to realise that customers can only continue to be customers that it pays us to have, so long as they also are working under advantageous conditions. If, by superior skill, we could secure all the profits that there are to ourselves, for how long do you think we should have any solvent customers to trade with ?

Fifty years or so ago, mankind—and particularly business mankind—seem to have been obsessed with the idea that in future everything would be done by machinery. Machinery was then (so to speak) a new toy, and it is hardly surprising that its general employment should have given rise to an age of materialism. Machinery has not merely come to stay, but with every year we find that it is being still further utilised as a factor, not merely in the creation of commodities but also in the creation of services. Even in connection with Accounting much that was formerly done by hand, or by head, is now done by machinery. But we have, I think, now lived sufficiently long in a world of mechanism to realise that mechanism is not the whole work ; but merely a means adopted by human beings to enable them to achieve desired results with greater speed, or greater certainty, than was formerly possible. The factor that the business man is too apt to overlook, even at the present time, is that this is not so much an age of machinery as it is an age of human beings operating machines. To far too small extent does the ordinary Accounting of to-day attempt to take cognisance of this fact, to provide us with really reliable records, not so much of what machinery can do as of what human beings can do ; and in particular what they could be persuaded to do (or not to do) given certain surroundings. Still less does the ordinary Accounting system of to-day attempt to provide us with any reliable record as to how the material used might be altered with advantage, to enable us to get the best possible output from the human machine, taken individually or collectively—but particularly collectively. In so far as any attempt has been made up to the present to organise and systematise human knowledge upon these lines, it is at present not called Accounting, but Statistics or Social Reform. Whatever it may be called, if it is not to work in the dark, it has to depend for its facts upon Accounting and Accountancy methods. While in the nature of things when working under human conditions we cannot hope to attain to absolute perfection, or absolute completeness, we ought, I think, at least to recognise that in Accounting we have the science of observing human effort, and recording it in such a form that it may be made available to enrich our experiences, as being not merely correct so far as it goes, but also complete in all essential details to cover the field then under investigation. It should be not merely a record of human

indebtedness inwards and outwards, not merely a record of outstanding transactions awaiting completion, but a record of all pertinent factors, both great and small. Nothing is too big, practically nothing is too trifling, to come under its cognisance ; and inasmuch as all human progress is based upon a proper utilisation of past experience which would have been lost if not recorded, it is, I think, very clearly the purpose of Accounting—and particularly of Modern Accounting—to see that all material facts are fully and faithfully recorded from every possible point of view.

My time is up, and (as you would doubtless have noticed) I have given you very little information indeed as to what Accountancy is, or how it achieves its purpose. But, as I told you at the start, that has not been the purpose of my lecture to you this evening. All that I have tried to do has been to arouse in you some interest in a subject that is popularly regarded as being quite uninteresting and somewhat unprofitable. That it can be made interesting, if taken the right way, I hope I have proved to your satisfaction ; as to whether it is "worth while" from the standard of mere money-making, I think we may safely say that, in the future, business efficiency (which, of course, in the long run means business success) will be with those whose accounting record is not merely the most complete, but above all the most intelligently applied—provided (and this, of course, is a big proviso) they have the ability to read and understand the record when it is before them, and thus learn to profit by experience—to take advantage even of their past mistakes.

MACHINERY
AS AN AID
TO ACCOUNTANCY

Lawrence R. Dicksee

Machinery as an Aid to Accountancy.

By L. R. Dicksee, M.Com., F.C.A.

A LECTURE delivered before the Chartered Accountant Students Society of London, on Wednesday, April 5th 1916.

So far as I am aware, the subject of my present lecture, "Machinery as an Aid to Accountancy," is one that has not hitherto been dealt with by any lecturer at this or any other Students' Society; but there can, in my opinion, be no doubt that it is one of great and of increasing importance. Even if we were still living under normal conditions, the necessity of at all times keeping up to date, and of adopting the best, the quickest, and the most economical methods of performing all kinds of work, would—or at least should—tend to impress upon us the importance of utilising machinery as far as practicable in connection with accounting records. But, at a time like the present, when something like 60 or 70 per cent. of those skilled in accounting methods are serving with the colours, or are in some other way engaged upon war work, the problem of producing the best possible results with the very limited amount of skilled labour at present available for the purpose becomes one of paramount importance. It would seem that, in some directions at least, these facts are beginning to be appreciated at their proper value, but in other directions there is still room for a good deal of improvement—room for more modern ideas than are yet very generally observable; and (I might add) room for a more enlightened view of the whole situation on the part of the accountancy profession generally, which in such matters should lead opinion, rather than follow unwillingly in its wake. Accordingly, I make no apology for selecting for the subject of my paper this evening "Machinery as an Aid to Accountancy."

I take it that I am not overstating matters when I say that we, most of us, entertain the view that there is a marked difference between mankind and the rest of the animal world. But if any one of us who accepts this proposition were to be asked off-hand upon what he based this assumption, he might perhaps be a little hard put to it to find an adequate explanation upon the spur of the moment. Probably the majority of us would take the line that, whereas animals go through life merely making the best of those faculties with which nature has endowed them, humanity has been able to achieve a far higher claim to civilisation, mainly as a result of its mechanical ability—its power to bring to its aid the forces of nature, as exemplified in tools and other mechanical devices. So far at least as tools and weapons are concerned, there would probably be hardly any hesitation whatever in accepting this as a true statement of the position. We can all appreciate the skill with which a man handles a weapon or a tool—or, for that matter, any implement connected with a game or form of sport; but—for what reason it is not altogether easy to see—there appears to be a very general hesitation about adopting the same view with regard to machinery. There appears, indeed, to be a somewhat widespread prejudice against machinery—an inclination to regard it as being, if not an invention of the enemy of mankind, at least something that can be (and is) exploited by those who are not the friends of mankind to their own personal advantage; and accordingly—inasmuch as there is nothing to be gained by blinking at facts—I propose, to begin with, to make some brief survey of the historical aspect of my subject, with a view (if possible) to disabusing your minds of the idea that the growth of machinery is a social evil, which, however inevitable it may be, it is the duty of all right-minded persons to put off as long as possible.

The best and most concise summary of this aspect of our subject with which I am acquainted is contained in "The History of the Royal Society of Arts from 1784 to 1880," by Sir Henry Trueman Wood, in which it is stated:—

"The history of the introduction of textile machinery, by which millions of operatives now make their living, is a record of the attempts of the progenitors of these operatives to wreck the new machinery; if possible, to murder the men who designed it. As long ago as 1710 the Spitalfields weavers rose in riot and smashed their frames, in protest against the introduction of improvements. A hundred years later, in 1816, the Luddite riots, after a wholesale destruction of factories and machinery in the Nottingham district, were only suppressed by the stern expedient of hanging a number of the ringleaders. In the first half of the nineteenth century the hatred of the new machinery was combined with strikes, often justifiable enough, for better pay; but certainly for nearly three centuries—since James Lee invented his stocking-frame in 1589—the workers of the textile trades have done their very best to prevent any improvement in the tools of those trades. If the spinners and weavers had had their own way, all yarn would now be spun by the spinning-wheel, and woven on the hand-loom. The artisan fought for the ancient system of economic organisation for domestic industry and handicraft. Forces were too strong for him. The growth of capital and its systematic industrial application conquered in the end, but only after a long struggle against excusable ignorance and natural incapacity to appreciate the inevitable.

"And the opposition did not come from workmen alone. Manufacturers a hundred and fifty or two hundred years ago were no more anxious to change all their methods, and scrap all their machines, than they are now. When an invention had proved its value, and had been taken up by the more enterprising manufacturers, the rest had perforce to follow suit. But in the meantime the original

inventor had had but a poor time of it, and in all proba
bility had died a pauper.

" Nor did the inventor, as a rule, get much sympathy
from the general public, or even from those members of
the public who might have been expected to know
better . . .   there can be hardly any great invention
which has not been condemned or depreciated by a competent and well-qualified authority. The working of the
same spirit may be traced from the beginning of the
industrial revolution down to our own time. When Dr.
Lardner demonstrated beyond cavil that no steamship
could carry coal sufficient to take her under her own steam
to America, the statement was accepted as the opinion
of one of the best authorities of the time. The heads of
the Admiralty declined to consider the use of the electric
telegraph because the excellent and efficient semaphore
arrangement fulfilled all their needs. We might have had
mechanical transport on roads fifty years before it was
accomplished, but for the opposition—partly interested
and partly ignorant—to the early constructors of road
locomotives. A year or two before the incandescent fila-
ment lamp was perfected, the best authorities were agreed
that the ' subdivision of electric light ' was impossible.
The internal combustion engine found but small favour
among the older mechanical engineers (there was one
brilliant exception). The idea of a ' rotary steam-engine '
was regarded with derision before the steam-turbine was
perfected. The members of the old Aeronautical Society
were for years looked upon as harmless visionaries. When
the first paper on the basic process of steel-making was
offered to the Iron and Steel Institute, the Council of
that body—a competent tribunal, if ever there was one—
declined to accept it."

Sir Henry might have added that, only about twelve
months before the first practical aeroplane was constructed,
a very celebrated engineer had stated, with a considerable
amount of confidence, that it would be absolutely impossible to produce a practicable heavier-than air machine
until some new metal, lighter than any then known, had
been discovered.

But mere incredulity as to the possibilities of new ideas
is only one of the obstacles that practical inventors have
at all times had to face. Another—and a far more
important one—has been self-interest, or what was thought
to be self-interest. Thus, in the reign of Edward VI, a
statute was passed that prohibited the use of gig-mills in
this country. In 1621 a memorial was presented to the
Sovereign by the weavers of London, complaining of the
competition of foreigners, and especially of the fact that
they had " made so bould of late as to devise engines for
" working of tape, lace, ribbin, and suchlike, wherein
" one man doth more among them than seven Englishemen
" can doe." In 1663 the first saw-mill was erected in
England by a Dutchman, near London; but this was
very speedily abandoned in consequence of the determined
hostility of the workmen. In 1802 a gig-mill that had
been erected in Wiltshire gave rise to a good deal of
rioting. According to Cunningham (" Growth of English
Industry and Commerce ") it is not quite clear whether
these new machines were identical with those that had
been prohibited in Tudor times ; but we get some evidence
here of a dawning enlightenment, in that we are told that
the attention of the Parliamentary Committee on the
subject was chiefly directed to the quality of the work
done. When the members were once convinced that
machine work did not injure the fabric, and wrought as
well as, or better than, the hand, they were entirely dis-
inclined to support the workmen in their demand for the
enforcement of the old prohibition of gig-mills, or to
recommend that action should be taken. Matters did not,
however, by any means proceed smoothly from this date
onwards; for when, in 1767, the second saw-mill was set
up in England, by a London timber merchant named
Houghton (which, it may be noted, was driven by wind
power), " no sooner had the mill been erected when a
mob assembled and razed it to the ground."

I must, however, pass on from the historical aspect of
our subject, or we shall have no time left wherein to
deal with its present-day application to accountancy,
which, after all, is the matter now immediately under
consideration. But, before we leave it altogether, I
should like to point out to you that the illustrations that
I have mentioned are merely a few out of very many,
all of which go to show that there has been singularly
little encouragement in this country to the inventors of
machinery of any kind whatsoever ; and that such
machinery has, as a rule, been introduced in spite of a
very active and determined opposition on the part of
those whose work it was designed to replace by something
better. For us the importance of this historical inquiry
lies in the fact that it should serve as a warning to us
that interested parties are rarely impartial critics ; and,
further, that, however insistent they may be, it is absolutely impossible for them altogether to arrest the tide of
progress. My suggestion to you this evening is that the
man who utilises a rising tide to drive a water-wheel is
a more practical person than he who sits upon the sea-
shore and defies the waves to wet his feet.

There is at least one office machine which has
undoubtedly already " arrived," and that is the typewriter. By this time, I take it, we are all familiar in
general terms with the advantages of a typewriter, but
those whose experience does not date back prior to its
general introduction can perhaps hardly appreciate what
a very real improvement it was; nor, probably, are they

particularly interested in considering all the very strenuous arguments that were put forward against its introduction into offices during the "eighties" of the last century. It is probably now very generally (if not universally) recognised that it is always a convenience that business documents should be of such a character that they can be read without any hesitation whatever; but apart from the great convenience of not being continually called upon to decipher all sorts of different handwriting of varying grades, it will, I take it, readily be appreciated that whereas practically everybody can learn to typewrite in a comparatively short space of time, with the result that their subsequent work would in almost all cases be up to a very fair standard of efficiency, the number of clerks who can ever be taught to write a really legible and rapid long-hand is, and always was, extremely limited. Another great advantage of typewriting is, of course, the facility with which copies of original documents can be multiplied by the aid of carbon sheets, thus opening the door to modern methods of accounting, which were quite unthinkable until this process became practicable. Yet again, the fact that even a moderate typist can operate at fully twice the speed of the long-hand writer is a consideration, not merely from the point of view of the quantity of output, but also in that it permits much correspondence, &c., to catch the post under modern conditions which formerly would inevitably have had to be held over until the following day. Speed is always, of course, an important factor of working cost; but speed is of special importance in matters of special urgency.

But I did not ask you to come here this evening to hear me talk about Typewriters, with which probably the great majority of you are at least as familiar as I am myself. My object rather is to suggest to you that there is a great and increasing field for the use of machinery in connection with offices in directions in which at present it is not by any means generally utilised. Professional accountancy is not nearly so much a mere matter of arithmetic as many outsiders seem to think; but, for all that, a good deal of arithmetic—and, in particular, a good deal of addition—has to be performed in most offices. At one time facility in rapid adding was regarded as an essential part of the education of all clerks. But, however that may be, I venture to think that you will all agree with me when I say that the educational value of this work is absolutely *nil*; that, save as a means of equipping the clerk to perform necessary work, the time occupied in acquiring a facility in rapid addition is really time absolutely wasted. Formerly there was no alternative process available, and therefore this facility had to be acquired—often with considerable labour. Under present conditions, it seems to me that this labour is very largely unnecessary. At the present time a considerable number of machines can

be obtained which will add far more rapidly, and far more reliably, than any ordinary human being; and of these, for general office work, there can, in my opinion, be little doubt that the Comptometer holds the premier place. The Comptometer is a calculating machine operated by keys, somewhat similar to those of the typewriter, save that the keys are placed in columns. It is not merely an adding machine, but a calculating machine in the widest sense of the term—that is to say, any form of calculation is equally easy upon it; but, speaking in general terms, the more intricate the calculation the greater is the saving of time involved by its use. The Comptometer also has the advantage of being comparatively light, so that there is no difficulty whatever about moving it from one part of an office to another, or even about taking it from one place to another. Like every other machine, it is, of course, necessary to study it in order to operate it to the best advantage, but it is not a difficult machine for any intelligent person to use. So far as the machine itself is concerned it can make no mistakes; but, of course, like every other machine, it is open to the disadvantage that the human being who operates it can make mistakes. It is a point worth mentioning, perhaps, that in contrasting machine work with mental work, it is important to bear in mind that no one would ever think of passing mental work as accurate until it had been carefully checked; similarly, machine work should in all cases be checked, for while a properly constructed machine cannot of itself go wrong, there is nothing to prevent the human being operating the machine from operating it wrongly, and thus producing a wrong result therewith. As one illustration of this point (which perhaps will cover the whole field), I may mention that no typewriter has yet been invented upon which it is impossible to mis-spell words; but I venture to think that hardly anyone would now be so unreasonable as to say that, until this has been done, the typewriter would remain a defective machine. Nevertheless, it should be noted that one of the old-time objections to the typewriter was that it "spelt so badly"!

Another, and perhaps even better known, calculator is the Burroughs Adding Machine, which not merely adds figures, but also lists them by the aid of a typewriting attachment in connection therewith. For some purposes this listing is no doubt a distinct convenience; but its advantages can easily be over-estimated, and in any event the listing attachment naturally adds somewhat materially to the cost of the machine. The Burroughs machine, however, is one that is perhaps better known in this country than any other office machine except the typewriter, and it is not without interest to note that since its introduction into the Bankers' Clearing House it has been practicable to close the "country clearing" appreciably later than was necessary when the clerical work was performed by hand. Something like ninety different types of Burroughs machines are made, to meet varying requirements, and it is obviously impossible for me to attempt to describe all of them to you in the course of this evening; I might mention, however, one very interesting machine which is used chiefly for the purpose of preparing monthly statements; while another type, the "duplex," contains within itself two distinct adding attachments, which might be used (for instance) for collecting the debit and credit balances respectively, when taking out a Trial Balance. The chief drawback to the "Burroughs" is undoubtedly that, on account of its somewhat considerable weight, it must for practical purposes be given a fixed situation in the office.

Another type of office machine which has many uses is the Addressing Machine, of which various types are at present available, as, for instance, the "Addressograph," the "Addressamite," the "Addressall," and the "Elliot." Naturally the method adopted in each case is somewhat different, but the result in all cases is very similar, viz. the production of any desired series of names and addresses (selected from a given list) on envelopes, invoices, statement headings, or any other similar form of business document, at a far higher rate of speed than would be possible under any other system, with the further satisfaction of knowing that the address must be complete and correct, assuming the original address filed was correct in itself. These originals are filed vertically in trays, like cards in a Card Ledger, and it is from them direct that the addresses to be used are printed, so that any discrepancy between the two is absolutely impossible. The machines operate at the speed of (say) 1,000 per hour upwards, so it will be seen that there is a considerable economy in the matter of speed, apart from the great advantage of being assured of absolute accuracy.

The Gammeter Multigraph may perhaps be best described as an office printing-machine. It is, of course, made in various styles, but the one, it seems to me, that is most likely to be generally useful in an office is one which produces letters that are an exact imitation of ordinary typewriting has. The type is set automatically without ever having to be handled, and accordingly the machine typewriting has. The type is set automatically without ever having to be handled, and accordingly the machine can be operated without soiling the fingers, which is an advantage not merely to the operator, but also to the employer, inasmuch as it saves time that would otherwise necessarily have to be occupied in washing the hands. In many offices there is considerable scope for the use of circular letters in quantities that cannot very economically be sent out to be printed; with the result that often there is a tendency to utilise one stereotyped form where

perhaps half-a-dozen different forms would really meet the case much better; or, alternatively, to go on using the same form when it would manifestly be of advantage to bring it more closely up to date. Any business house that makes much use of circulars would undoubtedly be able to make considerable use of the Gammeter Multigraph; but, apart from this, a very large number of offices would find that by its employment they were able to save very materially on their printing bill.

Other exceedingly useful office appliances are for the sealing of envelopes and for their stamping. It is true that neither of these operations involves any high degree of skill, and that accordingly a machine that can perform the work of an office boy is not likely to effect any very considerable direct saving; but it may be pointed out that the saving in connection with office salaries is by no means the only possible saving here. In many offices very considerable sums are spent upon late posting fees, which could be avoided altogether by the adoption of some labour-saving device which enabled those in charge to catch the post, instead of missing it. In any office with a heavy daily post there is probably a very considerable use for both these devices; while, so far as the stamping machine is concerned, it may be pointed out that it is a simple matter to have an automatic attachment to the stamping machine which registers the number of stamps used, and this naturally is a considerable advantage in checking the Postage Book, which is usually a matter that presents points of difficulty.

Another very useful machine in large offices is the Photostat, by the aid of which it is easily possible to obtain quickly photographs of any desired document— either the same size as the original, or larger or smaller, as may be preferred. These photographs are directly printed on to the paper, and developed and "fixed" within the camera itself, simply by turning a handle; accordingly the machine is able to turn out finished copies at the rate of two per minute, a rate quite sufficiently rapid for any ordinary practical purpose. Usually speaking, this particular method of copying written or typewritten documents is perhaps not very likely to commend itself for general use; but in the case of elaborate tabular statements, or diagrams, or maps, or for any document which it is desired to copy in facsimile, photography is, of course, the only possible method to employ. With the aid of the Photostat absolutely accurate copies can be turned out exceedingly promptly. Incidentally, I might mention that this method of multiplying Financial Statements, Statistical Reports, Cost Sheets, &c., for use at Board meetings, is probably the best and most convenient that has yet been devised. The machine also seems to have great possibilities for the multiplication of facsimile documents to be placed before a jury. You will, of course, understand that, in the nature of things, the first direct copy of the original document is a " negative," or reverse of the original in the matter of light and shade. For quite a surprising number of purposes these " negatives " are actually clearer than " positives " would be; but if positives are preferred, as being an exact reproduction of the original, all that is necessary is to take one " negative " first of all, and then to multiply " positive " copies by photographing this " negative " instead of photographing the original.

Another machine for which a use can be found in practically every office is the Dictaphone. This, as I dare say most of you are aware, is an improvement upon the old phonograph, which was the predecessor of the now ubiquitous gramaphone; but it has been specially adapted to the use for which it is intended, in that it takes a perfectly clear impression of the speaking voice without the speaking voice having to be raised in any way for that purpose; while, at the same time, it refuses to record any surrounding noises that are not intended for record. Accordingly, it can be used in a quite busy office, without necessarily interfering with other persons, and without the clearness of the record being in any way obscured by surrounding noises. The advantages of the Dictaphone, as compared with shorthand, are very clearly understood by all who have practical experience of it; but they are none the less worth mentioning on that account. The first, and most obvious, advantage is that, while the principal is dictating, the shorthand clerk is free to do other work. That is to say, the work of " taking down " in shorthand (which upon the average probably occupies four hours per day) is now cut out altogether, with the result that the shorthand clerk is available during that period of time for other work. In the second place, the principal can dictate exactly when he pleases, whether the shorthand clerk is in the office at the time or not—and for that matter, of course, it is not at all necessary that he should do his dictation in the office at all, if it should be more convenient for him to do it at home or elsewhere. The necessary motive power for the Dictaphone is obtained from any electric lamp socket, and the motor works on any voltage, so that a business man travelling from town to town can, if he likes, carry a Dictaphone with him, and set it up in any hotel that he comes to. The speed at which the Dictaphone works is the maximum speed at which the person dictating is able to formulate his ideas and to speak them with reasonable clearness; it is accordingly much faster than all but the most expert shorthand writers. Singularly little practice is required to enable the ordinary typist to transcribe from the Dicta-phone, and such transcription is, in the great majority of cases, far more rapid than transcription from shorthand notes would be. The cost of the current used is incon-

siderable, and it is said that the cost of the cylinders is so slight that it does not amount to more than the cost of pencils and note-books for shorthand purposes—a state-ment which (extreme as it sounds) I can well believe, as the result of practical experience, although I have never tested it accurately.

In manufacturing undertakings, as you are no doubt aware, the question of Cost Accounts is one of paramount importance; and in connection with Cost Accounts one of the most important matters is an accurate record of the time occupied in various operations. The Calculagraph is a time-stamping machine, which by an ingenious device will stamp upon job cards not merely the time when a particular operation was started, but also (subsequently) the time that it occupied. This, naturally, is a distinct improvement upon a mere record of the time when the job was finished, which would leave the time occupied to be calculated mentally.

An even more useful machine in connection with time records is, however, the Gledhill-Brook Time Recorder, by the aid of which it is readily practicable to stamp a series of time records upon the same card, with the certainty that these records will appear one under the other, in columnar form, without any uncertainty or unnecessary delay. This highly desirable result is achieved by means of an ingenious mechanism which clips off a portion from one corner of the card as each stamping is performed, so that the next time the card is put into the machine to be stamped it automatically goes somewhat further in than before, with the result that the next stamping is just the desired distance below the previous one. By the aid of the Gledhill-Brook Time Recorders it is a comparatively simple matter to design really useful forms of cards for all sorts of records in connection with costing. This machine does not automatically record lapsed time, although I imagine there would be no insuperable mechanical difficulty in the way of making it do so. At the same time it is not really a difficult matter to determine lapsed time with absolute certainty by means of a Slide-Rule.

It is probably the result of our present defective system of education, but it has always seemed to me remarkable that Slide-Rules should be so little used outside of the engineering profession. They are, as a matter of fact, invaluable for all sorts of calculations, but particularly so for stereotyped calculations—a special Slide-Rule being made, to fulfil the requirements of the particular office (or the particular branch of the office) dealing with calculations of one description. There is a popular impression that Slide-Rules are only approximate in their working. This is true only in the sense that all decimal calculations are apt to be only approximate; but, for all practical purposes, even decimal calculations may be made as accurate as need be, provided one goes to a sufficient number of places of decimals. The Slide-Rule will carry one into quite as many places of decimals as one would ever be likely to require for any practical purpose; but, naturally, the more elaborate Slide-Rules are less portable than those that are quite sufficiently accurate for many everyday purposes.

Another machine—or rather group of machines—that should be of special interest to accountants is the Hollerith, by the aid of which it is perfectly practicable to keep accounts in far greater detail than one would ever think of attempting under other circumstances, and that with absolute accuracy and with a very much smaller and less expensive staff than would be required for normal account-keeping purposes.

The principle upon which the Hollerith machines work is as follows :—Each separate transaction is recorded upon a separate card by means of a Punch, operated somewhat similarly to a typewriter, which punches circular holes in the card when required. The vertical position of the hole determines the magnitude of the record, the horizontal (right to left) position determines its nature. This part of the work, being done by human agency, must of course be carefully checked to insure its accuracy, in precisely the same way that (under the more usual conditions) first-entry records have to be carefully checked, or all subsequent accounting processes will of necessity be liable to error. Any reasonably intelligent person can soon learn to punch cards accurately at an average speed of about 250 per hour. The cards, having once been prepared, it becomes a quite simple matter, by the aid of the mechanical Sorter, to sort them out into groups on any basis of classification that may previously have been determined upon. This sorting into groups of the cards representing transactions, you will readily understand, corresponds with the process of classifying, or analysing, these transactions, which is usually performed by means of posting to appropriate Ledger accounts ; but the process is infinitely more rapid, for whereas a quite capable Ledger-keeper could hardly be expected to record more than (say) 10,000 postings in a month, the Hollerith Sorting Machine will sort at the rate of 15,000 cards *per hour,* thus opening out to us possibilities of development of detail which would otherwise be unthinkable But, in just the same way that Ledger postings are of but little value in themselves, until the entries under various accounts have been added up in order to ascertain their cumulative effect, so there would be little to be gained by sorting cards representing transactions into groups representing Ledger accounts, unless some means were available to arrive at their aggregate effect. This is performed by the Hollerith

Tabulating Machine. The sorted cards, on being put through the Tabulating Machine, will build up into totals representing their aggregate effect, not merely as regards the money value of the transaction, but (simultaneously) with regard to as many different features in connection with those transactions as may be found convenient. The normal form of tabulator works simultaneously in four columns ; but the number may be increased or reduced, according to the requirements of the individual case. The normal speed of working with the Tabulating Machine is at the rate of 9,000 cards per hour. That is to say, the machine does in one hour practically as much as the average Ledger-keeper could do in a month—and this notwithstanding the fact that these machines require no skilled attention, and use practically no electric current.

I think you will readily understand that, in the time at present available, it is quite impossible for me to attempt to deal exhaustively with the possibilities of the Hollerith machines. Suffice it to say that they represent an exceedingly convenient means of analysing transactions, and accumulating them into totals of a size convenient for posting them into the Ledger, without unnecessary detail therein. There is no difficulty whatever in securing an agreement of totals daily, and that indeed would be the normal course to pursue. The daily totals may be posted direct to Ledger accounts, or they might be transferred to intermediate tabulated sheets, for the purpose of there building up into monthly totals before any entries at all appear in the Ledger. But the great feature of the whole system—apart from the mere matter of speed—is, of course, that one is no longer limited to double-entry in connection with the record of transactions. From the same cards (representing original entries) we may build up records of all sorts and descriptions, representing, so to speak, different facets of our business operations, some of which may be embodied in the books of account ordinarily so called, and some of which may go to build up statistics for the use of directors or managers, upon a scale which has hitherto been regarded as impossible—with the enormous advantage that the statistics will be available practically hour by hour, instead of—as is usually the case—weeks (or perhaps even months) after the event.

By way of anticipating a possible objection upon your part, I should perhaps add that the Hollerith machines are no untried invention. They have been in use for a considerable number of years past, and (so far as I am aware) have invariably given satisfaction. Two installations that I have personally inspected—that of the Gas Department of the Birmingham Corporation and that of the British Westinghouse Company—appear to be giving perfect satisfaction to all concerned, and to be producing results which I do not think any of us would have attempted to achieve by old-fashioned methods. There is, to my mind, no doubt whatever that there is an enormous future in front of the Hollerith machines, particularly when it is borne in mind that their cost is only about £150 per annum—that is to say (approximately) the salary paid to an ordinary experienced clerk.

There is a popular impression that the general introduction of machinery has eliminated much joy from the life of the average worker. One hears of the "monotony" of machinery, of how its constant working tends to turn even human beings virtually into machines themselves. But those who take this poetical view of the situation apparently know so little about the facts that they assume that the life of the worker was all sunshine prior to the introduction of machinery. The fallacy of this idea is apparent directly one looks the facts in the face. Who do you imagine has the most joyful time of it—the girl in charge of a sewing machine, or the seamstress who laboriously stitches by hand hour after hour? How many telegraph boys are there who would prefer to walk, rather than to use a bicycle? And how many of them—if they had the chance—would not prefer a motor-cycle to a push bicycle? Instances could readily be multiplied; but the point that I want to emphasise is that it is not machinery that is monotonous, but, rather, work itself, and that, accordingly, when work has to be done, some degree of monotony is absolutely unavoidable. But the more rapidly the work can be performed, the less will be the feeling of depression resulting from the strain of being continuously occupied upon work with apparently but little result. Thus, we all know that practically the only feeling of exhilaration that could possibly be evolved out of adding (or checking the additions of) numerous columns of figures, is the contemplation of a considerable mass of such work actually accomplished, and accomplished within a very satisfactory period of time. This feeling of exhilaration can be obtained with one-tenth of the effort, if the work be performed by machinery.

But, even if this were not the case, the present war conditions with the great scarcity of skilled clerical and accounting labour that they necessarily involve—compel us to direct attention at the present time to the possibilities of office machinery; for, under present conditions, the choice really lies between doing work by machinery—or rather with the aid of machinery—and leaving it undone. In addressing myself to an audience of Accountants and Accountant Students, it is, I think, unnecessary for me to add that the latter alternative is simply unthinkable. Those of us whom age or bodily infirmities have compelled to stay at home during the present world-crisis have yet our work to do. With us rests the responsibility of keeping going," with greatly diminished staffs, the

business of this country, whether that business be the manufacture and transport of munitions of war, or the maintenance—and if possible the extension—of that trade upon which our prosperity and supremacy so largely depended in times of peace. So far at least as the accounting side of this last work is concerned, even in its humblest branches, the work is very largely skilled work; work which new-comers, no matter how willing, cannot perform with either speed or certainty until they have acquired considerable experience. But, up to the present, practically all of this work has been what might be called hand-work. We have yet to demonstrate, upon anything like a large scale, the enormous saving in human labour that is possible by the well-directed employment of suitable machinery. As I have briefly indicated in the course of my lecture, all necessary machinery for that purpose is at the present time really available; all that is required is that we should overcome our prejudice against using it, and turn our attention to the consideration of the problem as to how it may be used most extensively, and to the best advantage. In this connection I would like you to bear in mind that practically all the various devices that I have enumerated in the course of this lecture are already in general use. Probably most of them are better known to the average business man of intelligence than they are to the professional Accountant. Unless the Accountant is content to be pushed aside, and to be dispensed with, it behoves him earnestly to grapple with this problem of the application of machinery to office conditions; as rapidly as possible to make good use of his opportunities—the wasted opportunities of the past; and to approach the subject with an enlightened and open mind, thinking only of the best, the quickest, and the most economical means by which the most desirable results can be achieved. If what I have put to you this evening has awakened you to the importance of a serious consideration of the matter, my time and your time will not have been wasted to-night.

EFFICIENT ADMINISTRATION:
A PRIME ESSENTIAL
TO BRITAIN'S ECONOMIC RECOVERY

Lawrence R. Dicksee

Efficient Administration : A Prime Essential to Britain's Economic Recovery.

A lecture by Professor Lawrence R. Dicksee, M.Com., F.C.A., at a meeting of the London Branch of the School of Accountancy Students' Association, at Essex Hall, Essex Street, Strand, London, on Thursday, September 16, Mr. J. D. C. Mackay in the chair.

Chairman's Introduction.

Mr. Mackay said he was proud of the formation of this branch of the Students' Association, which had been attended with so much success. It was quite evident they had a most capable executive, consisting, as it did, of men who had organising ability and energy, and that was just as it should be. If his pleasure could be enhanced in any way this would be because Professor Dicksee was to lecture that night. They appreciated the honour he had done them. Accountancy was the youngest of the professions, and this was borne out when they realised that the men who made the literature of the profession were still alive and at the height of their mentality. Amongst those who had made the literature of the profession, Professor Dicksee stood in the foreground. The debt they owed him was a very large one. Education would be impracticable without textbooks, and those of Professor Dicksee were of the highest value and importance, and were valued, not only in this country, but in America and all over the world.

The Lecture.

Professor Dicksee said : The choice of the subject of my lecture to you this evening has been that of your Chairman, and I am particularly glad it has been so, because it struck me as one of the most useful subjects for a single lecture, where the aim is necessarily not so much to convey exact information as to inspire interest in a course of study. Our present subject—the vital importance at the present time of efficient administration—is a particularly happy choice for those studying accounts, because there is rather a tendency on the part of those in charge of the accounts of an undertaking to adopt the attitude of the disinterested spectator. This attitude is quite a proper one for accountants from one point of view, but the tendency is rather for the accountant to regard himself as someone cut off from the actual business, instead of being a co-worker. The place where the accountant does his work is called the office. The place where the outside people do their work is called the warehouse, the works, or the factory. In South America, the name given to the works or factory is " officina." The words " office " and " factory " really mean the same thing—the place where the work is done ; but the fact that we use the words " office " and " factory " as implying two quite different things, shows, I think, that we have got in our minds a sort of close partition between the accountant's work and the work of the practical business man. Few people realise that " office " is really the same as " factory." It is, therefore, worth our while now and again to try to get more closely into touch, in mind and in spirit, with the workers.

Efficient administration, as suggested by the title of my lecture, is a prime necessity for Britain's economic recovery. The use of the word " recovery " suggests that one has to recover from something ; that there has been ground lost, and that we have got to win it back. We all know that that is so, as compared with 1914. There has

been great wastage of property, many persons have been diverted from production, stocks of essential commodities have been brought low, credit and exchange disorganised, transport facilities rendered inadequate, and, worst of all, the morale to-day can only be described as deplorable. It may seem out of place, now that the war is over, to hark back to it, and call up painful memories by the use of similes suggestive of war. I will come to that point later, but at the moment I may say I am doing it deliberately, because I think it the only useful way to approach our subject.

When the Armistice came, the idea, as put forward in the newspapers, was that the men should come back and get to work, and achieve the economic recovery that we all felt was necessary. They came back —all but the best of them—but they have not done much else. The appeal made to them to get to work and repair the wastage of war was not so very absurd when we bear in mind the claim put forward for some years before on behalf of organised labour, as being the sole producer of all the wealth in the world ; but we have to take things as they are. Whatever our precise shade of political views may be, we must admit that efficient direction is not now conspicuous among the workers. If labour was now trying to do its best towards economic recovery, it might be reasonable to admit the claim that labour is the source of all wealth. But what at the present time is organised labour doing ? To a very large extent we must all agree that it is using its organisation to withhold production, with the result (whether it is intended or not) of creating further shortage. The appeal to labour to repair the wastage of war has so far had no good effect. My suggestion to you this evening is that to a large extent the failure is due to the appeal having been made, I will not say to the wrong parties, but in the wrong way —direct to labour, instead of being made through administration. Labour can do great things, but little or nothing without guidance. That guidance it is the function of administration to provide.

If we pause to consider for a moment what the word " administration " means, we find that it still further reinforces that idea. To administer is to render aid or service. Such administration will be efficient when it achieves a desirable result, and it will, in the main, consist of doing the right thing, in the right way, at the right time.

It seems to me that efficient administration has two aspects, material and spiritual. In each of these aspects it should be educative rather than directional. It suffers very often from the wrong assumption that authority of itself gives knowledge. If we take the view that administration represents the leading force in connection with all useful work, we shall see that it cannot be effective if it always operates from the rear. One can drive from behind, but one cannot lead from behind ; and, in so far as leadership is necessary, the rank and file, no matter how able they are, can do very little without leaders. Here you see I come across the military simile again. It is difficult to speak on the subject in any other way. Perhaps some of you may wonder why I use terms recalling these unpleasant things. It is because I think it is essential to Britain's economic recovery for us to remember that we are still at war, and that we shall always be at war so long as the world lasts. If we are not warring against one thing we are against another. Just now we are at war against ignorance and sloth, and without that kind of war there can be no progress.

If administration represents enlightened leadership, it may give very good value to the rank and file by enabling them to concentrate upon their own particular job. We all know that there are men in a small way of business who are never free from worry, who never make good ; men who would be far better off as employees, simply because they have no administrative ability. If we were to abolish administration, all employees would be in that position, save the few that had administrative ability.

One of the functions of administration is to find a job suitable for each member of the rank and file. By that I do not mean to find a job in the sense of creating positions that are paid for whether there is any use for them or not. I mean, considering the work that has to be done, resolving it into its constituent parts, finding out the qualities required for the performance of each separate part of the work and distributing that work among the workers in the best possible way—staff selection it is sometimes called. And hand-in-hand with staff selection goes, or should go, staff training.

The old-fashioned method of managing a business, I need hardly remind you, was—and to a large extent it still is—to call out for qualified workmen, and then to grumble at those who offer, and complain that they are deficient. The last thing the old-fashioned administrator ever thought of doing was to train his staff; he expected them to come to him ready trained. If it were possible for them—I do not mean exceptional individuals, but as a whole—to train themselves in the best possible way, that would be reasonable, but a little inquiry into facts is sufficient to show that it is not possible. It is only the exceptional man that can achieve any reasonable standard of competency by being self-taught in whatever line of activity we may choose to think of.

Being self-taught means picking up your ideas as you go along by observing others, and, in the vast majority of cases, without the possibility of observing the best people. It is a system which, under the most favourable conditions, serves to perpetuate mediocrity, and very often it does much less. That is what, as a nation, we have been very much in the habit of doing with regard to those kinds of things that, after all, make up the prosperity of our country. How little in our heart of hearts we believed it to have been an efficient system is shown by the fact that we never think seriously of adopting that method in connection with our games. Boys at school do not pick up cricket and football; they are taught them. The man who wants to play bridge without losing his money takes lessons. If a man wants to excel at golf he takes lessons from a professional. We always appreciate the importance of training and teaching in connection with our amusements. Directly a matter is in any way within the range of athletics we realise that training is something rather apart from teaching, and perhaps even more important, and we recognise that good results cannot be produced unless we live the life that makes it possible to produce good results.

Then another point. Directly we want to achieve something more than the mere passing of the time by these recreative pursuits, we take—and young people come to it instinctively—a very great interest in records. The average schoolboy knows a great deal more about the statistics of cricket, and attaches a great deal more value to them, than the average business man knows of statistics in connection with his own work. Of course, everything can be overdone. We can devote so much attention to burying our heads in figures and statistics that we really have no time left to look up and see what is going on; but it is very important that we should study what is happening, because only by that means can we possibly tell what it is reasonable to expect.

You will, I am sure, all bear me out, when you come to think of it, when I say that there is a general tendency for us all to be too easily satisfied with our achievements—not perhaps all our achievements, because we most of us probably have some particular thing that we are careful of

and doubtful about, and perhaps that is the very thing we do best; but with regard to most of the things we do, or ought to do, we are quite satisfied we do them well.

There are various ways, of course, of testing whether a thing is done well or badly. Some are easier than others, but just as an illustration—and only as an illustration—let us try the test of speed.

In connection with practical business it is obvious that in the long run the remuneration of the worker has to be provided out of the work produced, and it is clear, therefore, that speed of production is a matter of importance. It is not a matter we can afford to overlook, although, like everything else, it is an idea that can be overdone. In regard to this question of speed—because it is the one aspect of the matter that I can put before you in a more definite way than any other—I should like to draw your attention to a few figures. Men employed in shovelling coal from one place to another were found to average, doing it in their own way, 16 tons of coal per day, but when they had been taught how to do it they were able to shovel 59 tons per day with less exertion. Bricklayers, left to their traditional methods, were in the habit of averaging 120 bricks per hour, but when taught how to do it they could readily lay 350 per hour. Compare that with the number of bricks laid per day in this country at the present time.

Now let us get on to something perhaps more within the practical experience of many of you here this evening. Supposing someone is regarded as a competent typist; that very likely means he, or she, could average on fairly straightforward work from 40 to 45 words per minute. That is not bad typing. At the present time, to the best of my knowledge, the world's record is 143 words per minute. In shorthand, the shorthand clerk varies his speed more than the typist; it may be anything from 80 to 120 or 130 words a minute. The world's record is 322 words per minute. I am not suggesting for a moment that every worker could achieve a world's record; that would be as absurd as to suggest that everybody could run 100 yards, or a mile, in the record time; but beyond doubt a knowledge of what has been done by others is a most useful spur, and a very good corrective of that self-complacency we are all very apt to fall into.

I will give you another illustration which you can test for yourselves. Most of you shave in the morning; the probability is that the great majority of you have never counted the number of strokes you make with your razor in the process. The number of strokes you make is not necessarily an index of your ability—that is to say, the smaller number is not conclusive proof that you do it better or quicker, but you may be sure that the number is as large as it is mainly because you do not think beforehand what you are doing, but you just go on with a sort of reflex action of the hand without thinking what you are doing. Try the experiment next time, and count how many strokes you make; then make up your mind that that number can be reduced by half in a fortnight, and I am perfectly certain you will find you can do it. I have tried that with a number of students, and have never known it otherwise. In my own case I found I took as many as 320 strokes, which is certainly a large number. I got it down to 112 quite easily. Then the first time I put it to a body of students I found that, compared with their experience, 112 was quite a large number, their best being 52. That was rather a shock to me, but I was not to be beaten, and I got down to 52 within a week. From 320 to 52 is a big difference. The funny part about it is that if you do not count for a week you will find the number going up again. That is typical of everything; if we are not always on our guard, we find that we are always slipping back.

But administration, of course, does not consist in forcing the pace: speed, and nothing else. In so far as it is possible to increase speed it does so, in the main by studying precisely what motions are performed in the fulfilment of the task. Cutting out useless motions diminishes fatigue. In this matter we have been greatly assisted by the camera. We can get instantaneous photographs of the most rapid operations, and throw them upon the screen to get the general effect of how the thing has been done, or should be done, as the case may be. We can then reduce the pace at which they are thrown upon the screen, so that the movements may be analysed exactly. It is not to be expected that those who have been aiming at a high rate of speed in the past have accidentally stumbled upon the best possible method. Good results come only as a result of careful study. In the illustrations I have given you we have seen that there is scope for very considerable improvement. That is, scope for still further study.

Administration, again, does not consist merely of staff training, so as to speed up results; it also involves study of the psychology of fatigue. This is very necessary, if we are going to maintain these results, so that we may find out the conditions under which work can best be done. The average individual rank and file worker knows little about that. He is in no danger of smashing himself up by neglect of the necessary rests; but on the other hand there are casualties every year, probably every day, from this cause, and these casualties in the nature of things often occur in connection with the most promising workers. There is great scope for further inquiry in this direction, although during quite recent years a good deal of pioneer work has been done.

But we have to take a much wider outlook yet, before we can really claim that we have been administering to the needs of the worker. It is not merely enough to watch the individual worker at work and instruct him in the best way. We have also to see that he is supplied with the conditions which make for good results. This is classified to-day under the heading of Welfare Work. In all the large factories to-day are welfare workers, whose functions differ very materially according to the circumstances. The welfare worker may be anything from a domestic factory inspector on the one hand, to a games master on the other. Very often the welfare worker has the engagement of employees. Looked at from this point of view, we are dealing with what we may call the personal aspect of employment, and the aim is to supply that human factor in connection with employment which was formerly crowded out in large undertakings when the number of employees became so considerable that the management lost touch with the employees as human beings. There is much room for development on these lines, and much scope for administration; but nothing, it seems to me, can take the place of some sort of human intercourse, however slight, between the individual workers and the chief. My experience is that the more works managers, or managing directors, are able to keep in personal touch with all their workers, the better. They should not only know them by name, but be able to talk to them. We might regard that as one of the tests of administrative ability.

But that is not all there is to be said. There is such a thing as suitable housing, and provision for reasonable recreation, and education, and so on. And as regards housing, we have also to consider the position under which the worker operates while at his work. If we are expecting from A. and B., two workers, a similar output in quantity and quality we are manifestly unreasonable, unless we not only give them similar tasks to perform but also give them similar means of performing them and similar conditions. If we want to get the best results we must supply the best conditions for the production of them, and it is up to the administration to do that. In the ordinary course of events it is not reasonable to expect good results in the absence of suitable equipment, suitably placed.

It is up to the administration also to provide continuity of work, and that can only be done by very careful planning, which often involves thinking a long time ahead. We have got to consider, when we are deciding whether to take a particular order or not, how we are to carry it out.

In so far as it is the function of administration to guide, it can only guide, as distinct from driving, by pointing out the way—and pointing out that it is the right way—and keeping the rank and file informed of what they are doing. We want to be continually comparing what is with what should be. Competition has its uses in this regard, as was proved by the competition amongst rivetters in shipbuilding during the war, when one yard was competing with another as to the number of rivets that could be driven in a given time.

A very common criticism of any attempt at centralising administration is that it makes work monotonous. Don't believe it. The really monotonous or uninteresting job is always the job that is indifferently done. Whatever it may be, if it is really well done, you may be quite sure it is not uninteresting to the man who does it. If we can get workmen to take a really living interest in what they are doing they will never complain that their work is uninteresting.

But above all, administration means the inspiration of uplifting ideals, that brush away all clogging doubts and distrusts, and banish fatigue. It must be upon the right lines materially, because it has to deal with material things; but at heart it is essentially a matter of the spirit. Nothing can permanently succeed, if done in the wrong spirit. It is for the efficient administrator to renew a right spirit within us, so that we each no longer seek the welfare of ourselves, our families, or even of our class. So that we may strive in work not only to find our own soul, but rather the great One-Soul of all our race. Then, and then only, shall we be irresistible—because Efficient.

Do the Right thing, in the Right way, at the Right time.

A vote of thanks to the lecturer terminated the proceedings.

PUBLISHED BALANCE SHEETS
AND ACCOUNTS

Lawrence R. Dicksee

Published Balance Sheets and Accounts.*

By Lawrence R. Dicksee, M.Com., F.C.A.

(Sir Ernest Cassel Professor of Accountancy and Business Methods in the University of London).

It is often extremely difficult to estimate the true financial position of an undertaking from its published Balance Sheet and accounts. Professor Dicksee, the well-known author and lecturer, makes some suggestions as to the arrangement and form of a Balance Sheet which will be easily intelligible and at the same time convey all the necessary information to the general public.

I have chosen as the subject of my lecture to you this evening, " Published Balance Sheets and Accounts," partly on account of its importance and partly because it is not a highly technical subject and is, therefore, not unsuitable for consideration at the beginning of a session, but chiefly because of the widely divergent views as to what a published Balance Sheet ought to be. We may, therefore, I think, very usefully consider the question in its various aspects, and also consider how far the criticisms which are sometimes passed upon published Balance Sheets and accounts are reasonable, and how far they are unreasonable as being really impracticable. We find that it is said upon the one hand—and this, perhaps, of the two is the view more widely held—that a Balance Sheet should be a statement showing exactly the financial position of an undertaking, containing facts and nothing but facts, showing exactly how that undertaking would pan out if the business were to be discontinued and the affairs of the business wound up. At the other extreme we find it suggested that a Balance Sheet means practically none of these things, and that it is simply a statement prepared by the bookkeeper when he has finished his work at the end of a year, or some other period, and then simply puts together in the form of an annual statement a sort of list of the uncompleted transactions.

If we take the first view as being our standard of what a Balance Sheet ought to be, it might be regarded more or less as a statement of fact, although even then there might be widely divergent views as to what certain kinds of property would realise if sold, before any attempts had been made to find a purchaser for them. If we take the second view, it is possible to regard the Balance Sheet as a statement of fact, again up to a point; but of a different kind of fact. We must then regard it rather as a statement showing on the one hand what the undertaking has received and has not repaid, and is, therefore, liable to account for; and on the other hand a statement of what it has done with the moneys so received and not yet refunded. There again, to some extent, matters of opinion must crop up, and our Balance Sheet even on that basis cannot be regarded as a cold statement of absolute facts. Whichever way we look at it, we must

---

* A public lecture delivered at the London School of Economics and Political Science on 9th October, Mr. Wilson Potter, Vice-Chairman of the Shipping Sub-Committee for Commerce Degrees of London University, in the chair.

expect to find questions of opinion, so to speak, mixed up with our state-ments of fact, and the opinion must in the first instance clearly be the opinion of those who are rendering this statement of fact—the accounting parties.

When the Balance Sheet is audited, it becomes the duty of the auditor not to " certify " that the Balance Sheet is a true statement of fact, because that, as I have just said, would be impossible as regards at least a part of it ; but he is called upon to express an opinion as to whether the statement as put before him by the accounting parties properly discloses the position of affairs. If his opinion differs from theirs, it is his duty to report in what respect it differs ; but it is important to bear in mind that the auditor's report is to a very large extent a matter of opinion and that the expression " auditor's certificate," which is so very commonly used, is a misnomer. One can certify facts, but one cannot certify matters of opinion, and as a matter of fact the law does not require a Balance Sheet to be certified, but it does require the auditor to report whether in his opinion it is properly drawn up.

Supposing we were to take as our standard of what the ideal Balance Sheet ought to be the view that it ought to show what the position will be if the business is disposed of and its affairs are wound up, then clearly, if its possessions are at the time when we prepared the Balance Sheet likely to be sold at something appreciably above their cost price, we are looking forward to a profit on realisation. We are expecting that the position will turn out better on a realisation than it would have done had there been no rise in prices. If we frame our Balance Sheet upon those lines, it must necessarily result in its showing a profit up to date which includes a profit that has not yet been realised, and is, therefore, not at present available to be divided in money. In so far as that profit may be expected from the sale of what we may call the general equipment of the undertaking—what is technically spoken of as the " fixed assets " of the undertaking, the things that it does not try to turn into money in the ordinary course of business, but has acquired with the object of using them in their existing form as a means of increasing the profits of the undertaking—in so far as we include possible profits on the realisation of equipment, we shall be including as profits actually already made profits which there is no intention whatever of ever making on the assumption that the business is not being disposed of or shut down, but is to be continued.

Accordingly, when, as at a time like the present, the tendency is for prices to rise and to go on rising, a Balance Sheet so prepared would show very large profits which would be largely, if not entirely, illusory. At other times it might be that, with falling prices, Balance Sheets so prepared would show serious losses ; that is to say, the existing equipment might perhaps only be saleable at a price very considerably less than what it originally cost, even after making due allowance for the fact that it is partly worn out and, therefore, that we should not regard it as being to-day worth the original cost. Its realisable price might be less still. If we were to be debarred from dividing profits derived from the practical working of our business merely because equipment could be bought more cheaply to-day than when we purchased our equipment, this would certainly not make it easy for us to find new capital for expansion : it would not make it easy for other similar undertakings to find new capital for new enterprises. But, apart from that, these losses which a Balance Sheet so framed would show would be just as illusory as the profits would have been after a period of rising prices ; that is to say, they would be hypothetical losses which would be sustained if we were to dispose to-day of something which we have no intention whatever of trying to sell. In our attempt, therefore, to produce

579

a Balance Sheet which will get into close touch with actual facts, we find that we have entirely defeated our purpose and have got right away from the true facts of the position, the essential fact being that the business is a going concern which we are going to continue to carry on so far as we can anticipate, and which we have every reason to suppose that we shall be able to continue.

Then there is another point. If we frame our Balance Sheet so that it may show as profit increases of wealth which, even if turned into money, are manifestly of a non-recurring nature (and a profit derived from the sale of one's equipment clearly could only be made once, and not annually), the effect would be to encourage by this form of accounting the payment of very large dividends after a period of rising prices and no dividends at all after a period of falling prices. We should find that not even the soundest undertaking could maintain anything like a uniform rate of distribution among its proprietors by way of dividend, and that again would make it very difficult for us to get capital for new enterprises.

Then, again, if we keep to this first ideal of a Balance Sheet which represents absolutely realisable value, we have got to cut out altogether a number of items which, if we adopted the second ideal, we should certainly include in our Balance Sheet along with our possessions, or "assets" as they are commonly called. In almost every kind of business activity certain kinds of expenditure occur, the full benefit of which is not received entirely within the year (or other accounting period) in which the expenditure takes place, so that at the date of the Balance Sheet the whole of the advantage to be derived from that expenditure is not exhausted; there is still a surviving value in that expenditure which, with varying degrees of confidence, according to circumstances, we expect will be received in future years—sometimes a few years, sometimes many years. Now, clearly, expenditure the benefit of which is entirely exhausted within one week, is a proper charge against the profits of one week. Expenditure which is entirely exhausted within one year is similarly a proper charge against the profits of that year. Expenditure which is not entirely exhausted, until, let us say, the end of 20 years, is equally properly chargeable over the longer period of 20 years. Theoretically at least, we ought to ascertain what benefits will be received from this outlay in each accounting period during which it is any advantage to us whatsoever, and charge the corresponding portion of the cost against each accounting period. That is what is commonly done in practice with such items as plant and machinery and the like, which we know will last very much longer than one year, and the cost of which is spread over a longer period—a period approximately as nearly as one can tell, and as nearly as experience will help one to determine, to the time during which that plant and machinery continues to be useful as equipment, and, therefore, to serve its function as a profit-earner. It we accept that as a reasonable way of dealing with expenditure of this character, it necessarily follows that in each successive Balance Sheet prepared during the time that the effective life of that equipment continues, we must bring in such part of the original cost of the equipment as we consider is not already worked out or worn out—that part which we consider survives and for that reason is more properly chargeable against future profits than against current profits. If we work upon these lines, it necessarily follows that from time to time such outlays will appear in our Balance Sheets at figures quite different from the then realisable values of the articles represented by the outlay.

We cannot possibly frame a Balance Sheet which will carry out both ideals; we must choose which of the two is the one that we propose to adopt. In every case where we are proposing to continue the business and there is no reason to suppose that we shall not do so, and no reason, humanly speaking, to suppose that the future profits of that business will not be able to bear the burden that we are throwing upon them. that seems to be a perfectly sound method, and it has at least the advantage of charging against the gross earnings of each year their fair share of the burden that has to be borne by all of the years. The system, therefore. tends in the direction of producing statements of profit from year to year that will be as uniform as the varying circumstances of the case would permit or justify. At least, we are not going out of our way to make the profits fluctuate more widely than the conditions of trade necessitate.

Shareholders, in the nature of things, for the most part prefer uniform dividends. They are quite willing that distributions out of profits should tend to increase, but they are always inclined to be disappointed, and frequently inclined to grumble, when the rate of dividend falls. Accordingly, those who are responsible for the preparation of accounts, and for the successful conduct of a business, very naturally adopt in the main a procedure that tends in the direction of avoiding large distributions of profits which they know it will be impossible to maintain in the future. But although shareholders as a body like uniform dividends, as representing fixed income, they are not always very consistent, and, accordingly, we commonly find that where the dividend that it is proposed to declare is markedly less than the amount of the undivided profits available to be divided, pressure is brought to bear by the shareholders for the dividend to be increased, and directors as a rule endeavour to resist that pressure where in their opinion the standard of distribution proposed is too high to be maintained. To assist them in resisting that pressure, it is a very common thing to transfer a certain (or rather an uncertain) part of the profits actually earned to a reserve, thus reducing the amount of undivided profits shown. The device, although exceedingly thin to the initiated, seems to serve its purpose quite well in practice. We rarely find shareholders clamouring for a dividend to be paid out of reserve, although at times, when the reserve gets very high. they may look forward to, and expect, a free distribution of shares out of reserved profits; but the practice of transferring what we may call " surplus profits " to reserve is generally effective, as permitting current dividends to be kept within the safety limit. Nevertheless we do not always find that this particular method is employed by directors to keep dividends within what they consider to be desirable limits. Instead of transferring profits to a reserve that is clearly shown upon the face of the Balance Sheet as something which has to be accounted for in the future—or what is called a liability—the practice has grown up, and during recent years appears to be decidedly upon the increase, of piling up what are sometimes called " internal reserves," sometimes " undisclosed reserves," and sometimes " secret reserves." The term " secret reserve " does not seem to be much used save by those who oppose this particular kind of policy and regard it as being highly undesirable.

The effect of the policy is to withold from those to whom the Balance Sheet may be sent the fact that the undertaking has made certain profits which have not yet been divided. The directors do not " account " to the extent of such reserves. On the face of it that might seem to be entirely improper and highly unjustifiable. but it has been held that there is nothing whatever illegal about such a practice so long as it is not contrary to the regulations of that particular company. Most companies in their regulations take power for their directors to make such reserves as they think fit, without specifying whether those reserves are to be shown upon the face of the Balance Sheet or not. The only thing that the Courts have so far objected to in the matter is that they have decided that the existence and the extent of these reserves must not be concealed from the company's auditor. They throw upon the latter the grave responsibility of determination whether he shall make any disclosure to the shareholders with regard to the matter. This seems very clearly to suggest that the auditor will not do so without good reason, so that as long as the directors are acting in good faith these internal reserves are apparently recognised as being a reasonable business policy.

Such reserves may be made in a great number of ways, all of which will indirectly affect the published Balance Sheet. Excessive sums may be charged against current profits to provide for contingencies, such as the wear and tear and obsolescence of equipment, possible future bad and doubtful debts, the deterioration in value of stock in trade or investments, and so on. Almost everybody applauds the systematic and drastic writing down of goodwill in the case of a successful company. The policy is, no doubt, excellent in itself, but we have got to remember that the more successful the undertaking may be the more valuable does its goodwill become. Although, therefore, we may write goodwill off against profits, and out of the Balance Sheet as rapidly as the earning capacity of the undertaking will permit, we are deliberately preparing a Balance Sheet which under-estimates the value of that particular asset. The policy may be justified on the ground that even in the most successful business the value of goodwill is subject to wide fluctuations, because even in the most successful business profits fluctuate; but, however that may be, the effect of writing down goodwill is to state this particular asset in our Balance Sheet at less than we believe it to be worth, and to leave a corresponding amount of money (if the profits are realised profits) in the control of the directors for future purposes.

We may also build up internal reserves by overstating the total amount of our liabilities, by including reserves for possible future claims or in excess of what we really believe to be the actual extent of our commitments at the present time. Again, various kinds of outlay, which result in acquiring new possessions, whether by way of buildings or plant or investments, or what not, may be and sometimes are charged direct against profits as a working expense, with the result that that which has been acquired as a result of this outlay does not come into the Balance Sheet as an existing asset at all. The result of this kind of policy is that it leaves us without any formal record in our accounts of the property that we have purchased, the existence of which ought to be carefully verified from time to time.

The strongest argument in favour of reserves, whether disclosed or undisclosed, is the impossibility of saying with absolute certainty what the future has in store for us. We are only justified in putting into our Balance Sheet as assets that which we think we shall in the future receive real value for, either when it is disposed of and turned into money, or as the result of using it in its existing form. We can never say with absolute certainty what future benefits we shall derive from our present possessions. We must, therefore, leave a wide discretion in the hands of those responsible for the management of the business as to the value that they put upon these items as being fair and reasonable. Similarly, although not as a rule to such a great extent, it is not practicable in the case of a going concern to say with absolute certainty what claims may be made upon it in the future arising out of events that have already happened. We must permit the management, therefore, to provide an adequate and even a generous amount for future contingencies which, in their judgment, not only are likely to happen but also may happen. We cannot, and ought not to, complain, but rather to congratulate them if their general policy is always to be upon the safe side, and to aim at disclosing a position in their published Balance Sheets that is certainly not better than the true position.

We see then that we must give the accounting parties a very wide discretion as to how they frame their accounts, and that in the nature of things

Published Balance Sheets and Accounts.

they cannot put before us a statement of facts in connection with things that have not yet happened, and that things which may happen in the future will react upon what is, or is thought to be, the present position, in so far as they have not been provided for or have been over-provided for. In spite of all this we must draw the line somewhere, or we shall find that we are driven to the conclusion that the Balance Sheet may mean little or nothing, and would, therefore, be useless.

It is only shareholders who have a statutory right to see a Balance Sheet. On the other hand, most companies go much further than that and issue copies of their Balance Sheets to practically anybody who likes to ask for one, and some even go to the extent of advertising their Balance Sheets so as to make them as far as possible common knowledge. There must clearly be some responsibility resting on those who publish Balance Sheets for the information they contain, even although you may not find their responsibility defined in the Companies' Acts. We find it mentioned, however, in a rather forceful way in the Larceny Act, where it is provided that it is a misdemeanour to publish a Balance Sheet with intent to deceive a member or a creditor, or with intent to induce anyone in the future to become a member or a creditor, so that the Balance Sheet is not a purely domestic document.

In ordinary practice Balance Sheets seem to b eused, and to a surprising extent to be relied upon, not merely as a means by which the rank and file of the shareholders may test the degree of success with which a board ot directors has conducted the affairs of the undertaking, but also as a means of enabling the initiated to determine what is the true value of the company's shares from time to time. It is very doubtful whether a Balance Sheet can be of much use for this latter purpose. The true value of the shares in a company depends, no doubt, to a certain extent upon what return would be likely to be made to shareholders in the event of the company being wound up, but it depends certainly to a greater extent upon the income derived from the possession of the shares and the degree of probability of that income being maintained. The Balance Sheet as ordinarily prepared gives very little idea as to what shareholders may expect to receive if the company were wound up. It will give some idea as to the probability of the business being successful in the future, and it should enable us to determine whether the resources of the undertaking are sufficient to enable it to meet its debts as they fall due. We may, by looking at a Balance Sheet which has been prepared with reasonable honesty, satisfy ourselves that it is not likely that the company will be obliged to discontinue operations because it is unable to pay its debts, or we may form the conclusion from looking at the Balance Sheet that there is a greater or a less probability that it will be obliged to stop for want of money; but we can form no very useful idea from looking at any Balance Sheet as to whether the profits of the next few years will be as great as those of the last few years. You must remember that perfectly sound undertakings sometimes carry on for a year, or even more, with very little profit, or perhaps even at a loss. The existence of sufficient reserves will, however, enable them to tide over lean years, and still to go on paying dividends. That we may form a useful idea of the position of an undertaking from its Balance Sheet is all that we are able to say.

The Balance Sheet should show in reasonable detail the grouping of its assets. Most Balance Sheets do that. Some certainly do not; and as an illustration of one that does not, I should like to read you an extract from a Balance Sheet of a well-known company. Explaining an outlay of upwards of 5¾ millions sterling, it does it in five lines of print, as follows :—" By " land, water rights, reservoirs, effluent works, buildings, plant, machinery, " office furniture, goodwill, designs, engraving, and sampling, as per last

" account, £5,776,212 19s. 8d. Further capital expenditure at cost (less " sales) for the two years ended 26th June 1920, £14,922 16s. 11d.," making a total of £5,791,135 16s. 7d. I suggest that that is not an ideal way of disclosing to interested parties what the main resources of the undertaking consist of. Another example of how not to do it I should like to give you : The Balance Sheet of a shipping company having total assets amounting to £1,305,000 odd, explains £1,073,811 of that amount by simply describing it as " Stock in steamships and investments, book value at 31st December 1918, after deducting depreciation previously written off." At the annual meeting of that company the chairman was asked whether he would state how much of that figure represented steamships and how much represented investments, and he said that it was not in the interests of the company to give that information. At that time the £10 shares of the company stood at about £45. A little later the ships were sold and the company was wound up, and the return to the shareholders is now expected to be about £130 per share. One wonders whether it really was in the interests of the company that shareholders should have no information which would suggest to them that their shares were worth a very great deal more than the current market price.

I put these matters before you, but I have no time this evening, and I do not think that I have any particular inclination just now, to suggest a remedy. I have merely tried to point out to you that the question of what a Balance Sheet ought to be, and ought to contain, is not a very simple one that can be answered offhand, and yet that it is a very urgent one, in that clearly there are cases where shareholders and other interested parties do not get the information that would be of great use to them from the published accounts, and seem at present to be entirely without a remedy.

Printed and Published by GEE & Co. (Publishers) LTD., 14 Queen Victoria Street, London, E.C.4.

COSTING

Lawrence R. Dicksee

Costing.

By L. R. Dicksee, M.Com., F.C.A.

In the following valuable paper Professor Dicksee considers the main principles of Costing and the main points that have to be borne in mind in connection with all costing methods.

Costing, although it may be supposed by some to have been invented in the United States and brought into this country after the outbreak of the war by an American accountant for the benefit of Government Departments, has of course been in existence, at all events in this country, for almost countless years past. It is anything but a new idea, but like many other old ideas it has remained in a more or less primitive or chrysalis stage until comparatively recently, and it is the modern development of industry upon a large scale that has doubtless given it its greatest impetus. Undoubtedly its use in connection with munitions during the war gave it its greatest advertisement, but we cannot do better, I think, than look at the primitive ideas of what costing consisted of, and follow them up and see how they have developed, because there we shall find the very root of our subject.

We find at all events one idea that is very well worth bearing in mind in the mere word itself. The root of the word " cost " is apparently exactly the same as the root of the word " cash," and the root of the word " cash " conveys the idea, not as one might expect, of money, but of Fact. And it is well worth our while, I think, to bear in mind that the root meaning of the word " cost " as being facts is something that we cannot afford to disregard, and that we have got to hang on to for all time.

The next idea in connection with primitive costing methods that I the want to suggest to you comes from what I believe is the earliest use of word in this country, which was by solicitors. Now, when solicitors talk of their costs they do not of course mean the cost to them of the work they do for their clients, but the cost to their clients of the work they do for them, and that reminds us that the term " costs " can have no really accurate meaning unless we are quite clear as to the person or body that we have in mind when thinking of " costs." Quite a good deal of confusion of thought seems to arise out of the fact that the cost to the purchaser is inevitably the selling price to the seller, and therefore not what we understand by his costs. That, again, is a point we do not want to lose sight of, because we find the cost of commodities is frequently spoken of in a loose way without defining to whom that cost is supposed to relate.

A lecture delivered before the School of Accountancy Students' Association, at the Memorial Hall, Farringdon Street, on 26th September 1922.

Costing.

In anything like the modern sense of the term I think we may all agree that every system of costing aims at giving detailed information as to working which is not given in the usual annual or other periodical accounts, and at giving it sooner than it could be obtained from those sources. Very often people talk and think of costs as though they exclusively related to industry or manufacture, but it is just as well to bear in mind that they are not necessarily limited to industry. It is practicable to prepare costs—and just as useful to prepare them—in any kind of business activity, such as transport, or trade, though the problems are less complex in connection with trade. Any kind of service is capable of being costed, and, as I dare say many of you know, since the war there has been established a Corps of Military Accountants who are engaged in connection with the costs of various military operations, and particularly the costs of the upkeep of various units of troops.

When we bear in mind that the aim of costs is to give something more detailed and prompt than is obtainable from the ordinary financial accounts, it is pretty clear that at some time or another it must have been realised that something more detailed and more prompt than these financial accounts is required, and a recognition of that fact, and the giving effect to it, perhaps very naturally resulted in the actual work of preparing a costing record being given to persons other than those in charge of the ordinary accounting records. However that may be, we very commonly find that the two are quite distinct, and that very often the costing records—such as they are—have been introduced by those responsible for the administration of an undertaking because they could not get what they wanted from the accounts department and therefore set about getting it as best they could in their own way. That no doubt explains to a very large extent the fact that the methods employed were not always the best possible. We have a group of persons who for a great number of years have been specialising in connection with accounting records whose services were not utilised in connection with what after all is simply another way of handling those records for a slightly different purpose, and to this day the point seems to remain quite unsettled as to who really ought to be in charge of the costing records. Very commonly it is the person whose administration the costing system is designed to keep a check upon, but that of course is quite counter to what we all know to be the fundamental principle of accounting : that the accounting party ought not to keep his own records.

When we ask ourselves how costing methods, as we find them, grew up, I think we shall find the inquiry useful, amongst other things, as showing a certain amount of weakness in the way in which ordinary financial accounts are kept : a weakness which perhaps we might otherwise have not thought of suspecting. Costing systems, particularly the early ones, seem to have been based upon the earliest known systems of keeping accounts by double entry, which we very often speak of as the Italian method. As you no doubt know, we first hear of double entry definitely towards the end of the 15th century. The problem which had to be faced was to keep a record of what was being done by Merchant Adventurers. That was the class of business to which double entry accounting was then applied, and it presupposes that the operations that had to be recorded consisted of a series of distinct adventures, very often overlapping each other—various adventures going on simultaneously. Each separate adventure, however, came to an end in due course. The medieval idea was that each adventure should be kept separate, so that the results of each particular adventure should be manifest. We find a parallel to that in connection with existing systems which divide costing operations into separate jobs or contracts, or what not.

Like many other branches of knowledge, accounting seems to have had its ups and downs over a period of roughly 300 years preceding what we call the industrial revolution—that is to say, approximately from 1550 to 1850. Instead of progressing it seems to have gone backwards. We find that practically no text-books were published giving evidence of any original thought, or any new departure in practice worth commenting upon, that indeed the only development seems to have been in the way of forgetting a good deal of what was formerly known and well understood, so that that abomination which came to be known as "single entry" had to a large extent taken the place of double entry in connection with accounting, and during that time the conditions under which business operated were, of course changing considerably from those applying to the early Merchant Adventurers. The operations tended to become far more numerous—so numerous as to become for all practical purposes a continual series of transactions in buying and selling or in manufacturing and selling ; so numerous that it became no longer practicable to keep a separate account of each ; no longer practicable in many cases to keep effective track of the material handled so as to see when each separate purchase was brought to an end, so that a Profit and Loss Account in connection with each separate purchase should be practicable. We get instead the form of Trading Account with which we are all now familiar, a form which differs fundamentally from the old-fashioned Adventure Account in that it is never brought to an end so long as the business continues. For convenience the accounts may be balanced yearly, or at other intervals, and at such time the result of the business is shown, and the balance of unsold stock is brought down. But this form of accounting never provides us with a definite report of business completed and the result of such business, and of course it does not attempt to give us that information earlier than we could get it from the annual or other periodical accounts. We have, therefore, lost something and we have gained nothing in exchange, except that by substituting a short cut for the more cumbrous method of record we have saved a considerable amount of time. But we have lost touch with a definite system of reporting upon business completed, and the results of such business.

A further development of modern accounting from this centralised trading account which, as I have said, was continuous throughout the whole life of the business, was in the direction of departmentalisation, sub-dividing the trading account as a whole into a number of separate accounts proceeding simultaneously, each to keep a record of one shop

Costing.

or department of a composite business. By this means we are able to get more detailed results, but we are no nearer getting a systematic report on completed business, and the advantage of departmental accounts lies solely in the fact that where the operations are partly conducted by one administrator or manager and partly by another, by sub-dividing the trading account we may indicate, as well as a trading account can, how each administrator is dealing with his allotted task. But the real value of a trading account, whether departmentalised or otherwise, is but little unless we can assume that all the operations comprised in that account are so similar that the gross profit, or the result of the operations taken as a whole, may reasonably be taken as being at all events approximately the result of each separate operation of which the whole consists—and we all know, of course, that in practice that is not so.

But perhaps, even more, the departmentalised trading account can never satisfactorily solve the demand for effective cost accounts because it provides us with such information as it does give too late to be of practical use. We cannot shorten the period covered by a trading account as much as we might like for the purpose of getting prompt results, because we cannot prepare any trading accounts without first taking stock, because we have to remember we are still discussing the days when no attempt was ever made to keep stock accounts, the balance of which would actually show the value of the stock independent of any stock-taking. Accordingly it is very natural that we should find that something approximating to our modern idea of cost accounts should first be evidenced in connection with those occupations where the stock at the beginning and close of each successive period was least important as a factor in the figures as a whole, either by reason of being practically uniform in amount or by reason of its smallness as compared with the other figures, and we have to remember that the shorter the period the larger proportionately would be the stock in relation to the purchases or sales.

It is perhaps natural, therefore, to find the first serious attempt at costing, as we now understand the term, in connection with mining industries. Cornwall, I suppose, is one of the districts where mining has been carried on in this country for the longest period, and here was developed a more or less primitive system of accounting very fairly suited to its requirements, which goes by the name of the Cost Book system ; but the " cost book " of the Cornish tin mine is not what we should call a cost ledger to-day by any means, but is simply a cash book. But we do find that the Cornish cost book system recognises the importance of accounting at comparatively short intervals—normally six weeks. Every six weeks the proprietors were called together and had submitted to them a summary of the cost book—that is to say, all the receipts and payments in connection with the working of the undertaking, and, as in this case the undertaking was not of a complex character but of a simple character, the records here lend themselves to being expressed not merely in respect of money received and paid but also in terms of the actual output of the mine ; and here we get what we now realise to be a most useful factor in connection with any costing system—a systematic record, prepared at frequent intervals, reducing the working results to terms of some unit of production. But cost accounts prepared upon these primitive lines in the nature of things can only be found approximately satisfactory when we may suppose that the actual receipts and payments under each separate heading recur sufficiently frequently for the actual receipts and payments of any particular period to correspond at all events very closely with the actual incomings and outgoings of that period—that is to say, if the outstandings remain constant or negligible. So that from the very first we have got to supplement our bare statement of receipts and payments in money, and modify it at all events to the extent of seeing that instead of including expenditure upon consumable stores that happened to be paid for in that particular period we substitute for the cash figure a statement of the value of the consumable stores actually consumed, and that means we have got to keep an account somehow of the consumable stores, and substitute the correct figure of stores consumed for the incorrect figure of stores paid for.

Naturally in some cases that adjustment is a much simpler matter than in others, but this is not the only adjustment necessary, for there will be other kinds of payments which, in the nature of things, occur only quite infrequently, and which, therefore, working upon a purely cash basis, would be omitted altogether from some periods, while they would be included in other periods at too large a figure. If we adhere too closely to actual cash receipts and payments during a particular period, we are also in considerable danger of overlooking a number of transactions that are of vital importance as affecting working results and yet materialise so rarely, or so indirectly, into actual receipts or payments of money that we may, I think, conveniently think of them as "imperceptible."

I will give you one or two illustrations of what I mean in order to make my point clear, but I am not going to make the list exhaustive. Some undertakings may operate in works—in buildings, or on land—that they hire or lease from the true owners. When that is so the outlay arising from this source materialises into a cash transaction as often as they pay the rent or royalty that is due from them under the terms cf their hiring. It is, therefore, under no particular danger of being overlooked. Others, on the other hand, may operate on their own property. Now, a factor of that kind does not affect the cost of the operation. The cost of the operation depends upon the value of the property necessary to carry it on, whoever owns it, so that even if we have our own freehold property we have got to bring something into our costs as representing the proper and fair charge for the use of the property, or else in comparing our costs with those of other people less happily situated we shall get an entirely wrong idea of what our costs are. It may be that because we own instead of hiring we are able to operate at a slightly less expense, because the owner naturally wants his profit, but it is only by reason of the profit of the owner that there will be any difference in the costs of the two undertakings.

Costing.

Then again some undertakings operate exclusively with their own capital, some almost entirely with borrowed capital. That, again, cannot really affect what it costs them to do what they are out to do. I think we must take it that the costs ought to include a reasonable charge for interest on all capital employed, even although the interest on part or all of that capital may never be paid to anybody. On the other hand it is quite conceivable that an undertaking which at first was very unsuccessful may have had to raise loans to cover past losses on which it still has to pay interest. If we want to find the true cost of what we are now doing it is clearly not fair to load our figures with interest on loans that are not represented by any available assets used in connection with production.

Then with regard to the question of equipment of all kinds. Equipment, we know, does not last for ever, and therefore from time to time, but probably quite infrequently, expenditure upon renewals becomes necessary. We commonly meet that problem, both in connection with our costing records and in connection with our financial accounts, by providing for what we call depreciation of wasting assets, but for costing purposes it is, to say the least of it, an open question whether the proper charge under this heading should be based upon what the wasting assets happened to cost when we purchased them. We may have paid too much, or we may have been able to acquire them at an unusually low price. When these assets have to be discarded as no longer suitable, and replaced by others, the expenditure that will have to be incurred will depend upon the price at which we are able to replace that which we discard ; it would seem, therefore, that the cost of renewals, rather than the original cost of that which has to be renewed, is the more correct figure. In theory, at least, we may concede that, but in practice it may be so difficult to determine what the cost of renewals at an uncertain future date may be, that we prefer deliberately to adhere to the original cost as the basis of our charge under this heading, even although we can show that it is theoretically incorrect. But if we do, we have got to remember that from time to time, as we make expenditure upon renewals upon a very large scale, we must expect to find our costing results for similar operations fluctuating.

Then there is the cost of the management of the undertaking. If the undertaking is carried on by the proprietor it is very likely that in the books there is no charge against profits for the value of the services he renders, and considerable likelihood therefore that this factor will be left out of account altogether in the costing records, and the costs will show up favourably as compared with another undertaking owned by a limited liability company that pays suitable salaries to its managing directors. In the case of a private company we may find, on the other hand, that the remuneration of the managing directors is far in excess of a reasonable remuneration for the work that they do, because, the undertaking being owned almost exclusively by the managing directors, they prefer to vote themselves remuneration at a liberal rate rather than pay a high dividend, and in that way they may be able to effect a saving in income tax which is certainly more

393

legitimate than some methods which come to light from time to time in the Criminal Courts.

Then there is another point—I can illustrate it best perhaps by reference to a manufacturing undertaking. It is a common experience here that certain parts or articles will be spoiled in the process of manufacture, with the result that the real output is less than the theoretical output as judged by the quantity of materials issued for manufacturing purposes. If the manufacture be a complex process, and if for that reason we sub-divide the accounts to show the cost of the successive operations, we have to remember that these results may be made very misleading if we do not treat properly this question of loss arising from spoils. *Prima facie* it is the operation which has done that work that made the article useless—perhaps from some mistake in machining—that ought to bear the whole of the loss, which, of course, includes the cost of the preceding operations; but, on the other hand, in some cases the spoil may arise from a defect of material which could not have been foreseen, which only came to light when this particular operation was being performed, and then it is manifestly unfair to saddle that particular operation with the whole of the loss. But it is very important, if we are attempting to divide the cost accounts into successive operations at all, that the question of spoils should be handled properly, because otherwise we shall not be showing correct results upon any of those successive operations, and, what is perhaps even more serious, we shall not be bringing home to those whose fault it is what is the loss arisng through the mistake of their particular group or department, and we may be quite sure that under such conditions the losses arising from spoils will be higher than they need be.

Then, again, there are two other points I want to touch upon as adding further to the complexity of cost accounts that are going to prove a real help. Whatever the nature of the operations may be it is very likely the case that the product or output will not in all cases command an equally high price, that is to say, that although we may be aiming always at turning out articles of a particular quality, inevitably in the process of doing so we may have to turn out larger or smaller quantities of lower grade articles, saleable and therefore not spoil or scrap, but not saleable at anything like the price obtainable for the best quality. In these cases the problem that we have got to face is how to distribute the cost of production as between the two, or it may be the number of different grades or qualities of articles produced and sold. That is, perhaps, only one aspect of what seems at first glance to be an entirely different problem.

In connection with many kinds of manufacture associated directly or indirectly with chemistry, it is practically impossible to make one thing without at the same time necessarily making other things. These other things may in the first instance have been regarded as waste products, in which case the whole of the costs have to be borne by the one thing which we are really trying to make. In proportion as we are able to find uses for our waste products and turn them into by-products, we are able to reduce the cost of the main article we are

Costing.

trying to make. When the by-products are entirely subordinate we may very conveniently regard the amount we are able to realise upon their sale as merely a reduction of the cost of manufacturing the main article, but the tendency of modern times is to multiply by-products and to increase their relative importance, so that in some cases, and at some times, what was formerly regarded as a by-product may be even more important than the main article itself. As, for instance, you will remember that during the war certain by-products of gas manufacture were so important in connection with the manufacture of explosives that the gas companies and the munici-palities manufacturing gas were allowed to lower the standard of quality of their gas for the purpose of improving the production of those so-called by-products. While we have our conditions changing in this way it is, of course, impossible to standardise for all time the most suitable costing methods, and there will probably always be more than one way in which the problem may be looked at, and various methods may commend themselves to different men, perhaps of equal ability. The important thing perhaps in other cases is that there should be consistency in the method adopted in any one place, so as not to interrupt the ease with which the results of successive periods may be compared.

I said just now that the problem of costing was made more complex from the point of view of keeping the records by the fact that some of the items that have to be brought into account occur far less frequently than others, and it is very obvious, I think, when we come to consider the matter at all, that the modern tendency has always been in that direction. The multiplication of machinery, the employ-ment of mechanical power as far as possible instead of human power, all tends in the direction of large items of cost occurring as actual payments at less frequent intervals, and these facts perhaps explain why it is that for so long many of those who endeavoured to keep cost accounts were content with what we now regard as accounts of prime cost or first cost ; that is to say, they confined their records to those items of cost that could be handled conveniently because they occurred at frequent intervals, and tended to leave out those items which were more difficult to handle ; and although it is, of course, far simpler to deal with problems of what we now call direct costs than to deal with the indirect costs, or over-head as they are very often called, there is at least this point that we must not lose sight of, that the modern tendency, in very many cases at least, is to stabilise prime costs, that is to say, to make the cost of one business house very similar to another. The cost of labour is mainly determined by trade union rates, which individual houses cannot alter. The cost of materials is mainly determined by world prices of commodities, and it should not be a difficult matter for each separate business to buy practically as well as every other—at all events the tendency is in that direction. It is really in the matter of the overhead that the costs of different business houses performing similar operations, tend to vary most, and it is therefore on the overhead that one wants to concentrate most attention. If we stop short at the prime cost stage we are really regarding the job as finished before it is well begun.

Just let us consider for a moment what are the various objects for which cost accounts may be wanted, the various uses that may be made of them so long as they are available sufficiently promptly and are sufficiently accurate. They will assist those interested in the management to reduce costs by cutting out every kind of loss arising from waste or delay which the accounts may show, and we have to remember that one of the most fruitful causes of rising costs is failure to adhere to a definite time-table as to when the different operations are to be finished. They will assist the management to determine what kinds of output are best and most profitable at the moment; when it is worth while to push production to its maximum, and when, on the other hand, it is wiser to restrain production. They will assist the management to choose between alternative methods of operation, by showing in a far more realisable way than any person can tell by mere observation what the costs of these alternative methods or processes may be. It is not every invention which is going to revolutionise production that really reduces costs in the way it is expected to do. Then they assist in building up a reliable staff capable of estimating costs of future operations, and without such definite records of facts accomplished we have to remember that all estimates arᵉ mere guesses. They assist—or at least under ideal conditions they would assist—in the comparison of operations between different undertakings doing similar work, if only these different undertakings could be persuaded that it was really to the advantage of all that they should pool their results and thus render them available for comparative purposes: that would be quite practicable, in the case of every organised industry, if the results were submitted to the association which represented their organisation, and this could be done without disclosing anything that it would be detrimental to disclose.

Cost accounts represent the only really reliable method of valuing work in progress upon the basis of what it has cost, as distinct from measuring it up and estimating what it ought to have cost. They enable the management, among other things, to determine the desirability of doing things themselves or placing them out with others who perhaps can do them better. They determine when it is desirable to subcontract, when it is desirable to make and when desirable to buy. They instantly enable one to verify in many important respects those items of the ordinary financial accounts which are perhaps the weakest in the matter of verification. Wages—perhaps one of the commonest leakages—if all outlay in wages has to be charged up to some definite operation there is a far better chance of detecting payments of wages that were not due, because they will be perceptible when charged against a particular operation over a short period of time, but imperceptible as merely part of a yearly total of wages paid. They provide similarly a check upon stores consumed. And we may summarise it, perhaps, by saying that cost accounts provide the only reliable guide to business for the future. In the absence of cost accounts the only guide available is the impression of somebody trying to keep in touch with what is going on : a possible task perhaps in the days of very small concerns when one person was sufficiently vigilant to oversee everything, but an impossible task in connection with the mammoth undertakings of to-day, where no one person can hope to cover all the ground and all the details.

I would like to call your attention, by way of contrast, to one point where I consider that cost accounts have a definite limitation. It is, I think, a mistake to suppose that cost plus a fair profit—assuming we may agree as to what is a "fair" profit—is necessarily a fair price to charge. The mistake of that came out very clearly in connection with the legislation about profiteering when statutory limits were proposed upon the rate of profit that traders were entitled to. That operated in two ways, first of all it cut away everybody's incentive to buy or produce at the lowest possible price. By paying more than was absolutely necessary for a particular article the trader acquired the right of selling at a higher price, and being satisfied he could sell at that price there was every inducement to buy at the higher price. It helped, moreover, to multiply the number of business houses through which goods must inevitably pass before they reached the ultimate consumer. There was nothing to prevent the multiplication of the hands through which goods passed, and accordingly companies came into existence whose express purpose was to pass goods on to those working in groups at an enhanced price. No one need charge more than the statutory rate of profit upon that which it cost him to buy the goods that he sold, but he might have a proprietary interest in those from whom he bought them, and in that way, of course, his profits might be multiplied. Again we have to remember that if, by taking trouble, by good organising and adequate capital, any particular business house finds itself in a position to buy more directly than is usual, and thus eliminate one profit, it is not necessarily fair and reasonable that the whole of that advantage should go to the customer. If it did, we should leave no inducement for anyone to effect economies. It is generally easier, as a matter of fact, for traders and manufacturers alike, by organising, to put up prices than, by careful administration, assisted by good costing, to reduce costs. Cost accounts can be most valuable if properly prepared, and if properly used, as enabling costs to be reduced by pointing out at what precise stages costs seem to go up unexpectedly, and therefore quite likely in a preventable way. But until we can get those who are to use the cost accounts interested in getting costs down, any time and trouble devoted to framing our system of cost records upon the best possible lines is likely to be time wasted.

My time is up now, and I have only been able to touch upon these bare points of principle, and have left quite untouched the methods by which we may carry those principles into practice, but I hope that I have not altogether wasted your time or trespassed too much upon your patience. In conclusion I would just ask you to take away with you this one fact, that I am sure you will always find useful : and that is to remember that costs are money facts, and that the ultimate basis of all transactions, the test of their reality, is as to whether they will ultimately crystallise into something which, in terms of accountancy, may be described as an actual " transaction."

THE TRUE BASIS
OF EFFICIENCY

Lawrence R. Dicksee

The True Basis of Efficiency.

By Prof. Lawrence R. Dicksee, M.Com., F.C.A.

(Professor of Accountancy and Business Methods in the
University of London).

*" Individual self-culture is the essential prelude to all
collective progress. Let us begin at the beginning, and each
one be willing to do his bit, striving not for something at other
people's expense, but striving each to do his best to develop all
that is best within himself."*

The Chairman, Mr. A. Clifford Ridgway, F.C.A., in introducing
Professor Dicksee, said the process ought to have been reversed, as
the lecturer's reputation was world-wide. He was the writer of
more text-books on accountancy than any man living. He (the Chairman) well remembered attending lectures he gave at the Birmingham
University ; he was the first Professor of Accountancy there (applause).
They considered it a high honour to have Professor Dicksee with them,
as he was so busy with his duties as Professor of Accountancy at the
University of London that he could rarely make it convenient to leave
the metropolis.

Professor Dicksee, who was heartily received, said he would like to
tell them how glad he was to be in a position to come down to see them.
As their President this year he was very glad to find that there were
so many men and women of various ages in Birmingham endeavouring
to make themselves efficient in Accountancy. He was down to speak
to them on " The True Basis of Efficiency." He wanted the members
to know that the title was not his own selection. He had been wonder-
ing why that particular subject had been chosen, and the conclusion
he came to was that when he gave a lecture to the London Students
in 1920, the subject he then dealt with was " Efficient Administration—
a prime essential to Britain's Economic Recovery," and that what he was
then able to say apparently met with a certain amount of acceptance, and
therefore something of the same kind was asked for now. The present
subject, " The True Basis of Efficiency," was the title of a book he
published last year, and his lecture to the London Students in 1920 was
the first chapter of that volume. Probably whoever had selected the
title of that night's address had read this book. He hoped he might
be able to say something that would be of advantage to them, but he
was endeavouring to condense into a single lecture sufficient to form
half a dozen addresses, and he wanted to give them something which
was not exactly an abridged edition of a book which they could buy
and read. He would therefore approach the subject from a slightly
different point of view.

A lecture delivered to the members of the Midland Branch of the School of Accountancy
Students' Association at the Chamber of Commerce, Birmingham, on Tuesday, 25th September,
1923.

On a previous occasion he had emphasised the point that we could only hope for real efficiency where we got first-class team work. He did not want to go back upon that, but he did want to point out that we could not hope for efficiency in any considerable body of persons associated together in business if each and every one of them expected someone else to provide the efficiency. That was something we had to do for ourselves ; it was hopeless to expect the other man to do it. Only when there was all-round efficiency could we begin to get to work. We all knew that the chain was no stronger than its weakest link, and in the same way an organisation could not be efficient if it was a mere assembling of inefficients. All progress must begin with the individual ; without individual progress real collective progress was impossible. All that one could do in the way of the organisation of a rabble was to get them in some way to become soldiers.

It was the fashion to-day not to want to become soldiers ; we had all had enough of that. But there were different kinds of soldiers. There were soldiers of peace as well as soldiers of war, and if they wanted efficiency they must cease to be a mob and become an army. That meant that we had all to be ready to subject ourselves to discipline.

There were many people who thought that efficiency was another name for good organisation. Some even thought it another name for good equipment. Some manufacturers seemed to pay heed to furniture advertisers, and were under the impression that when they had paid for their office desks they had secured efficient organisation. That was not what he (Professor Dicksee) meant by efficiency, and he hoped it was not what they meant by efficiency. It was not human efficiency, and if there was no human efficiency, you could not go very far.

But how many wanted to make a start towards efficiency by beginning at home ? It was the curse of the time to believe that organisation could take the place of individual effort. "Believe me," said Professor Dicksee, "it can't." It had been said that the average man no more wanted to be made efficient than he wanted to be made good. There was no doubt a good deal of truth in that. He did not know how many of them claimed to be 'average men' in that sense, but if there were any, they would go away sorrowful, for he had nothing to offer them if they would not offer themselves in exchange. "But," said the lecturer, "if you realise that it is up to you, that you have not yet done your bit, and already earned eternal rest—if you agree with the Prince of Wales, who said last July : 'We can never really be ex-service men, in peace or in war, for every one of us still owes service to his fellow men as long as he has strength to give it.'—let us see what this cult of Efficiency means for us, and what it can do to help us to become more useful to our fellows. And even if we doubt our ability to establish a new heaven upon earth, let us at least remember that it has always been the few that have been able to make comfort possible for the many ; whereas all, even the least of us, has the power to make things uncomfortable for others. In the nature of things, few of us can be leaders ; but we can all be loyal followers, and not put sand into the wheels of progress. Let us realise at the start that what we

The True Basis of Efficiency.

think and feel is at least as important as what we do ; that no great movement is purely material.

" A little knowledge is a dangerous thing. We are all—or almost all—dabblers in science to-day. And because science always tries to solve one problem at a time, by separating it from its surroundings and examining it upon its merits, we are apt—dabblers that we are— to think that life itself is but an assemblage of watertight compartments, each of which can be solved independently of the rest, and often that the solution of the rest is someone else's job. Believe me, there are no watertight compartments in real life. If we are going to make any- thing of it, we must realise it as a whole, and realise it as something that does not cease when we ' go West.'

" But," said the lecturer, " Efficiency was undoubtedly based on material things. He would run through the more important of these very briefly :—

First there was the matter of Motion Study, as it was called. The whole object of motion study was to reduce the number of physical movements to a minimum, so that work might be as rapid, as little fatiguing and as healthy as possible. Motion Study was excellent as far as it went, but how far did it go ? Was it not like old-fashioned gymnastics ? Let them compare gymnastics, as in vogue thirty or forty years ago, with the physical culture methods of to-day; and more particularly with those associated with the name of Sandow. These brought mind and heart to the aid of the body, and called in scientific breathing to help. Breathing, properly done, was essential to develop- ment upon the right lines. Anyone who knew anything about singing would tell them that one of the absolute essentials to success is a right method of breathing ; yet the physical effort of singing was slight as compared with the physical effort of many other kinds of work But there was spiritual breathing as well as bodily breathing—just as breathing good air was good for the body, and breathing bad air was bad for the body, and just as deep breathing was essential to physical development, so breathing the bad air of hate and bitterness led to spiritual death, but the deep breathing in of cheerfulness and love brought life—the only real life there was.

Next to Motion Study came the question of speed. Speed was important in practical business affairs, because in the long run remunera- tion depended upon output ; but he would not stop to labour that point. But a high rate of speed, ill-directed, was impossible without great fatigue. Nevertheless, high speed was not necessarily unnatural ; indeed, some speed was essential ; it was a matter of comfort. In walking a certain speed was necessary to obviate a suggestion of fatigue, and in bicycling a certain minimum of speed was essential. Then again, an objective was needed—a walk with a definite objective was always more enjoyable and interesting than an indefinite stroll. The capacity to work at a good rate of speed was generally a matter of training. When we improved our capacity we found that we could work at a far higher rate of speed than we had formerly thought possible. This question of speed had nothing to do with what was termed ' nigger-driving.'

Then the question of emulation was important. The game of golf afforded a remarkable illustration of the value of this. When a man was on the links playing against bogey, he had something that exercised a remarkable effect upon him. He was not merely playing a lone hand ; he was fighting against an opponent. He was in competition with bogey. There were people to whom the word ' competition ' was something in the nature of a red rag. He did not know why, because ' competition ' was, at root, exactly the same word as ' competent.' Both meant seeking together. There was nothing antagonistic about competition. It was often a valuable incentive. Emerson was one of the earliest apostles of Efficiency in the United States, and some of his ideas in regard to expressing the performances of individual workers in terms of a percentage of a theoretical ' efficiency ' were decidedly interesting. But it was always dangerous to talk about 120 or 150 per cent. of efficiency, because it was a pretty certain way of causing people to get swollen heads ; if you told folk they had more than 100 per cent. of efficiency you were always running that risk. That showed how necessary it was for you to be right with your data before you started. One hundred per cent. ought to be the achievement of the super-man, who had never existed and never would exist." (Laughter.)

Then there was the question of Fatigue. Continued overwork was bad in the long run. It had been found, as the result of experiments carefully made, that somewhat frequent rests from strenuous physical work were beneficial. It had also been found that the length of the rests was not so important as their frequency. Short rests at frequent intervals were better than longer rests at longer intervals. It always seemed to those who thought most about the subject that the fact that large numbers of people should often be found working over-time suggested inefficient management. The heads of a business ought to be able to arrange something better than that. In the long run too much over-strain in the matter of work inevitably led to physical exhaustion, to a reduction in output, and a falling off in its quality—in fact, to the reverse of efficiency. Elementary school teachers had established the fact—it was rather the fashion now to criticise elementary teachers, but they were quite right on this point— that there must be intervals of rest if they were to get the best results. But, here again, it had been found that it was far more essential that they should be frequent than that they should be long. There was still a good deal of scope for enquiry as to precisely how the balance should be kept between the frequency and the length of the intervals of rest, but at least the principle had begun to be realised as one of importance. On the other hand, they must beware of going to the opposite extreme. Fatigue was not a disease ; it was the natural finish to a day well spent.

In the nature of things any group organisation must be directed by a head ; if the head were inefficient, or the response to its commands half-hearted, then there could be no true team-work and no efficiency. The functions of the head were in the direction of training and planning. Training meant organising, recruiting, educating—i.e. ' fitting.' Planning was virtually traffic control—internal and also external. " But," said the lecturer, ' the house that is built of rotten bricks is a rotten house, and so personal efficiency is the true basis of all efficient organisation.'

Personal efficiency was often spoken of as if it were another name for fitness—this is to say, ' fitting your job.' It was as a matter of fact fitness, plus a willingness to use that fitness—be it bodily, mental, or spiritual—for a cause. ' It is the sanctity of the cause that encourages, uplifts, ennobles, and creates enthusiasm : the faith that moves mountains. Wherein lies the sanctity of the cause, if it is just ordinary business, as too often conducted ? There is nothing ennobling about trying to score off others, or trying to extract money out of other people's pockets. We must get far above that level before we can hope for real efficiency. One of the most hopeful signs of the times is that the key-note of so many business houses to-day is ' Service not Self.' Self-preservation may be the first law of nature, but there is nothing ennobling about it. Self-culture is good, because it may be turned to good account. But we have not begun to live, still less to live efficiently, until we realise that we are each of us here, as units, to carry forward at least some stage further the welfare of some group of which we are but a part. That each of those groups is not a separate entity, but rather a unit in some other larger group, and so *ad infinitum* up to God. But there can be no short cuts—the origin of all evil. We must each, as far as may be, develop himself before we are fit to do even the duty we owe to the group that is nearest to us. Otherwise that group will fail in its duty to other groups.

Individual self-culture is the essential prelude to all collective progress. Let us begin at the beginning, and each one be willing to do his bit, striving not for something at other people's expense, but striving each to do his best to develop all that is best within himself; building slowly, faithfully, warily—if need be with the sword in one hand and the trowel in the other—with infinite patience and infinite hope in the abiding outcome. This is The True Efficiency that all can learn. No new cult, but the old, old story, told for nigh 2,000 years : ' Only Believe, and Ye shall See.' " (Applause.)

The Chairman said they had heard a most excellent address. He would not like them to bombard Professor Dicksee with questions. He would like to throw a bone of contention or two into the arena. He could never understand why so many manufacturers worked in dingy and uncomfortable offices. Considering that they spent two-thirds of their time—their waking time, at any rate—in their offices, it struck him that they might just as well have them comfortable. It was not a question of money, for many of them were wealthy persons. In regard to frequent rests : Were these essential ? Might they not mar efficiency, by causing delay in taking up the task again ? We lived for something else besides efficiency, and he personally felt that he had done a good and efficient day's work without feeling " dog tired." That might sound heretical, after what the lecturer had said, but it was so. " However," said the Chairman amid laughter, " I merely want to draw the badger."

Professor Dicksee, in replying to this criticism, said it might be all right for the employer himself to work in an office of the kind mentioned if he really thought that his most suitable environment. It might suit him and convey a sense of homeliness to him, but it was not a good principle when other people had to be considered. Dingy surroundings re-acted upon them, and possibly increased their inefficiency. He was disposed to think that the matter of colour affected people very much. A gardiner did not take the same view of things as a collier or an ironfounder. By the way, why was machinery usually painted black ? might it not serve a useful purpose to have it painted a brighter colour ? Colour in a factory had an influence on the workers. Since women had taken to work in offices, one frequently found flowers there ; sometimes the girls paid for them themselves. They liked to have them there, and they thought that their presence rendered them more efficient.

In regard to frequent intervals of rest. These were not so necessary in respect of mental work, but in regard to heavy physical tasks they assuredly were. After all, they were merely concerned in finding the most economical way of spending time. It had been found better to have the rest time allowed split up into three or four intervals, instead of having it all at one time.

In regard to what he had said about fatigue. No one ought to get " dog tired," as the expression went, but a feeling of tiredness at the end of a day was surely natural. They did not normally expect to be as fresh at the end of a day as they were at the beginning.

Replying to a question as to the strength of a chain being the strength of its weakest link (the query was as to how that weakest link could be strengthened), Professor Dicksee said that sometimes the only effective way was to cut the link out. " I know no other way in some cases," said he tersely.

Mr. G. R. Griffin, F.S.A.A., proposed a cordial vote of thanks to Professor Dicksee, and eulogised the principle of dicipline to which he had alluded.

Mr. A. W. Billington seconded the resolution, which was adopted with acclamation, and Professor Dicksee briefly responded.

SOME ECONOMIC ASPECTS
OF OFFICE MACHINERY

Lawrence R. Dicksee

The Office Machinery Users' Association.

(The Accountants' Journal is the Official Organ of this Association.)

Some Economic Aspects of Office Machinery.

By Professor L. R. DICKSEE, M.Com., F.C.A.

Economics has been defined as the study of business in its social aspects, and in this paper Professor Dicksee discusses the social aspects of the introduction of office machinery.

I want to draw your attention to what I have called " Some Economic Aspects of Office Machinery." It is rather a high-sounding title perhaps, but it really expresses the particular point that I want to direct your attention to : Economics is sometimes defined as the study of business in its social aspects, and I want you to consider with me the social aspects of office machinery.

Of course this view of economics is an utterly different one from the view that is sometimes put forward that economics is an absolutely cold-blooded and non-human science. It recognises that we are here dealing with the actions and re-actions of human beings upon each other, and it will be just as well, I think, for us all to realise that it is not possible to divorce economics from the humanities.

Obviously, it must be admitted that tools of some sort are an absolute necessity to civilisation. We cannot imagine humanity, even in its most barbarous condition, getting along at all without the aid of some kind of tools. In fact, it seems to be one of the most important distinctions between human beings and the rest of the animal world that they do contrive for their use tools of some sort to assist them in carrying out the work that they have planned to do ; and, as civilisation becomes more complex, of necessity those tools tend, in adapting themselves to the requirements of more complex conditions, to become more and more complex also.

I do not know, really, that there is any essential distinction between a tool and a machine, except that what we dignify by the name of " machine " strikes us as being more complex than what we call a tool. For instance, we may admit for the sake of argument that the ordinary writing pen is

---

A lecture delivered under the auspices of the Office Machinery Users' Association at the London School of Economics.

a tool. Whether a fountain pen is still a tool, or whether it is sufficiently complex to be called a machine, is, perhaps, rather a fine point; but however that may be, we should find it very difficult in practice, I think, to draw an absolutely hard and fast line between what we agree to describe as tools, and what we agree to describe as machines. And the reason why I put this point is that anyone who has any work to do must realise the necessity of having suitable tools for the purpose, and recognise the necessity of learning how to use those tools in the best way. Commonly, we find that the skilful worker gets on the very best terms with his tools; conversely, we have a proverb that it is the bad workman who complains of his tools. We want to establish something like the same good terms between the machine and the worker of the machine, and I do not see upon the face of it any particular reason why we should attempt to distinguish between the two.

But with regard to office machinery in particular, it is worth while remembering that by no means all office machinery is quite modern. For instance, however you distinguish (if you think of distinguishing) between tools and machinery, I think you would have to call the old-fashioned copying press a machine, rather than a tool. I cannot say exactly how long the old-fashioned copying press has been in existence, but certainly it is not a particularly modern invention. One can hardly imagine anybody seriously suggesting that the introduction of such a machine as an old-fashioned copying press would revolutionise office work, and lead to any appreciable extent to unemployment in office work. We will go back to that question in a moment.

If we want to find a convenient place to draw the line between tools and machinery, it seems to me that perhaps the most reasonable place at which to draw the line would be to limit the term " machinery " to those kinds of mechanisms which are driven by some kind of power other than human agency—electricity, or whatever it may be. And certainly there is this to be said about the power machinery we employ in the office or elsewhere, that it does undoubtedly save an enormous amount of human drudgery—pure drudgery—and leaves human beings free to do work which we may more reasonably associate with human beings than the mere movement of matter from one place to another, or moving it in a particular direction.

But in order to popularise office machinery I suppose really the first thing that we have to do is to face, and try to dispel, a belief which seems to be fairly widespread, that the wholesale introduction of machinery into an office will make for a considerable amount of unemployment. That, no doubt, is what people have always thought about the introduction of machinery for purposes which were then novel. It is one of those superstitions that are very prevalent, but in point of fact it appears to be the merest bogey.

When dealing with the question of office work you have to remember, first of all, that any attempt to reorganise the methods by which the work of an office is done is never a matter that can be undertaken lightly or effected very rapidly; it must of necessity be a very gradual process, or the result will be chaos. We shall not commonly find that the reorganisation is undertaken, save very gradually and piecemeal, and when so conducted it rarely leads to any serious reduction of the staff. What it does lead to is a change in the form of employment rather than a discontinuance of employment, and so far as there is any discontinuance of employment at all it would simply be the discontinuance of employment of those who are unable to adapt themselves to the new conditions—that means either those who are so far advanced in life that they have not many years of working activity before them, or those who are so unteachable, or unadaptable, that in any event probably they would have dropped out of the race pre·ty soon, even if there had been no question of the introduction of the new methods. And, of course, in every office there are likely to be new methods introduced from time to time, whether machinery is introduced or not.

But the general effect, and the main effect, of the introduction of machinery into the office, as elsewhere, is the greatly increased output of the workers with less toil to the workers themselves. If it does not achieve that result we may, I think, safely say that there would be no particular point in introducing it. Increased output in the office, as well as in the factory, necessarily means greater prosperity. It should mean greater prosperity all round. If it does not, the fault lies, not with the machinery, but with the distribution of the advantages of the increased prosperity—which, after all, is an entirely separate proposition.

In the office, of all places, the increased accuracy of machine work is to be valued, for we have to remember that accuracy in office work is of all qualities that which is the most important. But, as a matter of fact, although accuracy in office work is infinitely more important than speed, speed itself is also of very considerable value, because information that can be obtained promptly is often worth compiling, which would be utterly useless if it could not be obtained promptly. Thus the introduction of office machinery, which gives us the possibility of reaching results more quickly than would otherwise be possible, opens the door to the possibility of more information being compiled, and stimulates the demand for more information being compiled as an aid to management. It is in this way that we may reasonably assume that under all normal conditions there will be found enough work to be done to absorb all the workers already employed, so that the general effect of introducing office machinery—and the introduction, of course, will be gradual—is that the same number of workers are employed in producing more information, more records, and not a smaller number in producing the same quantity of information or records as before.

The whole object of accounting, of course, is to build up information used in connection with the conduct of business. There is no real limit to the amount of information that can be used in that work. In the past Management had to contend with imperfect information, solely on account of the prohibitive cost of the information and the delay in preparing it, and had to be content with the bare minimum that was absolutely essential ; and this partly because (as I said before) much information that would have been very useful if it could be obtained promptly is useless if it can only be obtained with great toil and delay. We do not yet know, and we are probably still a long way off knowing, all the information that could be compiled for the aid of Management, and could be utilised by Management if available sufficiently quickly. There is still room for a great deal of investigation on these lines, and the mere fact that perhaps at present some of those in charge of business affairs do not realise how beneficial further information might be to them, prevents an earnest inquiry as to what more is possible in the way of information, now ﹙hat the means of producing it are so readily available.

For the most part, of course, office machinery is of comparatively recent introduction, and it may be difficult, therefore, to do more than form the merest estimate of its future outcome, but at least in connection with typewriters we can say that office machinery of this particular kind has been in general use for quite sufficiently long to let us form some idea as to how its general employment works out in practice. It would be interesting to know, I think, whether anyone seriously suggests that the introduction of the typewriter into the office has caused any large measure of unemployment. I think, on the contrary, it would be more reasonable to say that the use of the typewriter has led to a vast increase in the number of business letters written, and has led to those letters being longer, and more full, than they otherwise would have been—longer and more full than they were in the old days when they had to be laboriously written with the pen. If that be so, we can take it as an illustration of the way in which the demand for the use of a machine increases, as it is found that the machine is capable of producing a larger output than was otherwise available at the same cost, or anything like the same cost.

If we are going to put forward doubts as to the way in which a more extensive employment of office machinery is tending, I think it might perhaps be better to look in a different direction altogether. One might wonder whether the abolition of drudgery from the office by the introduction of machinery might not lead in the long run to what we may call mental atrophy on the part of the worker. We all know that human qualities are developed by exercise, and that in the absence of exercise they tend to dry up, and drop out of being altogether. It may be that the introduction of calculating machines, instead of calculation being a mental process, may deprive present and future generations of the opportunities of developing mentality that have been open to previous generations. If, however, there is anything in that argument, I think we must recognise that it might be applied equally well as an argument against the introduction of the metric system into this country. The abolition of the somewhat cumbersome and complicated tables of weights and measures, and the introduction of a system of decimal coinage, would no doubt greatly simplify many arithmetical calculations. Following the same line of argument, we might say that the introduction of the metric system is to be deprecated, on the ground that it would deprive workers of opportunities of working their brains.   It would, of course ; but the question is not as to whether certain kinds of work, or drudgery, should be done, or not done, so much as whether we cannot find a better means of using one's time, if one can cut out a certain amount of unnecessary work, and devote one's energies to higher things.

After all, if there be any serious fear that life is going to be made so easy for the office worker by the introduction of this machinery that there is nothing left for him to exercise his mind upon, the natural antidote for that would seem to lie in the direction of a more intellectual use of the larger measure of leisure rendered available to the worker by the increased output of the machinery and the accompanying reduction of working hours which experience shows always accompanies the general introduction of machinery in the place of hand work.   Any movement that tends to make people realise that the whole of their activity in this world should not be concentrated upon business and money-making alone must, I think, in the long run be useful, and justify itself upon economic grounds —upon grounds which recognise that, whatever our precise form of activity may be, it has its social aspect : that we have duties to each other as well as to ourselves.   (Applause.)

AN AUDITOR'S RESPONSIBILITY
FOR BALANCE SHEET VALUES

Lawrence R. Dicksee

An Auditor's Responsibility for Balance Sheet Values

By Professor L. R. DICKSEE, M.Com., F.C.A.

The sad state of many a company's finances in recent years has led to auditors being blamed for many things by people who do not realise their real position and functions. The accounts of a company are not the accounts of the auditors but of the directors, and while the auditors may criticise them, they cannot alter them. Professor Dicksee makes some suggestions as to the way in which the law might be strengthened in the direction of protecting shareholders.

My subject this evening is "An Auditor's Responsibility for Balance Sheet Values." I think we must all agree that this is a subject upon which it ought to be possible to say something, because when we find that companies in the course of a single year admit in their published accounts losses running into, say, £8,000,000 or £12,000,000, it is certainly disquieting, and one cannot help feeling that losses of that kind can hardly be made as a mere result of ordinary trading operations, and that there must be something in the values attached to the balance sheets of the different periods to explain so very large a discrepancy.

Let us start by pulling our title to pieces and considering each part of it separately. First of all, what is an auditor ? We need, I think, deal this evening only with auditors of companies. We know, I think, that the basic idea in having an auditor of the accounts of a company is that owing to the large number of shareholders in even comparatively small companies, it would be quite impracticable to give to each individual shareholder the right which every partner naturally possesses of making his own investigation of the accounts of the undertaking whenever he wants to do so. Thus we get the idea of an auditor, acting as agent for all the shareholders in making such examination of the accounts as may be thought necessary on behalf of them all. In the early days the auditor or auditors were, I think, invariably shareholders, and the practice of appointing auditors who are shareholders has not entirely died out up to the present time.

Let us ask ourselves what we mean by " responsibility." That word, I think, does not necessarily mean anything quite so strong as saying that

A lecture delivered before the Metropolitan Certified Accountants Students' Society on 9th March 1927.

an auditor is absolutely liable. The word "liable" is a little stronger, I think, than the word "responsible." To be responsible does not mean much more than to be answerable for or open to be called to account if the need arises, whereas the word "liable" is a very strong word indeed ; it implies being bound, and goes back to the times when debtors who were unable to pay were liable to be bound and sold into slavery. In modern conditions debtors are dealt with in a different way, and sometimes it is highly profitable to go through two or three bankruptcies, but the original idea was that a liability was taken very seriously indeed.

Now, as to a balance sheet, perhaps half the trouble in connection with our subject arises out of the fact that not everyone has the same opinion as to what a balance sheet is or ought to be. We who are versed in accounts know, of course, that a balance sheet is a summary of the balances appearing in a ledger after the Profit and Loss Account had been closed, and that, if the Profit and Loss Account has been properly prepared, it follows that the items which come into the balance sheet are items which are properly excluded from the Profit and Loss Account, because if they are credit balances, they are not profits, and if they are debit balances, they are not outlays properly and fairly chargeable against the operations of the current period.

It does not follow as a matter of course from that that everything which goes into the balance sheet is either a debt capable of being extracted from the company by legal process immediately, or, on the other hand, an asset capable of being turned into money to an amount equal to the figure appearing against it. A balance sheet, we at least know, is not precisely the same thing as a statement of affairs which would be placed before the creditors in an insolvency, but many persons certainly seem to think that a balance sheet ought to be a precise statement of assets and liabilities based upon realisable values, and I think that a great deal of the criticism which has been directed against balance sheets has arisen out of that misunderstanding.

Lastly, as regards our title, we come to the word "value." Now, that word merely represents "worth" or "strength." It has not necessarily a meaning absolutely tied up with money, or something capable of being expressed in terms of money. If a thing is of value it must be of worth, and it implies the idea of strength. That is quite all right from the point of view of balance sheet values. The possessions or resources of a company are, of course, the measure of its strength, but there is a difference between a concern being strong in the purely static sense of possessing property, and "going strong" in the dynamic sense of being possessed of a valuable and profitable undertaking.

There are many different ways in which values may be computed. One method is to base them on cost price, on the assumption that at least it was a measure of value at the time when they were acquired, and that, perhaps, nothing has happened since of a sufficiently definite character to provide us with any better basis for a revaluation, which, of course, may or may not be true, according to the circumstances. An alternative basis of valuation is the estimated cost at the present time of replacing the article in question. It would differ from the original price to the extent to which prices had varied in the meantime, and also to the extent to which the condition and general utility of the article in question had been affected by the lapse of time.

Another basis of valuation would be the price at which the article in question could be sold, and another would be the price at which we should be willing to sell it, which is not necessarily the same thing. If we are very anxious to realise, we may be content to accept a lower price than that which we might be able to obtain if we were in no particular hurry. Finally, there is, as a possible basis of value, the actual prices at which such things are being currently sold, a basis which is valuable, of course, only upon the assumption that there are considerable quantities of precisely similar things which are being readily dealt in and for which, therefore, we have, in fact, a current market price.

These different bases of values are not by any means all capable of being ascertained with precision, and some of them, as you will not have failed to notice, are based upon what it would cost to acquire such an article, while others are based on what one might expect if one were a seller instead of a purchaser. There would always necessarily be a difference between the buying and the selling price, that difference being the basis of trading profits. Apart, however, from any question of how we are going to value the individual assets comprised in a balance sheet, we need to remember that in the case of a business which is going on and which there is every reason to suppose will continue to go on, the value of the assets as they stand is not necessarily the same thing as the value of such assets if the business was being discontinued and sold piecemeal. Whatever basis we may select for our valuation, there will be a difference between an undertaking as a going concern and the individual possessions of that undertaking sold at break-up prices. Clearly, so long as there is no reason to suppose that the business of an undertaking is going to be discontinued, then the going-concern value, if we could arrive at it, is much more interesting for our purpose than a hypothetical break-up value. We might put it in a rather different way, and it is sometimes convenient to do so. If we have before us the balance sheet of any ordinary concern, and if we are going to accept the valuations placed upon the various assets, we may say that the company itself is possessed of wealth equal to the total of those assets, subject to the payment of its proper debt—what it owes to outside creditors—and we may call that new figure the aggregate free assets of the undertaking. That is what it has, or what presumably it would have, after providing for the payment of its just debts, and that is the measure of the property of the shareholders.

Theoretically, the aggregate amount of free assets ought to come to the same thing as the aggregate market value of the shares of the company. If it does not, there must be a discrepancy between the valuation placed upon the assets in the balance sheet, and the valuation placed upon the shares by those whose opinions have determined the current market price of the shares. It does not necessarily follow, of course, that the balance sheet is wrong and the market price is right. It is just as likely that the reverse is the case, or that both are wrong. We should. in practice, invariably find a fairly wide discrepancy between the two.

That discrepancy is often so wide that although we know that market prices are not always right and that they vary from day to day and even from hour to hour far more violently than the actual position of the company can possibly be varying, yet if we find a permanent discrepancy between the two, it does suggest that a balance sheet is of little if any use to those who wish to derive from it some information as to the value of the shares. After all, that is one of the uses to which balance sheets are commonly put, whether it be reasonable or unreasonable, that they should be employed for that purpose.

There is another aspect of that, which it is well for us to consider. I referred just now to fluctuations in the market price of shares of companies, which obviously cannot be explained by alterations in the general condition and prospects of those companies as measured in terms of accounts. They can sometimes be assigned to a definite cause, such as the death or retirement of a director, which might have a very adverse effect upon the price of the shares. It is not easy to see how we can make any accounting entries to correspond with that in the books of the concern, but at the same time we should be forced to state that something had happened which altered the value of the undertaking as a whole. It looks, therefore, as if we should have to admit a paradox—that the value of an undertaking as a whole is not necessarily the same thing as the aggregate value of its different parts, in spite of the mathematical axiom that it is.

Now, let us pass on to consider the assets of companies a little more in detail. You are all, of course, familiar with the broad distinction between fixed assets and floating assets, so I need not stop to labour that point beyond reminding you, perhaps, that it is not possible for anyone to make two lists of articles and say that list A contains always fixed assets, while those in list B are always floating assets. It is not a matter of classifying the articles themselves, but of inquiring for what purposes they are held by a particular concern. If they are intended to be retained in their existing form and used as equipment to facilitate the earning of profits, then, of course, they are fixed assets. Use is the essential thing that we have to look for. That suggests that we have to discriminate between a thing being used and a thing being used up. Most things in the process of being used tend to become used up, and, therefore, in any just valuation we have to take into account the fact that they are in process of being used up, and that we do in the ordinary way by the process which we call " providing for depreciation."

I think you will agree with me that, if our accounts are prepared as they should be, the object of providing for depreciation is not primarily to revise balance sheet values with a view to restating them according to current prices (whether buying prices or selling prices), but it is rather a method of spreading over a series of years, each of which has had or will have the use of the articles in question, that loss which will ultimately be found to have resulted from the marked difference between what it will be possible to sell the fixed assets for when discarded as no longer useful and what it cost us to acquire them in the first instance. The whole of the difference between the original cost and the ultimate scrap value is part of the working expenses of the period during which they are in use, and the aim of providing for depreciation, even though it may not always be achieved, is to spread this loss properly and equitably over the whole series of years.

That we have to make the calculation in advance makes it, of course, always liable to error, but, if the calculation be made carefully by competent persons—by which I mean persons competent to be trusted with the buying of those articles in the first instance—they should know sufficient about them and about their enduring qualities to be able on the average to form a very fairly reliable estimate in advance of the length of time during which they will be useful. Otherwise it would have been impossible for them to form any opinion as to whether they were worth buying at that price or not. It is one thing, of course, to say that directors and managers of companies ought to be able to estimate provision for depreciation in advance with some approach to accuracy, and it would be another thing altogether for the law to make them liable for any mistake in their estimate, and that, I think, without doubt is the reason why the law (as represented by legal decisions from time to time) has been so very chary of laying down any dictum compelling even an honest attempt to be made to provide for depreciation where directors have thought fit not to make such a provision. But we must not lose sight of the fact in our criticism of balance sheets as commonly prepared that, if and when they do make provision for depreciation they are doing something more than the law compels, and, therefore, if it be done imperfectly, that is apparently only what the law anticipated would be likely to happen.

If we make our provision for depreciation upon the usual business methods of aiming at spreading the ultimate loss equitably over a series of years, it must, of course, inevitably follow that that portion of the original cost which we carry forward from year to year—the " written-down value " as it has often been called—will be a figure entirely different from any figure which we might expect to arrive at arising out of a revaluation of the assets, considering them merely from the point of view of their present values as distinct from spreading the depreciation loss.

So far as I can see there is no means by which it is possible to spread the depreciation charge equitably over a series of years so as to arrive at a reasonable statement of profit year by year and at the same time produce a balance sheet which will give a revaluation of assets year by year based on current values, even supposing that we thought we would like to have a balance sheet on those lines. On the question of the possibility of a revaluation of assets from time to time, according to their then actual value, as distinct from a written-down value arrived at by some process of calculating provision for depreciation, it would be necessary to take into account not merely the deterioration in value arising from depreciation, but also alterations in prices of such articles from time to time. Those alterations might be upwards or downwards, or upwards as regards some items and downwards as regards others. For instance, during the war you will remember that current prices of anything in the nature of machinery tended to soar upwards. If we were to revalue plant and machinery to give effect to those new prices, and if we allowed for depreciation arising from wear and tear, we should probably have been able to show a profit for at all events a couple of years on the possession of equipment in the form of plant and machinery. Again, at all times there is a tendency for business premises to increase in value to an extent which very often more than covers any deterioration in the fabric of the building arising from wear and tear.

Any attempt at revaluation could hardly ignore price fluctuations, and, if that valuation were to be brought into the Profit and Loss Account, the Profit and Loss Account would no longer afford us any reliable index to the actual results of what we might call the legitimate business operations of the concern. We should therefore be losing one of the main things which it should be the function of the accounts to show.

Floating assets, on the other hand, I suppose everybody admits, must be revalued for balance sheet purposes, but the revaluation there is not always carried out in its entirety, particularly if the result of a revaluation would be to write up the book figure, as it might be if the prices of certain commodities, which are being dealt in, had risen appreciably or, in the case of investments, if there had been a general rise in prices as compared with those existing at the date of the previous balance sheet. We usually find, therefore, that the revaluation of floating assets is limited—and, I think we are all agreed, properly limited—to taking account of any decline in value, while deliberately ignoring any increase in value. That more or less brings us to a state of affairs such as we normally find in the balance sheet of every really prosperous concern—that the true position of affairs is not represented by the assets stated in the balance sheet, and the true position is more favourable than the position shown upon paper, because there have been improvements in value which have been deliberately excluded.

Now let us turn to another aspect of the matter—the extent to which we are able to form any idea of the real value of the possessions of the company by looking at its balance sheet. It is clear that those possessions or assets must be stated in such a way that we really can get an intelligible idea of the position from reading the balance sheet. In this country a balance sheet is never published which is a complete list of all ledger balances; it is always in summarised form, but while it is the invariable rule and while it is, I think we shall agree, perfectly legitimate to summarise the items in the balance sheet, those items must at least be stated in sufficient detail in order to enable us to get the desired general impression from the balance sheet itself.

The different kinds of assets must be properly grouped so that different kinds of things are shown separately. Not only that, but before the impression which we obtain from the balance sheet can give us any clear idea at all it is necessary that somehow we should have the means of knowing on what basis the figures stated against those items have been arrived at. It will not necessarily be the same basis in all cases, even apart from the broad difference between the bases of valuing fixed assets and floating assets. Not all fixed assets will necessarily be valued in the same way, and perhaps not all floating assets either. There should be no uncertainty as to the basis and, if we are going to avoid uncertainty, it means that in some cases at least it is necessary to state by whom the valuation has been made.

Certainly, a very much more definite impression would often be obtained if that information were forthcoming. It is sometimes forthcoming, but much more frequently it is not. For instance, an item in the balance sheet, " Business premises, less depreciation," so much, informs us that something has been deducted to cover depreciation, and that is all. It does not even tell us who arrived at the amount to be deducted for depreciation, except by inference, the inference being that, as the balance sheet is signed by the directors, they are responsible for the way in which it is prepared. If, on the other hand, we were told that the amount of depreciation had been assessed by so-and-so, we should at least know that those figures were backed by the opinion of that individual, and, if we were able to form any idea of the value of his opinion, we should be nearer a clear idea of the use of the information which we had obtained.

Alternatively, if we have a note added to the effect that the business premises have been revalued by Messrs. So-and-So, a well-known firm of valuers, who now value the premises at so much, even although it may be an entirely different figure from the effective one in the balance sheet, the information becomes very much more definite in consequence. Similarly, with regard to the valuation of stock-in-trade, if those responsible for the valuation had their names disclosed—if not on the face of the balance sheet, in the directors' report—they would, I feel sure, in the vast majority of cases, feel their responsibility more acutely than if they knew that they were going to remain anonymous. The source of the basis on which the valuation is made can hardly ever fail to add to the use of the valuation itself.

We in this room all know that when anything goes wrong in connection with the finances of a company it is the fashion to blame the auditors for everything. The auditor is always responsible for the due performance of his duties, but he is not responsible for everything, and he is certainly not responsible for the skill or want of skill with which the affairs of the company are managed. We want to remember—and we want,.I think, as much publicity as possible given to the fact—that the accounts of a company are not prepared by the company's auditors and that the auditors have no power to alter those accounts other than by bringing influence to bear upon the board to induce them to modify something which the auditors think ought to be modified or might be modified to the general advantage.

The auditor is simply a critic of the accounts as stated by the directors, and the accounts are the accounts of the directors, who are the parties liable to account to the shareholders. An auditor is not an insurer or a valuer. He does not guarantee the results of a company. He does not even guarantee that there is no error in the accounts put forward by the directors, even though he has reported upon them. It is no part of his duty to value assets. Indeed, in the majority of cases he would not be competent to make a valuation any more than anyone else concerned; neither has he the means of getting at the sources of information necessary to enable a proper valuation to be made.

For what it is worth again, we want to remember that the auditor is the agent of the company and not the agent of each separate shareholder. The duty that he as agent owes to his principal is therefore a duty to the company rather than to the individual shareholders. That being so, there must obviously be a limit to the extent to which he can be expected to go out of his way to disclose to individual shareholders a weakness which is the weakness of the company, his principal. He must, of course, perform the duties that he has undertaken to perform by the acceptance of fees, but he must be careful not to exceed those duties out of an excess of zeal.

Although the auditor has no special duty to individual shareholders, and still less to members of the public who are not shareholders, but may be thinking of becoming shareholders, he has, of course, a very important duty to perform to the company in reporting upon the balance sheet as presented to him, and it is, I think, quite worthy of serious consideration whether the Legislature, in providing what we may call a statutory form of formal report for an auditor to make to the shareholders, has not done something rather to encourage a perfunctory view of the auditor's real responsibility. When we have got a statutory form, that form, of course, must be used unless we are able to give full chapter and verse for departing from it. If the position were more elastic and the auditor left to select his own form of words, we should, I feel sure, in most cases, get better and more really useful reports from the auditors to the shareholders of companies. But, whatever we may say under that heading, I want to suggest to you the possibility that, apart altogether from an auditor's position in connection with the issuing of company balance sheets, there are other bodies that might do something towards strengthening the shareholder's position and making him less helpless in the hands of a board of directors.

There are four points, I think, for instance, in regard to which the Legislature might help. Speaking generally, I am no advocate of Parliamentary intervention in business affairs, but there are four points which might be altered, and I think that the alteration in each case would be entirely beneficial. First of all, I think that the very common practice of directors, when issuing accounts to the shareholders, of enclosing a stamped form of proxy in favour of some of their own number should be forbidden by law. While that practice is permitted, it is almost inconceivable that a board should fail to obtain a majority of the voting power, even although they might be quite unworthy of the trust. From such inquiries as I have made among shareholders who are not business people—and we have to remember that the vast majority of shareholders of most companies are not business people—I find that there is a very widespread impression that this stamped form, which they are asked to sign and get witnessed, is a receipt for the dividend which they are going to get after the meeting is held. They do not read it, and do not realise that it is a proxy form at all. If directors want proxies, I do not see why they should not tout for them at their own expense as other people have to do.

My next point is that I do not think that companies should be allowed to frame a provision in the articles of association as a result of which the holders of certain classes of shares are deprived of all voting power. That means for all practical purposes that they have the disadvantages of being shareholders and none of the safeguards. It is difficult to see what useful purpose is served, except that it makes it wholly unnecessary for the directors to trouble about securing a majority of votes save in those limited classes of shares which are not subject to this restriction.

In the third place, I think that when a company goes into compulsory liquidation—and I think we shall all agree that no company ever does go into compulsory liquidation unless there is something radically wrong with it—every director of that company should submit to a public examination somewhat analogous to a public examination in bankruptcy, and, until he has obtained the Registrar's certificate that he has passed that examination, it should not be competent for him to sit as a director on the board of any other company.

Fourthly—and this is perhaps the most contentious of the four points—I want to suggest to you that at all events in a very large number of cases—probably in the great majority of cases—no real difficulty would be experienced in prescribing a statutory form of published accounts that would be a very great improvement upon the vast majority of published accounts that one gets under present conditions. Statutory forms of accounts are at the present time provided for only a very limited number of different kinds of undertakings—railways, gas companies, electric light, and so on—but the idea is certainly capable of being expanded. By the provision of, say, half a dozen different statutory forms of account, I think it would be possible to provide something suitable to almost any conceivable kind of company.

Then, again, I think that both the Stock Exchange and banks might do a little to protect the unsuspicious public from many of the wildcat schemes that are inflicted upon them. Speaking generally, I think that professional accountants do not allow their names to appear on the prospectus of a new company unless they are satisfied as to its respectability and as to its having some reasonable prospect of success, but it is not so difficult to get the names of brokers or bankers upon the prospectus of a doubtful company, and there is less excuse for them, because brokers and bankers always insist upon a fee, whereas auditors commonly do not. If they are going to be paid a fee, for that fee they ought to be able to make adequate inquiries. They will, of course, be mistaken in some cases and misled in others, but I think something more might be done than is done at present. In the same way I think that the conditions under which the Stock Exchange allow dealings to take place in the shares of a company might be tightened up with advantage.

As suggestions coming in under a somewhat different heading, and which perhaps are less contentious, I should like to suggest to you that, without any kind of legislation, and without attempting to induce any kind of public body to take action, it is open to individual accountants as and when the opportunity arises to suggest to individual boards of directors that in the long run they might with considerable advantage to their companies do one or all of three things:—First of all, in all cases, publish something in the nature of a Revenue Account or a Trading and Profit and Loss Account—something which shows, however inadequately, how the profit has been arrived at, instead of merely giving us the bare figure and leaving us to guess as to its source. Many companies, of course, do publish Profit and Loss Accounts, but the majority of Profit and Loss Accounts published are far too meagre to serve any very useful purpose. There is a stock argument against that—that the publication of such figures which give information to competitors. It is very difficult to see what information that would be of any use to competitors can be given from any kind of Profit and Loss Account that one would suggest should be published.

Secondly, I think that many companies might with advantage follow a practice of issuing accounts more frequently than once a year. In some cases the expense of so doing might be prohibitive, but in many cases quarterly accounts are actually prepared for the use of the directors, and when that is the case, it is not very easy to see why the rank and file of the shareholders should not have the advantage of the same information.

Thirdly, if it be thought desirable to meet in some way what is undoubtedly a rather insistent public demand, even if it is not a very well informed demand, for balance sheets that are really statements of affairs —revaluations of assets from time to time—that might, I think, best be met by the publication, not necessarily every year, but, say, every five years, of something in the nature of a valuation report like that which life assurance companies provide, quite independently of the annual balance sheet and not necessarily in any way linked up with it, but a quinquennial statement which would aim at showing the true position at the then current values as far as is reasonably practicable. It would not be impossible to prepare a valuation balance sheet of that kind, and it would certainly go a long way towards meeting this criticism which is so frequently levelled against balance sheets that the values placed in them are illusory, because they are not current realisable values.

In the long run, of course, the welfare of the investing public does not depend—perhaps it is fortunate—upon any Act of Parliament or similar regulation. It depends in the main—I think we shall all agree— upon the honesty and capacity of individual professional men who may be employed to audit the accounts of different companies. Where the selection has been wisely made the results will be as satisfactory as any kind of regulation or enactment could make them, even although auditors suffer, as they do, under the disability of having only limited powers to deal with the position.

ACCOUNTING METHODS-YESTERDAY, TODAY AND TOMORROW

Lawrence R. Dicksee

ACCOUNTING METHODS— YESTERDAY, TO-DAY AND TO-MORROW—I

By Lawrence R. Dicksee, M.Com., F.C.A.

Emeritus Professor of Accountancy and Business Methods in the University of London

During the past twenty-five years, considerable alterations have taken place in accounting methods, partly in consequence of the introduction of cards and loose-leaf systems in place of bound books, and partly as a result of the introduction of mechanical methods. Twenty-five years represents something like a generation ; at all events, a very large proportion of those actively engaged in accounting to-day have had no practical acquaintance with bookkeeping methods as they existed with surprisingly little modification or improvement between 1494 (when Lucas Pacioli's monumental treatise was published) and (say) 1904, which is approximately the date when card and loose-leaf systems began to be at all general in this country.

Far exceeding the exploits of Rip Van Winkle or the Seven Sleepers of Ephesus, bookkeeping succeeded in hibernating for something like 410 years ; but since it came to life again and took its place as a living rather than a dead art, it has been doing its best to make up for loss of time, and the strides that it has made have been literally enormous. The object of the present articles is, however, to suggest that the present day pioneer has been so preoccupied with making progress that he has failed to see the forest for the trees ; that is to say, he has been so concerned with improvements of method and improvements of detail, that his work is largely in the nature of a highly ornamental superstructure reared upon a foundation originally intended for something very much more modest. The time, I think, has come when at all events some attempt should be made to co-ordinate the modern methods upon a rational basis which will serve to render further developments possible without a wholesale re-casting of methods each time a new advance is contemplated.

If we endeavour to get down to first principles, and ask ourselves what really are the objects to be aimed at in keeping accounts, a wholly satisfactory answer may, it is thought, be found in the following quotation :—" There are two objects to be aimed at, (1) It is necessary that the record be so explicit that at any subsequent time the exact nature of the transaction may readily be perceived without the aid of the memory ; (2) It is necessary that the transactions should be so classified that at any time the combined effect of such transactions during any given period, or at any given time, may readily be ascertained."

This quotation has been selected because, although it was written as long ago as 1891, it is just as satisfying to-day as when originally penned. If we regard it as a statement of basic principles, from which no departure can be permitted, it may prove of considerable interest to inquire how far short-cutting methods yet evolved have respected the principles here laid down, and also what (if any) further development in short-cutting is possible which does not infringe these principles and is therefore admittedly legitimate, not in any pedantic sense but in the purely practical sense of answering every reasonable requirement at all times.

Every reader of *The Accountant* knows, of course, that medieval methods of accounting were cumbersome in the extreme. Probably, however, few know that so recently as fifty or sixty years ago it was a common thing to find City business houses regarding the journal as their most important book of account. All transactions were journalised, and in some cases it was not until the end of the year that the posting from the journal to the ledger was begun ! We seem to have travelled a very long way since then, but it remains to be seen whether we have travelled quite so far as we think we have in the direction of moulding our accounting methods to our actual needs, rather than regarding them as some form of ritual which must at all costs be observed.

The transactions that fall to be recorded as such under accounting systems may be divided broadly into two classes : (*a*) those between a business house and the outside world, and (*b*) those between one branch or department of a business house and another department or branch. Under whichever of these two classes transactions come, some communication is necessary between the parties, either setting out the particulars of the transaction, or confirming the particulars as stated by the other side. Until comparatively recent times, these communications were built up as separate and distinct documents, hand-made copies of which were inscribed by each party in so-called " books of original entry," thus fulfilling the first of the two basic principles already mentioned that it is necessary that the record be so explicit that at any subsequent time the exact nature of the transaction may readily be perceived without the aid of the memory.

In order to fulfil the second requisite, that the transactions should be so classified that at any time their combined effect during any given period, or at any given time, might readily be ascertained, the traditional practice was to " post " from books of original entry to appropriate ledger accounts. When everything was journalised, each transaction had literally to be posted twice over, thus giving rise to the familiar term " double entry " ; but with the substitution of specialised journals for the old-fashioned " omnibus " journal, it was possible to effect a very considerable saving by posting group totals, with the result that in many cases " double entry " might be more accurately described as being (say) " 1.05 entry." But, even as far as we have gone, it will be seen that a record of the original transaction had to be made by pen and hand at least three times, with the possibility of copying errors creeping in at every stage.

ACCOUNTING METHODS— YESTERDAY, TO-DAY AND TO-MORROW—II

By *Lawrence R. Dicksee, M.Com., F.C.A.*
Emeritus Professor of Accountancy and Business Methods in the University of London

As transactions multiplied, an ever-increasing difficulty was naturally experienced in effecting an exact agreement of trial balance totals, with the result that sectional balancing became absolutely necessary if indeed the idea of an exact balance was not to be given up altogether. This need for sectional balancing naturally increased the difficulty of reducing the number of ledger entries by group posting ; but the difficulties, although considerable, were not insuperable. The columnar book of original entry provided one possible method ; the late Sir John Craggs, M.V.O., F.C.A., evolved another;

while yet another (the exact origin of which seems very uncertain) is what is called the " Check-Number Method." Each of these devices aims at localising such errors as may creep in as the result of continual re-copying. The Check-Number Method is no doubt the most effective localiser, but it is cumbersome and has never come into general use. The Craggs system, on the other hand, may be focused, so to speak, so as to localise errors within a fairly narrow compass, and is easy of application when once its methods have been mastered. Sectional balancing, on the other hand, only localises errors within quite wide limits; and therefore in practice its advantages are limited to setting free for new work those clerks whose work in the past has been found to be without error, while leaving those who have made mistakes to continue to hunt for them as best they can.

The general introduction of the typewriter, combined with the employment of carbon sheets for the purpose of multiplying mechanically prepared facsimile copies of original entries, effected an enormous advance (a) By cutting out all possibility of discrepancies between the original documents passing from one business house to another, or from one department or branch of a business house to another, and the records of the same transaction preserved at the source of the transaction ; (b) When each transaction recorded was entered upon a separate slip, as a distinct unit, further economies became practicable by sorting out the unit slips and handing to each ledger clerk those slips representing transactions affecting the accounts of which he, and he alone, was in charge ; (c) The flexibility of the unit system was also of enormous advantage, in that with the aid of adding machines it became a very simple matter to arrive at group totals for sectional balancing purposes. But at this stage the actual posting of transactions to ledger accounts was still a pen and hand proceeding.

The next step was the introduction of ledger posting machines. Some of these may best be described as a development of the typewriter, so modified as to enable it to build up the totals requisite for sectional balancing purposes ; and in the later examples, by means of a subtracting device, to arrive at net totals which were of course equivalent to ledger balances. The other method of approach was along the lines of elaborating adding machines, so that in addition to handling and printing figures, they might be made to attach to the record such abbreviations of dates, particulars, etc., as were reasonably necessary to make the record suitable for a ledger account. These two separate lines of approach seem to have met in the Burroughs Moon-Hopkins Ledger Posting Machine, which combines the ordinary Burroughs Adding, Subtracting and Listing Machine with a standard keyboard typewriter.

In the meanwhile, typewriters had evolved automatic tabulators and automatic returning carriages. These improvements applied to the ledger posting machine made it quite practicable to build up ledger accounts and statement sheets simultaneously, and at the same time construct a continuous list of postings known by various names such as a "proof strip," an "audit strip," etc., which would give the automatic total of postings actually effected in the course of a given running period for comparison and agreement with the previously (or subsequently) prepared machine total of the unit slips that had been handled upon the posting machine. If there should be any discrepancy between these two totals, inasmuch as the items would be in the same order upon each strip, a calling over of one strip against the other would enable the error to be localised with a minimum expenditure of time.

In some cases it is possible even to go one step farther, and to make the ledger record contemporaneously with the typewritten record of the original transaction, either by carboning the posting on to the ledger sheet at the same time that the original entry is being typed, or alternatively by filing away a set of unit forms under the account numbers as constituting each a separate ledger account. The present generation may well look with some complacency at the enormous strides that have thus been made in the course of a single generation ; but just because the advances gained have been so very marked it has seemed desirable to emphasise the fact that the *Ultima Thule* has not yet been reached..

ACCOUNTING METHODS—YESTERDAY, TO-DAY AND TO-MORROW—III

By Lawrence R. Dicksee, M.Com., F.C.A.

Emeritus Professor of Accountancy and Business Methods in the University of London

At this stage, it may perhaps be convenient to repeat what has already been stated, that the second main object of accounting is " that the transactions should be so classified that at any time their combined effect during any given period, or at any given time, may readily be ascertained."

So far as we have traced the evolution of modern accounting methods up to the present, it will be seen that all that has been done is to speed up the interval between the occurrence of the transaction, and the time when its record (duly classified) finds its appropriate place in the ledger accounts affected. The ledger accounts may be typewritten, instead of being written with pen and ink, and the employment of group totals has to an enormous extent reduced the number of detailed entries necessary upon some of the nominal accounts ; but in other respects, with the single exception of the slip ledgers—which, for obvious reasons, have only a very limited application in practice—ledger accounts are in very much the same form as they were in the Year of Grace 1494. A reference to any individual ledger account (provided that account has been posted up to date) will enable one to ascertain the balance of that account by the process of casting up the debits and credits and striking a balance between the two ; or if the account be machine posted, by reference to the last entry in the balance column. But if we want to ascertain the total of all the balances, or all the balances of a particular group, we still have to list them ; and if the busy man wants to scrutinise balances, he will naturally wish to have them in list form rather than turn over the pages of the ledger and consider them one at a time. Using slips for first entry records, and cards or loose leaves for ledger records of course reduces to a minimum the weight of dead matter that has to be handled every time a living fact is sought for, but there is surely still room for improvement in the classification of business transactions so that their combined effect may be reached. This is true, even if we limit ourselves to such information as is absolutely essential for purely accounting purposes. If we extend our requirements so as to cover other information that may be vital for the purpose of preparing management statistics, the incompleteness of the results so far achieved becomes even more marked.

It is for these reasons that it seems to me that future improvements in accounting methods must lie along the lines of employing perforated cards as full and detailed records of original transactions, subsequently handled by mechanical sorting, counting and tabulating machines, so that any desired result may be reached at any desired moment with a minimum expenditure of time and trouble. It is clear that, so long as we retain the ability to build up our transactions in any desired form with any desired volume of detail, whenever we want infor-

mation from any particular view-point, that is really all that is necessary. The laborious construction of ledger accounts merely for the sake of enabling them to be listed into a trial balance is surely but a relic of medieval superstition. Such an assertion may seem revolutionary to some. If so, it may be pointed out that not every form of revolution is undesirable. Many of the most important forms of movement are essentially revolutionary. In a mechanical age to veto revolution would be almost the same thing as vetoing motion itself !

Probably the majority of my readers have heard of the Wheatstone Bridge used in telegraphy, which is known to be the fastest telegraphic converter of punched holes into figures or letters that exists. Precisely the same description applies, and precisely the same principle is employed, in connection with the Hollerith and similar machines in accountancy. The main difference is that in the case of the Wheatstone Bridge, everything has to be reproduced, whereas in the case of the Hollerith, we have the remarkable and particularly interesting feature that we can at will suppress just as much of the detailed record as we do not happen to want to use at the moment, and only reproduce that part which is wanted. There is accordingly no system capable of treating transactions with anything approaching the same degree of speed, while the accuracy with which they are handled is unchallengeable. Just as much of the information as may be contained on the punched cards, and no more than is required for the particular purpose in view, may be printed. Accordingly, it becomes a simple matter to classify transactions from any desired point of view, and to compress the results into the smallest possible amount of space. In this way, actual ledger postings may be reduced to one posting per day on each account—or, of course, one posting per month, if one is content to wait for a monthly total—and thus the actual ledger accounts of even a very large concern may be kept within strictly moderate proportions.

But, unlike most accounting systems, the Hollerith does not insist that the designer should make up his mind in advance precisely what information he will need in the future, and strictly limit him to information framed upon those particular lines. If at any stage in the development of an undertaking it should be desired to ascertain any sort of information whatsoever arising out of the transactions that have occurred, the Hollerith can supply the information with unerring accuracy, and in a space of time that is negligible as compared with any other conceivable method. The information, whatever it may be, is on the punched cards, and only the sorter and tabulator are needed to draw it out and set it up in printed form in just as much detail as may be wished for, and no more. Thus, if a trader should wish to know the quantities of any particular commodity that he had sold during a stated period to each separate customer, the Hollerith could give it to him unerringly. If he wished to know the quantity sold by each separate traveller, or in each separate district, the information will be given with equal facility, and any information not needed would be automatically suppressed, so that the facts when reached would be in a form really useful to the busy man.

Going back to the question of ordinary personal ledger accounts, as every reader of *The Accountant* knows, in the majority of cases a balanced account is never referred to again. It was a recognition of this fact that induced me to describe a form of slip ledger in the first edition of my " Advanced Accounting," published in 1903. A very large proportion of the personal accounts of most business houses are balanced off as a matter of course month by month. So long as it is known that they do balance, it is pure waste of time to build up ledger accounts in the old way which is never likely to be needed for any future purpose. But there is, of course, always the possibility that reference to an old account may be necessary, or desirable, even although it be a settled account. Under the Hollerith system, if and when the need arises, the account can be built up practically instantaneously ; but unless and until it is wanted, it remains so to speak in embryo. Time is not wasted in compiling it, space is not wasted in storing it.

The future evolution of accounting methods upon these lines represents of course something entirely different to the gradual development from medieval methods through unit slip records up to machine postings in card or loose-leaf ledgers. Because it is entirely different, it will doubtless be some little time before its claims to consideration are generally accepted. In the meanwhile the new idea will have to battle against exactly the same interested opposition that all mechanical methods of accounting have had to face, and that manufacturers of card and loose-leaf ledgers, etc., had to face from the manufacturers of bound books. But, sooner or later, the best will prevail ; and enormous as are the strides that have been made by Hollerith machines in this country during the past twelve years or so, they are, in my opinion, even yet only upon the threshold of the recognition that awaits them.

(To be continued.)

ACCOUNTING METHODS— YESTERDAY, TO-DAY AND TO-MORROW—IV

By Lawrence R. Dicksee, M.Com., F.C.A.

Emeritus Professor of Accountancy and Business Methods in the University of London

I have found it necessary to supplement the three articles that have already appeared in *The Accountant** under the above heading because, since these were penned, I have discovered that what I there spoke of as representing the probable future evolution of accounting methods is already actually in being and giving very satisfactory results.

A few days ago I was taken over the head office of an undertaking having about a dozen branches, each with a number of selling depots, where the whole accounting system is centralised at the head office and operated in its entirety by means of tabulating machines.

Carbon copies of the original documents recording the selling transactions are sent to each depot daily, by the selling agents, together with a summary recording the nominal aspect of these transactions and totals. Each depot amalgamates the summaries from its selling agents, and the depot summary, together with all the original documents, is passed to the branch, which in turn collects its depots' figures for the purpose of rendering a branch summary to the head office. These branch summaries—again with the original documents relating to all the depots and selling agents within their branch area—arrive at the head office.

Cards are now punched for each item on every original document. When the punching process is completed, the cards are tabulated to agree with the various branch and depot figures, as summarised. It is not uninteresting to note that when the system began to operate this process immediately revealed a large number of previously unsuspected errors in both calculations and additions, the cards being found to disagree in a number of cases with the hand-recorded figures on the summaries. It should be, perhaps, explained that this result was obtained by sorting the cards under commodities at a given price, and then obtaining a total of quantities at each price, the bulk extensions of which should naturally (when totalled with all the remaining bulk extensions) agree with the total of all figures rendered. Once the reconciliation has been made between the various summaries and the cards—but not before—the accounting can begin. This is a basic principle of the system.

Similar procedure is followed with regard to all documents relating to expenditure and the incurring of liabilities in any form whatsoever by the depots and branches. Cards are also punched to denote all movements with regard to usage of materials in any form, i.e. plant, tools, repairs, &c. &c.

From the foregoing it will be seen that these cards contain the details of every single accounting transaction relating to the particular period under consideration, and at every geographical point of the company's business.

Turning now to the uses of these cards, these can be divided into three groups, in order of operation :—

1. Nominal Account Recording.
2. Personal Account Recording.
3. Statistical Analysis.

Nominal Account Recording.—The cards are sorted under the various nominal account headings, and the financial totals pertaining thereto provide the figures for posting into a control account summary; summary cards being punched for sub-totals or details, to await the compilation of weekly and monthly, and finally an annual trading account.

Following this procedure the cards are sorted under the groupings from the nominal aspect, i.e. sales, packages, cash, sundry charges, credits, &c., and filed away, each subsequent day's transactions being added to each file.

Personal Account Recording.—It should be mentioned at this point that the original documents, after the cards have been punched therefrom, are filed in datal order under customer for the purpose of answering any queries that may arise during an intermediate period. At the end of the accounting month, the cards are tabulated in totals to agree the control book. This, of course, is to provide a check that no cards have been lost or abstracted during the period.

The cards are now sorted, together with the balance cards which have been punched with the balances of each customer's account at the conclusion of the previous accounting period, under customer No., and are run through the tabulator to produce the statement on which the customer pays—this statement, of course, giving full details of every transaction, both debit and credit, recorded during the month.

As a check on the complete accuracy of the figures, cards called turnover cards are punched to record the totals relating to opening and closing balances, current debits and current credits, in respect of each statement. Obviously a tabulation of these cards will prove that the accounting during the period under review, when related to the preceding period, is definitely accurate, and furthermore in agreement with the turnover figures as shown in the control book.

The turnover cards are again used for the purpose of compiling lists for each traveller, to enable the balance in each case to be collected.

Statistical Analysis.—The cards are finally sorted under the various statistical headings to show such statistics as are necessary for the payment of commissions, increases and decreases in debtors' balances, expansion and contraction of sales by classes of commodity and by geographical districts, &c. &c.

It will be appreciated that it would be impossible within the scope of these notes to give full details of the procedure followed, but mention should be made of the fact that various periodical financial returns (which may be called, for the purpose of this article, trading account, profit and loss account, and balance sheet) are compiled entirely by means of summary cards punched at various stages within the procedure described above.

The question will no doubt be asked as to what books of account remain to be kept, and the answer to this is—in effect—none. At the same time, it must not be thought that in consequence of this no figures are available. They most certainly are available, and in far greater detail than could possibly be the case in ordinary books of account ; with this one vital difference, that no figures have in any case been produced by hand.

*The previous articles appeared in our issues of December 7th, 14th, and 21st 1929.—Ed.

A few notes at this point as to the equipment necessary for the scheme which has been outlined may be of interest. The approximate number of items per diem is roughly 10,000-12,000, and the equipment comprises :—three sorting machines, and three tabulating machines with a suitable complement of punches.

At the moment a separate department is in operation which may be called the experimental section, where a special sorter and tabulator fitted with the most modern devices are occupied in testing possible improvements in the system already outlined. Foremost among these experiments is one for the provision of complete daily control, both in total and in detail, of all credit accounts. This latter point, i.e. the provision of control in detail, is in my experience quite novel, in that by no other known means is it possible to produce daily, and without any clerical labour, a complete proved list of balances on every customer's account. The most important feature of this work will be the provision of a daily comparison —made entirely mechanically—of customers' daily balances with their authorised credit limits, showing excesses or unabsorbed credits, as the case may be.

ACCOUNTING METHODS— YESTERDAY, TO-DAY AND TO-MORROW—V

By Lawrence R. Dicksee, M.Com., F.C.A.
Emeritus Professor of Accountancy and Business Methods in the University of London

Having outlined as briefly as possible the general idea of the system, attention may appropriately be drawn to at least the most obvious of its merits :

First, it has been found possible to establish the most immediate control over branch, depot, and selling agents' activities with the minimum of time lag.

Secondly, the methodical entering of accounts' figures in books, where their presence is of but passing interest, has been entirely eliminated.

Thirdly, the statistical data provided, in view of its production from the same document as the cash statements, must be in complete reconciliation with the financial figures throughout, and therefore accurate.

Fourthly, the system is operated by a staff which can reasonably be estimated at approximately 20 per cent. of the requirements under any hand system, and furthermore it has enabled a less qualified type of clerk to be employed at the various decentralised points.

Lastly, amongst other advantages, may be mentioned the question of saving in floor space, filing space, stationery and books.

Any description of an accounting system operated by office machinery is apt to tend, perhaps almost inevitably, to the merits of the system being lost sight of in contemplation of the ingenuity and novelty of the mechanical means employed to carry it out. That being so, it is perhaps worth while to stress the point that office machinery is not a substitute for an accounting system ; that all the most ingenious and reliable machine can do is to carry out a system designed by the human brain. Machines can perform " donkey work " excellently, but the most that they can be expected to do is to produce results along the lines of pre-conceived ideas born in the human brain, and it is fatal to expect office machinery to take the place of human intelligence.

That this pitfall has been avoided in the case which I have been describing in these notes, is clearly demonstrated by the fact that the time of the better qualified staff is not wasted in pure routine, but is available mainly for critical and observation work. Another proof of this can be seen in the excellence with which the cash in the undertaking is controlled.

After all, when an organisation provides that all moneys received by the various branches and depots are to be lodged daily with local banks under an arrangement whereby the total amount paid in each day is automatically transferred to the credit of the bank account of the head office, much more has been accomplished than the mere avoidance of the keeping of a number of separate cash books, or of one huge cash book with an enormous number of columns, each representing the account of a different local bank. If charges for keeping the account are to be avoided, it is necessary for a minimum bank balance to be carried under all conditions. If interest is to be avoided, similarly overdrawn accounts must be eschewed. A floating balance that would be quite adequate for one centralised account would be hopelessly inadequate for a hundred, or even for a dozen, separate bank accounts. By centralising the bank account, accordingly, more is accomplished than the mere simplification of records. A very material economy in bank charges is the inevitable result. Moreover, those in charge of the head office records are compelled to scrutinise the daily receipts and payments more closely than would be at all probable if the finances were decentralised.

The possibility of using office machinery undoubtedly encourages centralisation ; but the converse of this is probably a greater truism, namely, that centralisation encourages the employment of machinery. After all, the principal object of centralisation is economy ; not so much in terms of establishment charges, but in terms of control.

Some emphasis has been laid in the preceding paragraphs on the control of cash and quantities relating to the same figures ; but as with cash, so with goods, in fact, in financial effect, these two words are synonymous. It is not denied that what may be termed the physical centralisation of cash is easier of achievement than the physical centralisation of goods in the form of stocks, but the same principles of control apply. It may be impossible to centralise goods, but it is never impossible to centralise the numerical and financial control over them. The system which has been described shows that the cash control is obtained by punching cards from various cash records, e.g. invoices, debit notes, credit notes, cheques, money orders, paying-in slips, &c. The equivalent documents exist in the case of transactions with goods in the form of purchase invoices, debit notes for expenses, requisitions, credit notes and journal entries.

The punching of cards from these, whether it takes place at decentralised points or at a central office, will enable the strictest control of movement in any direction to be obtained by passing the cards through the sorting and tabulating machines. Increases and decreases of stock, excessive purchases or excessive usage of material, are known by those in control with the least practicable delay. Without either machines or the employment at a central office of a staff which by comparison with machines would prove uneconomic, those in control can do no more than wait for the manager at each decentralised point to compile his figures and transmit them periodically, and the only power that head office has in the matter is to ask for explanations as to why these or those figures are abnormal. The greater the period between the incident and the explanation of it, the more plausible will the explanation become, and the greater the possibilities of a recurrence of it ! Surely one of the primary objects of centralisation should be to prove the truth of the adage that " Prevention is better than Cure " ?

Much more might, of course, be said upon this very interesting subject of centralised control, but in connection with the present series of articles, the matter is only of importance from the point of view that a well organised system, for the average undertaking will always be one that can derive the utmost assistance from the intelligent employment of suitable office machinery.

I hope that the comments I have made will have at least indicated that the logical ultimate development of the mechanical accounting idea is really actually in being. Some of the developments are quite new, but others—and in particular the keeping of customers' records—have been in operation for nearly 18 months, and as such can be considered as being well beyond the experimental stage. The undertaking in question is of sufficient magnitude and importance to demonstrate the fact that the system is suitable and entirely adequate for any concern, no matter how numerous or intricate its transactions may be, and yet its proportions are such that the conclusion should not be drawn that such a system applies to large undertakings only.

The earlier methods of ledger-keeping will never become obsolete in the case of quite small concerns, but the larger the operations of a business, the greater scope there will always be for the introduction of mechanical labour-saving devices.

It may be added, as the tendency of the times is undoubtedly in the direction of amalgamating under a unified control businesses which were formerly carried on independently, that this unified control can only be made really effective by means of centralised accounting, with office machinery as its servant.

In conclusion, readers may be interested to know that the foregoing system is operated on an installation of Hollerith machines, and I am quite certain that any who are interested and would care to see a demonstration of it will be able to obtain the necessary permission from the British Tabulating Machine Co., Ltd., who own the machines in question.

POPULAR FALACIES

Lawrence R. Dicksee

The Accountants' Journal

Vol. 47	January 1930	No. 561

Popular Fallacies—I

By LAWRENCE R. DICKSEE, M.Com., F.C.A.
(Emeritus Professor of Accountancy and Business Methods in the
University of London)

I.—The Nature of Goodwill

The belief seems to be widely entertained that goodwill is neither more nor less than the capitalised value of the surplus profits of a business— that is to say, of its profits in excess of a reasonable charge for interest upon capital employed and for the remuneration of those engaged in its management. It is no doubt perfectly true that upon those occasions when goodwill has to be valued, its value is usually arrived at upon the basis of some computation made in accordance with this formula ; but it is one thing to say that when a valuation is necessary, goodwill must be valued upon some such basis as this, and it is an altogether different thing to say that goodwill *is* the capitalised value of past profits. The purchaser of the goodwill of a business does not buy the past profits, and he is only interested in them in so far as they afford an indication of what the future profits may be expected to be. It is the future profits, and the future profits alone, that the purchaser buys. It is accordingly in the future profits only that he is really interested ; and if a prospective purchaser seeks to estimate them by any process of arithmetical calculation based solely upon past profits, it is submitted that his estimate will be entirely fallacious, because his calculation will be based upon a complete misunderstanding—or at best only a very incomplete understanding—of what goodwill really is.

It seems most unfortunate that so distinguished an authority as Lord Eldon should have been so widely quoted as saying that goodwill is "nothing more than the probability that the old customers will resort to the old place." Like many other quotations that have achieved an almost world-wide circulation, this is a mis-quotation, which altogether fails to do justice to its author. What Lord Eldon actually did say in 1810 in the case of *Crutwell v. Lye* was " The goodwill which has been the subject of sale (in this case) is nothing more than the probability that the old customers will resort to the old place." As the business then in question was that of a country wagoner, the definition was probably sufficiently comprehensive, but it is far too narrow to be applied seriously to modern business conditions.

In the first place it may be pointed out that all business profits fluctuate.

In so far as these fluctuations are seasonal, they may of course be disregarded for present purposes, as the profits will be taken over a period sufficiently long to afford a just average. But in so far as the fluctuations are due to causes external to the business itself—to causes which affect the whole trade, or even many trades—the period over which the profits are taken will probably be shorter than the period representing a complete cycle of fluctuations and when that is the case a so-called valuation of goodwill based upon the average profits of past years will be altogether fallacious. The average profits will appear highest at the close of a boom period, i.e. just at the time when it is only to be expected that there will be a fall in profits in the near future. Conversely, the average profits will appear at their lowest at the end of a slump, when there is every reason to expect that general conditions will improve and profits increase. It is common knowledge that new companies formed to take over established businesses usually buy them at the close of a boom period at prices which, in the light of subsequent events, prove to have been greatly inflated. One cannot altogether blame vendors for seeking the highest price they are able to secure ; but it is hardly believable that they would have been able to obtain so high a price, were the above facts more generally appreciated.

From what has been said it will be seen why an established business is likely to be of more real value to a purchaser in the near future if it is bought at the beginning of a boom period, rather than at the end. But, apart altogether from profit fluctuations arising out of general conditions, over a long period of time the fortunes of any individual business house, so far from being uniform are apt to wax and wane for reasons intimately connected with the manner in which the business is being carried on for the time being. These fluctuations, arising from purely internal causes, will affect the profits of any business altogether apart from general conditions. Sometimes the two causes will pull together, sometimes they will be in opposition. If the profits of a particular business are rising more rapidly than the profits of other similar businesses, that business is improving in itself and thus becoming more valuable ; but if the profits of a particular business are not rising as rapidly as the general profits in that particular trade, the business is actually receding in that it is failing to secure its due share of the general prosperity. Conversely, if the general conditions are unfavourable and one particular business is not doing so badly as its competitors, that business is relatively speaking advancing, and in all probability it will retain the lead it has thus gained during the ensuing period of prosperity, whenever it comes about. It may of course be said that, however true these ideas may be, they are altogether too nebulous to find a place in any serious valuation of goodwill. If there were any known method of accurately assessing the value of the goodwill in any particular business, there would no doubt be a good deal of force in this objection ; but the suggestion is that nothing could be more " nebulous " than to value goodwill upon the assumption that the future profits of the business will depend upon the profits in the past, and upon nothing else.

From time to time the various authorities, legal and otherwise, have attempted to provide a more satisfactory definition of goodwill than that already quoted from Lord Eldon, and these all seem to agree in one respect, namely, that they regard goodwill as a payment to acquire the right to receive the future profits of a business, and assume that the constancy of those profits is assured by the reputation which the business has succeeded in establishing for itself among its customers. This view seems to ignore altogether two very important, but widely different, factors.

In the first place, however desirable it may be that a business should be so conducted as to secure the esteem and good wishes of its customers, and to establish with them a more or less fixed belief that they will get what they want better or in a more satisfactory way by dealing with that particular business house than with any other, no honest observer can fail to notice that some businesses are quite profitable that fail altogether to give any kind of satisfaction to their customers, and that some business men are exceedingly prosperous whom nobody really esteems. Other things being even, everybody desires to do what business they have to do pleasantly, and accordingly the pleasing of the customer is an important factor in the build up of any so-called goodwill; but in many cases any genuine " goodwill " between the proprietor of a business and his customers is altogether absent, and these are precisely the cases where it might be expected that a change of ownership (or a change of management) would make the least difference to the profits, and therefore the transferability of the goodwill would be at its greatest.

The second point is that it is altogether a mistake to suppose that success in business consists solely in pleasing the customer. In the majority of cases that is probably the most important factor; but it is never the only factor, and is not always even the most important. Apart from the general public—actual and potential customers—two other forces have to be reckoned with, employees and supplying houses. Unless the active goodwill of employees has been secured, no organisation will run smoothly, and accordingly no organisation can be expected to give uniform satisfaction to those who deal with it. The truth of this assertion is now very generally admitted. It is indeed the basis of the whole " Peace in Industry " movement. But what is less generally appreciated, even at the present time, is that those business houses that have secured the goodwill of their suppliers have an enormous advantage over those less highly favoured. When there is no shortage of goods this fact is very naturally apt to be lost sight of, but if there is anything approaching a scarcity, even if it only be a scarcity of goods available for prompt or early delivery, the supplier is in a position to pick and choose whom he will sell to, and he will not be the less quick to take advantage of the opportunity because it only comes his way upon somewhat rare occasions. Speaking generally, the buyer who pays promptly and makes no unnecessary trouble with regard to discounts, allowances and returns, will always have the first opportunity of buying goods when goods are generally scarce. That is to say, he will be given an advantage over competing houses just at the time when that advantage will be most useful to him.

It is not suggested that any formula can be designed which will enable all these varying factors to be taken into account in assessing the value of the goodwill of a business as at any particular date, but it is suggested that they all have a definite bearing upon the matter, and that any valuation based upon the assumption that they can be ignored must of necessity be unsatisfactory, and can only cause disappointment to those who rely upon it.

The vagueness of some current ideas concerning the nature of goodwill is well shown by some correspondence that has recently appeared in *The Accountant*. It is there suggested that Section 124 (2) (*c*) of the Companies Act, 1929, probably means that, wherever possible, (1) Goodwill, and (2) Patents and Trade Marks should be shown as separate items upon a company's balance sheet. This *may*, of course, have been the intention of the Legislature, but in any case where a company owns Patents or Trade Marks of any value these are an essential part of its goodwill, and could not be sold without serious damage to the goodwill. No one would buy the goodwill of a business, if the integral patents or trade marks had already been sold to a competitor. How, then, can the two be separated ?

Popular Fallacies—II

By LAWRENCE R. DICKSEE, M.Com., F.C.A.

(Emeritus Professor of Accountancy and Business Methods in the University of London)

VALUE AND PRICE

It is a trite saying that the value of anything is what it will fetch; a statement which, if it means anything at all, implies that the terms "price" and "value" are synonymous—an assertion which is so contrary to all human experience that it would seem hardly worth condemning were it not for the fact that the most serious consequences often ensue from a failure to realise the essential difference between the two.

In a living—as distinct from a dead—language it is only to be expected that from time to time new words will be coined aptly to express ideas, or combinations of ideas, that have recently come to the front; and, similarly, old words from time to time acquire a new meaning, sometimes altogether at variance with their original one. Nevertheless, if one wants to get to the bottom of the meaning of a word, it is always as well first to search for its derivation, for in that way one can at least arrive at its original meaning, which in these days of hurry is sometimes apt to be overlooked.

The word "price" is akin to the words "prize" and "praise," and may thus quite reasonably be described as the reward that the owner of a valued possession is willing to accept as compensation for parting with it. The word "value," on the other hand, is akin to "valour" or "strength" and thus would seem to describe the inherent qualities of an article, as distinct from what anyone may happen to think those inherent qualities to be. The terms "exchange value" or "value in exchange" may perhaps be held to mean the inherent qualities as judged by possible buyers and sellers. It may moreover be argued that it is exceedingly difficult to form any opinion as to the inherent qualities of anything, or anybody, unless and until one contemplates having to part from him, or it. But the fact remains that, so far from "price" and "value" being words intended to describe precisely the same idea, if the words are still to be used in anything approaching their original meaning, we must regard "value" as an inherent quality, existing quite independently of our appreciation of its worth; whereas "price" represents an attempt to express in figures our idea of value at any particular point of time and place, from our own particular point of view.

If this were a purely academic problem, it would, of course, be as little concerned with human activities as academic problems always are; but the essential point it is desired to stress in the present article is that, so far from " price " and " value " being the same thing, they are essentially different things, and that most of the troubles that arise in practical business are in fact caused by this particular confusion of ideas. If " Price " were the same thing as " value," there could be no such thing as " a bargain " ; it would be inconceivable that one should pay too little, or too much, for anything. But we all know that business troubles are caused very largely by paying too high a price for something (more than it is really worth), because one has, consciously or sub-consciously, assumed that a thing must be worth its price—meaning thereby the price at which such things then stand in the open market.

Any inquiry as to what constitutes " value " must necessarily be pro-tracted, and there is probably scope for considerable difference of opinion with regard to the ultimate solution, but an inquiry as to what constitutes price is a very much simpler matter in every way. The underlying prin-ciple can probably best be followed if we limit our inquiry to some parti-cular commodity (or group of commodities) that are continually being dealt in in the open market as, for instance, commodities dealt in daily upon the Stock Exchange. It is important, however, to bear in mind that the precise nature of the commodity has nothing to do with the under-lying principles, which are the same in all cases. If the quantity of identical articles in existence be very considerable, the conditions will correspond roughly with those normal upon the Stock Exchange in con-nection with any so-called " active " stock. If the number of articles be small, and necessarily limited, the procedure will follow that commonly observed when the articles in question as those in which collectors take an interest (e.g. old pictures, &c.); but this latter is only an extreme ex-ample of what might be observed any day upon the Stock Exchange in connection with a particular security when the market is said to be " short " of that particular stock.

The first point to be noticed is that market prices are the consequence of buying and selling orders. When buying orders are in excess, there is a tendency for there to be a scarcity of that particular stock. When selling orders are in excess, there is a glut of that particular stock. Save on those rare occasions when there is an absolute equality of buying and selling orders it would be impossible for all the orders to be executed on any one day, were it not for the jobbers, who take in stock when selling orders are in excess and give it out when buying orders are in excess. It is so rarely the case that there is an absolute parity of buying and selling orders that normally it is the jobber who makes the prices, which remain unchanged so long as there is an approximate parity between buying and selling orders, but tend to change so as to induce selling orders when the jobbers are short of stock and to en-courage buying orders when jobbers are overloaded with stock. Accord-ingly, assuming that there is anything like an active market, the market price tends to fluctuate in accordance with the trend of buying and selling orders received from the outside. This remains the primary cause of such fluctuations so long as the actual quantity of that particular stock in existence remains constant. When, however, the quantity of stock in

existence is increased by further issues the effect is much the same as
though selling orders were increased to a corresponding extent, and
prices tend to droop.   On the other hand, if the quantity of stock in existence be reduced (as for instance by redemption), the tendency is for
the price to rise, whether the redemptions are effected by actual buying
orders placed upon the market or by drawings, as a result of which certain
existing holders are compelled to sell at a fixed price.

But although market prices are thus primarily the result of buying and
selling orders, duly executed, they will to some extent be " shaded," so
to speak, by contingent orders or " limits."   Thus, if the present price of
a particular security be (say) 85-85½ it may be that there are limits (or
contingent orders) outstanding for considerable quantities of stock to be
sold at 85⅜ and other considerable orders for the stock to be purchased at
about the same price.   Naturally, while these limits remain outstanding
and unexecuted, the price of that particular security cannot go beyond
these particular figures, for immediately the price falls sufficiently the
buying limit comes into play and has a steadying effect, and similarly,
if the price rises sufficiently the selling limit comes into effect, thus checking the upward tendency.   But this is, of course, merely a refinement of
our original statement, that market prices are determined by buying and
selling orders.

The next point to be appreciated—and this is all-important—is that
it would be quite wrong to assume that all these buying and selling orders
come from persons equally well informed and equally intelligent.   The
theoretical economist is very apt to assume that all the phenomena he
observes have been dictated by the " enlightened self-interest " of the
individuals originating them.   There is no justification for the adjective
" enlightened."   Even those who buy or sell such commodities as cotton,
wheat, jute, rubber, &c., are not all equally capable and equally far-
seeing, but the illustration of Stock Exchange securities has been selected
because in this particular case it very often happens that the bulk of the
buying or the bulk of the selling orders (or of both) received from day to
day, while they may be dictated by self-interest, are certainly not dictated
by enlightened self-interest.   On the contrary, they may be dictated by
the grossest stupidity.   Whatever may be the motive that dictated them,
they will be equally effective in modifying current market prices, save
to the very limited extent that when jobbers feel certain that the public
has lost its head, they will not be so intent upon undoing all their business
as they go along as they would be in more normal times.   To the extent
to which jobbers are running a " bull " or " bear " account against the
public, their action will tend to modify the effect that the public's action
would otherwise have had upon current market prices.   But jobbers are
not reckless gamblers, and therefore the effect of this modification will
usually be comparatively slight at the time.   Indeed, very likely it will
only be noticeable as a somewhat steadying effect in the subsequent reaction, when the " bull " or the " bear " comes into the market to cover
himself by selling or buying, as the case may be, in a market where practically all the orders from the public are in the opposite direction.

If then it be true as a general proposition that market prices are dependent upon buying and selling orders received from the public (who are very often acting upon wrong information or no information at all), it follows that there may be marked alterations in prices which have little or no connection with the inherent ability of the undertaking to provide by way of dividend or interest an adequate return for the capital outlay of those who have acquired shares or stock—i.e., with value. But an artificial demand based upon mere hearsay is like seed sown upon a shallow soil. It is at the mercy of every wind of rumour that may blow, essentially unstable, and can only be stabilised by results. If these results are not forthcoming, public opinion will veer round, and the price will fall as rapidly as it rose, or perhaps even more rapidly. Prices can only be maintained at a higher level where there is a real increase of value, i.e., strength.

But this, of course, is based upon the assumption that the motive—whatever its wisdom—which induced buying orders was to invest for an adequate return by way of income. In point of fact, as everyone knows, a very large number of buying orders are not instigated by a desire to find a satisfactory investment of a more or less permanent nature, but by the belief that prices will rise further, and that it will therefore be possible to sell at a profit in the near future. That is to say, many who buy are buying in the hope of selling again at a profit, in just the same way that the trader buys goods in order to make a profit on their subsequent sale. Whatever the motive of buyers may be, so long as the buying orders from day to day appreciably exceed the selling orders, the price of even the most worthless security will tend to rise. But sooner or later it is inevitable that a price should be reached which, in view of the future possibilities of the undertaking, is no longer sufficiently attractive to maintain the necessary stream of surplus buying orders, and then the inevitable reaction sets in. In the long run truth will prevail, and in the long run market prices, although still directly caused by buying and selling orders, will tend to coincide with prices that are justified by performance or yield—i.e., with " value."

It is not a little curious that while a man whose business is in cotton would probably quite frankly admit that he was no judge of furniture or horses, and while a dealer in horses would be equally modest about his attainments as a judge of pictures or literature, almost everyone seems to think that he is a judge of Stock Exchange values, and may therefore hope to take profits out of a market that he does not understand. The root of the whole trouble, it is submitted, is a confusion as to the essential difference between " price " and " value." " Price " is what a thing may happen to fetch at a particular time and place ; " value " is rather what a thing can reasonably be expected to fetch, if and when a reasonably fair-minded buyer can be found willing to make an offer. That the price of a particular security, or of any particular article, has increased is no more evidence that that article has increased in value than a shortening of the odds against any particular race-horse is evidence that that horse will win the race. As every Stock Exchange man knows, prices are sometimes below values and sometimes above values. The right time to buy is when prices are below value, and the right time to sell is when prices are above value. To buy a security at an inflated price, in excess of its value, is like buying a ticket for a sweepstake at a price greatly in excess of the price of the ticket. As a venture it may come off, but the odds are far greater against the purchaser of the ticket than they were against the original subscriber.

Popular Fallacies—III

By LAWRENCE R. DICKSEE, M.Com., F.C.A.

(Emeritus Professor of Accountancy and Business Methods in the
University of London)

BALANCE SHEETS

There is a widespread belief that a balance sheet is a statement of fact,
and that it is the duty of the auditor to " certify " its correctness.   Should
any reader be disposed to regard this as too sweeping a statement, he may
be referred to the thirty-sixth question set at the Intermediate Examination of the Law Society held in November last, which reads " Draw out the
form of certificate which should be given by the auditor of a limited liability company at the foot of the company's balance sheet to satisfy the
statutory requirements as to such auditor's certificates."   If solicitors
talk in this loose way about auditor's " certificates " in an examination
paper, is it surprising that the views of investors—and even of business
men—should be equally indefinite ?

It ought, perhaps, to be noted that, although the examination in question was held after 1st November 1929, candidates were not expected to
answer in accordance with the terms of the Companies Act, 1929 (which
came into force upon that day), but in the terms of the obsolete Companies
(Consolidation) Act, 1908.   The powers and duties of auditors were set out
in Section 113 of that measure, and provided that the auditor " shall make
a report to the shareholders " on the accounts examined by him and on
every balance sheet laid before the company in general meeting during his
tenure of office " ;   but there was no provision anywhere in the Act concerning a form of " certificate " to be given at the foot of a company's
balance sheet.   Indeed, the only statutory duty of auditors with regard
to certification was to be found in Section 65 (4) which provided that the
statutory report to be submitted at the first statutory meeting of the company, so far as it related to the shares allotted by the company and to the

cash received in respect of such shares and to the receipts and payments of the company on capital account, was to be " certified as correct " by the auditors (if any) of the company.

Attention is drawn to this particular fallacy of confusing a report with a certificate, not from any desire to be hypercritical but because the distinction which has been carefully observed by the Legislature is of vital importance, as emphasising the fact that whereas an account of receipts and payments is a statement of fact capable of absolute verification, and therefore capable of being certified as correct, a balance sheet is nothing of the kind. A balance sheet is neither more nor less than a summary of the uncompleted transactions of an undertaking at a given moment of time, to which money values have been attached which in the nature of things must in the great majority of cases be matters of estimation or opinion only, or alternatively historical statements based upon actual cost on some prior date which may or may not have any real significance on the date at issue. It is as though someone with a sharp knife cut through the threads of all outstanding transactions, and presented a momentary vision of the section thus obtained. But, even then, the section may present an altogether abnormal appearance owing to the process known as " window-dressing," by means of which the normal progress of certain selected transactions may be hastened or retarded at will.

Many ill-informed persons suppose that a balance sheet is the same thing as a statement of affairs, but of course every reader of *The Accountants' Journal* knows that it is nothing of the kind. There is no known system of accounting which would enable a statement of affairs to be prepared from the books of an undertaking without numerous adjustments of the figures therein contained ; and many—although of course not all—of the necessary adjustments to obtain a proper statement of affairs would altogether destroy the accuracy of the profit and loss account, because they would of necessity have to take cognisance of capital profits and capital losses which have no proper place in the profit and loss account. Theoretically, of course, it would be quite possible to frame accounts so that a proper statement of affairs could be prepared from the books at the appointed time, and a correct profit and loss account also prepared showing the earning power of the business during the accounting period now brought to a close ; but this would only be possible if a second profit and loss account were introduced, dealing with losses and profits on capital account—which, in point of fact, is never done, and would be of very doubtful utility.

Probably the confused ideas that are still so prevalent are in part at least a heritage from the dark days of accounting, when almost everybody kept his records by so-called " single entry " and was therefore quite unable to build up any profit and loss account at all. Just as the fox that lost its tail in a trap tried to convince his brethren that it was in every way better to dispense with that unnecessary appendage, so those who had lost the art of preparing a profit and loss account from systematic records urged—and apparently continue to urge—that the divisible profits of an undertaking may be computed better from a statement of affairs than from a profit and loss account. Any discussion with such as these is pure waste of time. One might as well discuss music with the deaf, or colour schemes with the blind.

Whether we like it or not, the fact remains that a balance sheet is a summary of those balances remaining in a ledger (or set of ledgers) after a just profit and loss account has been prepared by transferring thereto the balances of all those accounts representing earnings during the period in question or working expenses properly chargeable against those earnings. The result is that the balance sheet contains, in some form or other, all those balances which have not been collected together into the profit and loss account, and also the balance of the profit and loss account itself as representing the combined result of its constituent items. It is primarily an historical statement, based not only upon the obvious " transactions " that have occurred, such as the receipt and payment of money and the receipt, dispatch and manufacture of goods, but also upon those non-obvious (or as they are sometimes called " imperceptible ") transactions, such as wages, salaries, rent, rates, taxes, interest, &c., accruing due, depreciation of wasting assets and price fluctuations, so far as they affect revenue, but no further.

So regarded, a balance sheet is just as much an " account " as any of the more usual ledger accounts. It is the account submitted by the management to the proprietors, in which the former debit themselves with everything that they have received (whether from the proprietors or from the outside world) and have not already paid back, under the heading of " liabilities," and on the other side show what they have got in the form of assets to represent this balance of receipts for which they are accountable ; including as assets every expenditure which is more properly chargeable against future profits than against current profits (e.g. payments in advance, expenditure upon plant, machinery, &c.) as well as those more obvious assets which in the ordinary course of business may be expected to crystallise into money, e.g. book debts and stock in trade.

Any balance sheet compiled from a set of books kept by double entry must be built up upon these lines. The real trouble would seem to be that so few persons realise its inevitable consequent limitations. Because they insist upon confusing it with a statement of affairs, they attempt to read into a balance sheet more than it can possibly contain ; to derive from its perusal information which it is quite beyond the capacity of a balance sheet to reveal. From time to time a good deal has been written upon the " interpretation " of balance sheets, and by no means all of it is utter nonsense ; but the fact remains that it is quite impossible for any interpreter to derive more information from any balance sheet than that measure of information which those who compiled it desired should be extracted. A balance sheet is probably the most diplomatic of all business documents.

It may quite frankly be conceded that this is an undesirable state of affairs ; that shareholders have every reasonable right to information concerning their own property, and reasonable opportunities of forming an opinion as to the ability, as well as the honesty, of their paid agents the directors. The remedy would seem to lie, not in the direction of attempting to make a balance sheet serve purposes for which it was never intended, and which it is quite incapable of performing, but rather in the direction of requiring the directors of every company, when submitting a balance sheet, to submit therewith a report giving all such information as it may be reasonable to call for, and to make the directors as strictly responsible for the accuracy of every statement contained in this report as they already are for the accuracy of every statement contained in the prospectus on the strength of which they obtained applications for shares in the first instance.

A company audit serves many useful purposes ; but, like a balance sheet, it is not calculated to give shareholders timely information as to the ability with which their undertaking is being managed, nor does it provide them with any reliable data upon which either the price or the value of their shares may be assessed. To the trained mind, both the published balance sheet and the auditor's report thereon may at times be exceedingly illuminating, but to the average investor they are worth little or nothing. Indeed, perhaps all that one can say is that a statement of affairs would perhaps be even less helpful to the average investor.

The Accountants' Journal

| Vol. 47 | April 1930 | No. 564 |

Popular Fallacies—IV

By LAWRENCE R. DICKSEE, M.Com., F.C.A.

(Emeritus Professor of Accountancy and Business Methods in the
University of London)

INTANGIBLE ASSETS

It would perhaps be overstating the case to say that any "fallacy" underlies the employment of the word "assets" as commonly used ; but there can, it is thought, be no serious question as to the host of fallacies imported by the use of the qualifying adjective "intangible" in connection with the word "assets."

In its original sense, of course, the word "assets" implied nothing more than the idea of adequacy or sufficiency. When a statement of affairs is prepared, one first of all sets out the liabilities of the undertaking and then one sets out against them that which is available to meet those various liabilities. If this latter total be in excess, the concern is solvent—there is a state of sufficiency. The word "assets" accordingly,. thus used, implies that those things which are available to meet liabilities are more than sufficient for that purpose. If they were insufficient to meet the liabilities, strictly speaking there would be no sufficiency and therefore no "assets" ; but in common parlance that which is available to meet liabilities is spoken of as "assets," however insufficient it may be for that purpose. And this is now so well understood that it seems quite unnecessary to protest against the altered meaning of the word, which in this particular case at least no longer involves any real ambiguity

When we turn our attention to the word "intangible," however, we find that this word not only involves a considerable amount of ambiguity and uncertainty but also not a little essential fallacy. Strictly speaking the word "intangible" means "untouchable," "impalpable," "non-material" ; and many (who must surely be materialists at heart) have stated—and upon occasion continue to state in no unmeasured terms—that "intangible assets" are unsatisfactory items in any balance sheet. If we are to take such an assertion literally, it means, of course, that the only satisfactory assets are visible, tangible and material assets, such as land, buildings, plant, machinery and stock-in-trade. Apart altogether from such assets as goodwill, patents, trade-marks, copyrights, &c. (which we will consider shortly), book debts are quite "intangible" ; and, judged by this materialistic standard, it seems questionable whether investments or bills receivable are more than mere "scraps of paper." Even a bank balance is only a book debt, and therefore intangible! From the lawyer's point of view a bank balance, like book debts, is not property, but merely a *chose in action*. It seems quite clear, therefore, that however we may look at the matter this tirade against intangible assets is altogether over-stated, and must be modified considerably before it can be taken seriously.

Some such modification was adopted by the writer of a leading article in *The Times* some years ago, who after stating that " a goodwill is valuable only as long as a company is doing well, the directors cannot borrow on its security when bad times come, and if the worst comes to the worst and liquidation is necessary, its selling price will *ex hypothesi* have vanished almost completely," went on to say that " nothing should be reckoned as an asset which cannot be taken to a bank as security for an advance." Recent experience has shown that not everything that may be taken to a bank as security for an advance can safely be regarded as a good asset; but assuming that we are willing (as the writer of *The Times* article evidently was) to accept banks as the final arbiters on the question of what is an asset and what is not, it seems very doubtful whether the question can be, or ever is, decided upon a purely materialistic basis. J. Pierpont Morgan—probably one of the shrewdest bankers who ever lived—is reported to have stated that he lent money on character—usually upon character plus securities, sometimes upon character alone, but never upon securities alone—and recent events have abundantly proved the wisdom of such a policy, for in the long run it will pay nobody to have business dealings with unscrupulous persons. Yet, surely, character—the one thing above all others upon which bankers ought to make advances—is the most intangible of all assets!

These considerations, however, by no means exhaust the subject. Let us take it for granted that the reputation of a company and of its directors is such that bankers will not hesitate to make advances to that company against security; the suggestion, is, however, that the directors ought not to submit to the bankers a balance sheet of that company setting out good-will as one of the " assets," because " nothing should be reckoned as an asset which cannot be taken to a bank as security for an advance." If this means anything at all, it means presumably that in an approved case a bank may quite properly make an advance to a company upon the security of its business premises, plant, machinery, and stock-in-trade (and possibly also upon its book debts and uncalled capital, if covered by a floating charge), but not upon its goodwill, patents, &c., because " when bad times come, and if the worst comes to the worst and liquidation is necessary, the selling value ' of these intangible assets ' will *ex hypothesi* have vanished almost completely." The question which in these circum-stances a bank should ask itself would seem to be, not merely whether in the event of failure the goodwill, &c., of the company would have been found to have " vanished almost completely," but also whether the value of its business premises, plant, machinery, &c., would not have suffered to almost the same extent.

It is true of course that in some cases such assets as business premises, plant, machinery, &c., are of general utility; that is to say of such a nature that they will always find a ready sale without serious shrinkage of value, even in a forced market. But in the great majority of cases this is certainly not the case, and speaking generally the larger the undertaking the greater will be the difficulty of disposing of its " tangible " assets, save at a ruinous loss. If, therefore, *The Times* writer be justified in his contention that balance sheet items and balance sheet values should be based upon the amount which it is reasonable to expect that a bank would lend upon them, there are probably few companies, apart from the small minority that have abundant secret reserves, that ought not to write down their tangible assets by 50 per cent. in order to conform to this standard of perfection.

Readers of *The Accountants Journal*, however, will hardly require to be reminded that the accepted view with regard to balance sheet values is that one is entitled to assume that they have been taken upon the basis of a " going concern " ; that is to say, not upon the basis of what might happen if the worst came to the worst, but upon what is a reasonable allocation of expenditure and losses as between one year and another during a term of years, upon the assumption that the business will be carried on during that term. If this be a reasonable assumption in the case of so-called tangible assets (which, as has been shown, are subject to very great fluctuation), surely it is the merest cant to pretend to distinguish between so-called " tangible " and " intangible " assets, seeing that both alike are affected by the same causes, in very much the same way and to very much the same extent.

Lest this be thought to be too extreme a statement, it may be pointed out that it is quite conceivable that at some particular moment of time the plant and machinery of an undertaking may be fast becoming obsolete although its earning capacity—and therefore the value of its goodwill and patent rights—may be as great as ever. There are, of course, many excellent reasons why a prosperous company should make ample reserves before dividing its profits among its shareholders in the form of dividend ; but there is, it is submitted, no sound reason for writing down the value of so-called intangible assets which does not apply equally to the writing down of the value of tangible assets, which are subject to precisely the same risks.

Popular Fallacies
V

By LAWRENCE R. DICKSEE, M.Com., F.C.A.

(Emeritus Professor of Accountancy and Business Methods in the University of London)

FLUCTUATIONS

One of the few points upon which there will probably be a general consensus of opinion in connection with matters of account is the dictum that, in arriving at the profits of an undertaking available for dividend, favourable fluctuations in the value of capital assets (or fixed assets as they are technically called) must be disregarded, and especially is this point insisted upon with regard to goodwill. The object of the present article is to suggest that while practically everybody assents to this doctrine in the abstract almost everyone ignores it in practice, with results that are often little short of disastrous.

It has already been pointed out that the market prices of stocks and shares—including of course industrial shares—are in the main regulated by buying and selling orders which are by no means always based upon accurate internal knowledge. The result, as, of course, everyone knows, is that the market prices of industrial shares, in the absence of manipulation—i.e. in the absence of buying or selling orders inspired by those who have some "axe to grind "—tend in the direction of becoming the capitalised value of the income estimated to be receivable as the result of owning such shares, modified by popular expectation as to whether such income is likely to increase or decrease in the near future. No doubt many persons realise that the prospect of capital appreciation, even when it becomes an accomplished fact, is something radically different from an actual increase in earning power ; but perhaps for that very reason it is often regarded as the more attractive feature of the two, if only because a profit derived from this source is not subject to income-tax or sur-tax. But many investors who are not seeking an income " free of tax," but are quite content to retain an improving investment for the sake of the income they hope to derive from the distribution of its earnings, regard any improvement in the market price of their securities as an actual increase of wealth, and are bitterly disappointed if they find on some subsequent occasion (as they very likely will) that it is not permanent.

If we look at the published accounts of any reasonably successful and well managed company over the past four or five years we shall probably find surprisingly little difference in the figures shown upon the successive balance sheets. It may be that there has been some increase in undivided profits, which may be represented by external investments or by an increase in the stated value of equipment or stock in trade, but in many cases this increase will be negligible as compared with the advance in the market price of the shares. If the price of the shares has doubled, it is as likely as not that the increase in the accumulated undivided profits is not more than 20 per cent. of the capital. If we look at the matter in the terms of balance sheets, how then may this increase in market prices be explained?

A very little reflection will show that the only way to account for it is upon the assumption that, in the opinion of those whose views tend to make market prices from time to time, the goodwill of the business has in fact increased to an extent corresponding with the increase in market price. That is to say, those whose views make or mar market prices, who are popularly supposed to endorse the dictum that goodwill is an " unsatisfactory " asset to appear in any balance sheet, do in fact attach a most exaggerated importance to the value of goodwill—if not for balance sheet purposes at least for the purpose of settling the market value of shares.

But if the market value of goodwill increases as profits increase, so obviously does it fall as earning capacity decreases ; and if an exaggerated importance has been attached to the value of goodwill in prosperous times, the inevitable reaction will be more marked than it would have been had a more reasonable view of the situation been taken. Thus it comes about that while, in certain cases at least, it may be practicable to exclude goodwill altogether from the balance sheet of a prosperous firm, it is in practice quite impossible to exclude goodwill—and an exaggerated view of goodwill at that—from the market prices of shares.

The next point to be noted is that in the case of any person or persons whose assets include the holding of shares in such company, these shares, if they be valued at current market prices, will be valued upon a basis which in fact takes into account reputed fluctuations in the value of goodwill. Accordingly, if investments be valued at market prices in any year when the aggregate value of investments shows an increase, investments will be " written up " and credit taken for an assumed profit which has not been realised and quite possibly never will be.

It may be argued, of course, that neither private investors nor holding companies are likely ever to value their investments precisely in this way, but it is beyond dispute that many individuals do value their investments at current market prices from year to year, and that most companies if they do not actually write up the aggregate value of their investments because market prices are favourable, do at least refrain from writing down investments which are known to be unsatisfactory so long as the aggregate market price of all their investments is not less than the aggregate " book value " of such investments. That is to say, the common practice in connection with joint-stock finance is to refrain from writing down the value of unsatisfactory investments in profitable times, although a little forethought would have shown that, sooner or later, they would have to be written down when bad times came and the inflation of the more satisfactory investments had worked itself off.

Another unsatisfactory feature about the way in which the profits of investment companies are commonly computed is with regard to their profits on the underwriting of new issues. If and when a new issue is entirely successful, the underwriting commission is, of course, clear profit; but, even so, underwriters are expected by issuing houses to " take the rough with the smooth," and therefore a portion at least of such profits ought to be set aside to cover possible losses hereafter in connection with less successful issues. But when an issue is unsuccessful, and the underwriters are left with (say) 50 per cent. or 60 per cent. upon their hands, it is suggested that it is manifestly wrong to treat the underwriting commission as a profit and to take the shares or stock into the balance sheet at their issue price and describe it as " cost price." When an underwriter under the terms of his contract is compelled to take up part of an issue, and pay the issue price for what he takes up, the cost to him of the stock he thus acquires is, it is submitted, not the issue price, but the issue price *minus* the whole of the underwriting commission he received upon the issue. Thus, if the issue were at par at an underwriting commission of 5 per cent., and the underwriter is compelled to take up 50 per cent. of the amount he has underwritten, the actual cost of that stock to the underwriter, it is submitted, would be 90 per cent. of the issue price, and there would be no profit at all upon the transaction until the stock taken over had been disposed of at more than 90 per cent.

If these views were more generally accepted, and if the practice they involve were more generally followed, a good many quite unnecessary fluctuations in the market prices of shares from time to time would be smoothed out. But, of course, the trouble is that not everyone wishes to see a greater stability in share prices.

Popular Fallacies
VI

By LAWRENCE R. DICKSEE, M.Com., F.C.A.
(Emeritus Professor of Accountancy and Business Methods in the
University of London)

TRADE EXPANSION

There is a natural tendency for every well-conducted business to expand,
for real ability is always scarcer than the demand for it. Consequently it
is the common experience of those who are conducting any business with
real ability to find that there is an ever-increasing demand for such
services as they are able to offer. Hence there is a popular impression that
any business which succeeds in increasing the volume of its operations is
ipso facto a successful business, ably conducted ; but this, it is submitted,
is merely to confuse effect with cause.

The bureaucrat in charge of a department may perhaps wisely concentrate his energies upon increasing the work done by his department,
for it is only by this means that he is able (as he thinks) to demonstrate
the increasing importance of his office and his own ability to fill it ; but
the mere business man is usually content with a somewhat more modest
role. Normally, he regards his business less as a crusade against the ignorance, sloth and greed of his competitors than as a means of securing for
himself, for his employees, and for those who have entrusted him with
capital, a satisfactory return for their respective sacrifices. To such a
man, every increase in the sphere of his operations involves increased
difficulties all round, and as such can only be justified if it carries with it
a corresponding increase of profits. But in many cases it is exceedingly
difficult to ensure that every expansion of business shall carry with it a
corresponding expansion of profits.

Yet, to refuse new business, is to make a present to one's competitors ;
it is deliberately to stand aside in the race towards supremacy. And
therefore, whether he likes it or not, the business man often feels compelled to make his plans for the carrying through of a larger volume of
business than he would wish to be responsible for were the matter entirely
one of his own choosing. To be carried along the stream under such conditions is merely to follow the line of least resistance. The object of this
article is to suggest that here—as in most other cases—the line of least
resistance is probably in the long run not the most advantageous.

It is the easiest thing in the world to promote sales by reducing selling
prices, but if the net profit be only 10 per cent. of the sales, a cut of 5 per
cent. in the selling price would reduce the net profit by one-half, and it
would be necessary to increase the sales by 90 per cent. before the same

amount of net profit as before could be obtained. It is very questionable whether the turnover could be so increased without at the same time increasing the working expenses ; thus, probably the turnover would have to be increased very much more than 90 per cent. to produce even the same amount of profit as before ! But the difficulties of conducting the business, and the risks necessarily attendant upon it, would vary approximately with the turnover, rather than with the net profit.

If the rate of net profit on sales were more than 10 per cent., the effect of reducing selling prices would, of course, not be quite so disastrous. But even if the rate of net profit were as high as 20 per cent., a cut of 5 per cent. in the selling prices would reduce the net profit by 25 per cent., and the sales would have to be increased by at least 33 per cent. to justify the reduction. It will be seen, therefore, that the magnification of sales by the simple expedient of cutting selling prices is not one to be resorted to lightly.

As a general rule, any increase in the volume of a business as the result of attracting new customers, as distinct from inducing existing customers to spend more, will not pay unless those new customers can be persuaded to become permanent customers. It is of course easier to make an assertion of this kind than to prove it, for reliable statistics upon the subject are not generally available. At the same time it is suggested that some significance must be attached to the terms offered by the leading life insurance companies to their agents for new business. On a new policy, the agent is allowed a commission of 1 per cent. on the amount assured in respect of the first year, and thereafter a commission of 2½ per cent. on the annual premium. Thus, on a policy for £1,000, at age 25, the agent's commission for the first year would be £10, and in each subsequent year about 11s. only. Many offices have an alternative scale under which the agent's remuneration for the first year would be £3 7s. 6d., or thereabouts, and in each subsequent year £1 2s. 6d. Even if we disregard the first scale, and accept the second as a better indication of the cost of finding new customers as distinct from serving old ones, it would seem that the general experience of life offices is to the effect that it costs three times as much to attract a new customer than to retain an old one. But, in spite of this, many businesses are conducted upon the assumption that the attraction of new customers is all-important, and the retention of old customers quite unimportant. Yet manifestly it costs money to attract new customers, and it must be a waste of money to let them go again, by allowing them to be dissatisfied with the quality of the goods or the services they receive, or by allowing them to buy goods or services that they are unable to utilise to their proper extent.

It would be interesting to inquire how many of those who deliberately lay themselves out—often at vast expense—to attract new customers, pause to consider where the new customers are coming from. From the point of view of the individual business, it may be a very good thing to detach customers from a rival concern, as by that means one effects the dual purpose of enriching oneself and impoverishing a competitor ; but another quite possible, and indeed very probable, way of attracting new customers is by persuading them to anticipate their own needs—to buy now what otherwise they would have bought later on. To the extent to which we may succeed in accomplishing this particular result we are merely " pawning to-morrow in order to enjoy to-day."

This, of course, is one of the very natural results of the popularisation of the idea of buying goods and paying for them by instalments. The hire-purchase, or extended credit, system enables many to acquire and at once enjoy things which otherwise they would have had to wait for. But it also encourages many to buy things which otherwise they would never have purchased, as being entirely beyond their means.

If we look at the general effect of the system as a whole, and disregard the clashing interests of rival supplying houses, in so far as the effect of extended credit is to encourage people to buy now that which otherwise they would have been compelled to wait for and to buy later on, the effect is, of course, to stimulate an immediate demand which for the time being greatly increases the volume of trade that it is possible to carry through. But as soon as these increased facilities become generally known and are acted upon, the temporary increase in trade will have worked itself out. Thereafter many orders which in normal conditions might have been expected to materialise, will not be available because they have already been filled on deferred credit terms. The only orders available to take their place will be from a new wave of potential customers, in their turn ordering ahead of the normal because of the improved credit facilities provided, and after the first year or so (other things being equal) the demand for goods will have settled down again to the normal. All that will have been achieved by the introduction of extended credit facilities will be an increased demand during the early period when these facilities were available—when the demands of the " anticipators," so to speak, over-lapped the demands of purchasers for cash in the ordinary way.

To the extent to which extended credit facilities induce people to buy goods which otherwise they never would have bought at all, there will, of course (other things being equal), be a more or less permanently increased demand for the goods supplied by these particular houses. But inasmuch as the spending capacity of the individual is necessarily limited—and particularly so in the case of those persons to whom extended credit facilities are especially likely to appeal—this increased demand in certain directions must necessarily be counterbalanced by a reduced demand in other directions, and, therefore, while individual traders may benefit, trade as a whole cannot benefit as the result of the extended credit.

There remains to be considered the price which has to be paid by the supplying house. To sell for credit is always a more risky business than to sell for cash. To sell for extended credit is naturally a more risky business than to sell for credit over a much more limited period of time. The increased risk of bad debts has therefore to be set off against any possi-bility of increased net profits as a result of an extension of turnover. It is not enough for the extended credit customer to pay interest on the out-standing debt at a rate equal to that charged for good trade bills. A further loading must be put on to cover bad debts, and steps must be taken—probably very extensive steps—by advertising and otherwise to stimulate demand, in order to overcome the reluctance of the would-be purchaser to pay this loading in addition to the purchase price.

In many cases traders avoid the risks attendant upon this class of business by arranging for others to finance the hire-purchase agreements. When this course is resorted to, we may feel pretty sure that the loading for interest and risk approaches more nearly to a moneylender's idea of remuneration for risks undertaken than a banker's idea of interest for money lent upon good security. But this is by no means the only objection to such an arrangement from the trader's point of view. Directly a trader allows someone else to finance his extended credit business, he is losing all control of the way in which his customers are going to be treated in the event of their failing to meet their engagements with absolute punctuality. He is running the risk that, in cases where there is no real probability of ultimate loss, as well as in cases where a certain amount of latitude would undoubtedly be given to his customer by the ordinary business man, those financing the agreements will consider only what they conceive to be their own interests in the matter. There is accordingly a very real risk that, in some cases at least, those who have made themselves liable to pay periodical instalments for goods already supplied will feel that they have been harshly treated, or even taken advantage of. In so far as they may feel any resentment for such treatment, they will vent it not upon the financing house, but upon the trader from whom they purchased the goods. And, upon the well-known principle that one active enemy can easily undo the work of many friends in promoting goodwill, it is quite possible that the trader may find it would have paid him much better in certain instances to have made a bad debt rather than to have made an active enemy.

When employment is good, it is quite possible, with only reasonable care, to conduct an instalment business with a very little risk of defaulters. But the more common this class of business becomes, the more serious upon it will be the effect of bad times, giving rise to considerable unemployment. And if to these troubles and losses be added an active sense of grievance at the way in which defaulters have been treated, it may very well be that this particular method of extending a business turnover will in the long run prove to be one of the most disastrous that has hitherto been conceived.

Popular Fallacies
VII

By LAWRENCE R. DICKSEE, M.Com., F.C.A.

(Emeritus Professor of Accountancy and Business Methods in the
University of London)

UNEMPLOYMENT

There is a widespread belief that unemployment is caused by over-production, and that therefore the best remedy for unemployment is to curtail the output of the individual producer by artificial means. Like many popular fallacies this is not wholly untrue, but it is sufficiently far from the truth to produce very mischievous results.

It is quite true that if, by so-called " good salesmanship," let us say a tailor succeeds in selling six suits of clothes to a customer in a year instead of the usual three, it is quite likely that he will see very little of that customer in the course of the following year ; and in this way intensive salesmanship does undoubtedly tend to produce an inevitable reaction in the ensuing period unless it is accompanied by an equally intensive campaign for the widening of the market—which may be quite practicable in some cases, but is certainly not practicable in every case. If in the meanwhile the trader, encouraged by an unwonted influx of orders, has laid himself out to handle a much larger volume of business than ever before, the inevitable slump in orders comes upon him quite unexpectedly, and because he is loath to think that it has been brought about by any lack of foresight on his part, he is more than willing to accept the popular view that these fluctuations in demand are wholly beyond human control ; part of the inevitable risks of business. It is always possible to discount the future up to a point, and modern intensive methods of so-called salesmanship (for the real salesmanship is an entirely different thing) tend to make this easier than it used to be. But the truth is, of course, that the only kind of expansion that is worth while is that which is steady and continuous ; that in the long run hothouse methods do not pay.

But although what is often called " over-production "—and what would be better described as discounting the future—is to some extent responsible for unemployment, beyond all question, the two most potent causes are (1) that the demand for a particular commodity or service has ceased, or is on the wane ; (2) that the price which we are willing to accept in exchange for a specified commodity or service is unattractively high as compared with the price asked by other suppliers. Of these two causes the second-named is undoubtedly the most common.

As regards cessation of demand, this is caused in the main by the march of invention, by the discovery of new methods of reaching the same result in a more desirable way, or of new materials being found to be effective substitutes for those formerly in use. At the present time, the demand for horses, and for horse drivers and horse tenders, cannot be anything like as great as it was (say) 20 years ago ; railways are no longer the sole means of long distance transport ; and artificial silk has played havoc with the cotton and woollen trades. And these are only somewhat conspicuous instances of a tendency which is always in our midst—the tendency for things which were admirable in their day to be rendered obsolete by newer things performing the same functions either better, quicker or more cheaply. The tendencies in this direction are always with us, but the perceptible effects of these tendencies are not continuous but occasional, and for that reason are all the more violent when they do occur.

When a whole group of activities is thus rendered obsolete by the march of events, vast sums of capital sunk in equipment are lost, and large numbers of those who have hitherto found their livelihood in this particular form of activity have to look for it elsewhere.

As regards the obsolescence of equipment, readers of *The Accountants' Journal* will not need to be reminded that obsolescence is always to be regarded as one of the most potent factors in depreciation. Equipment that is not highly specialised is naturally not subject to quite the same risk of obsolescence as that which is very highly specialised ; and the matter is not quite so important as it would seem to be at first by reason of the fact that, as a rule, highly specialised equipment becomes obsolete before it is worn out, and also before the purpose for which it was constructed has itself become obsolete.

Theoretically, at least, the effect of the obsolescence of industries upon individual workers should not be very serious, for the great majority at least should be able to adapt themselves to changed conditions and become efficient workers in the new industries that have taken the place of those in process of supersession. It is hard to teach an old dog new tricks, however, and therefore there will always be a certain number of the more experienced workers who would find it difficult—or perhaps even impossible—to adapt themselves, and in any event they will find their previous experience thrown upon the scrap-heap, and to a certain extent at least they have to begin life all over again. But beyond all question, their greatest difficulty will not be the difficulty of self-adaptation to new conditions, but trade union regulations, which appear to delight in placing difficulties in the way of any such self-adaptation. If these difficulties could be overcome, most of the inconveniences arising from this particular cause of unemployment would at least be ameliorated.

Perhaps, also, it is permissible to suggest that " captains of industry " should get into the habit of looking a little further ahead ; of not assuming that because a particular course of events is likely to last " their time," it will last for ever. Neither motors nor artificial silk in a practicable form came among us unheralded. On the contrary, there was ample warning, and therefore ample scope for the man of vision to foresee the probable trend of events.

The other—and, as I have said, the most common—cause of unemployment is high prices. As I have already stated in these articles, price is not everything ; but while a retail buyer may sometimes be prepared to pay a somewhat higher price for the same article in a shop where he receives attentions that give him pleasure than he would be willing to pay in a shop which—for whatever reason—only causes him annoyance, it will always be very difficult to persuade people in very large numbers that they ought to " buy British goods," and pay more for them, unless they can be persuaded that they get some definite advantage in the way of quality or reliability. The only real remedy, if prices are too high, is either to reduce them, or—by means of protective tariffs or otherwise—to increase the prices charged by the competitor. Under first-class management, prices can commonly be reduced by multiplying output, but there are obvious limits to the practicability of reducing selling prices by the simple expedient of cutting profits, and when these have been exhausted, the only possible remedy is to reduce working costs, which in the main means increasing the output of the worker by placing at his disposal an ever increasingly efficient equipment. That is to say : properly understood, machinery properly designed and properly used is not a cause of unemployment, but the very reverse.

Perhaps one of the most widespread fallacies at the present time is that present-day unemployment is to a large extend due to the general use of machinery. The fact is, as Mr. Herbert N. Casson stated in a recent issue of " The Efficiency Magazine," that " machinery has done more to raise wages, shorten the hours of labour, and give workers a chance to develop their inner lives, than any other one thing in the world. Machinery has to a very large extent abolished drudgery and given us time to think and enjoy life, but perhaps the trouble is that we have not as yet sufficiently taken advantage of the time that is thus given us for thinking." In the old days, it used to be recognised that a shoemaker was the artisan who did the most thinking, because his job was one that did not call for any great physical exertion. It is impossible to do strenuous physical work and to think at the same time, but the mind of a competent machine operator is in the majority of cases free to follow wherever fancy dictates. The real trouble would seem to be that it so often follows unprofitable channels. Most people in this age of machinery are more willing to accept the ready-made ideas of others than to solve their own problems, with the result that some of the greatest fallacies are among those ideas that are most generally accepted, not the least of these fallacies being that unemployment can be cured by restricting the output of the individual worker without reducing his pay. In the long run a community subsists on its own labour, not upon an abstention from labour—however " scientific " that may be thought to be.

Popular Fallacies
VIII

By LAWRENCE R. DICKSEE, M.Com., F.C.A.

(Emeritus Professor of Accountancy and Business Methods in the
University of London)

REVENUE CHARGES

From Adam Smith until Marshall the view appears to have been
generally accepted that rent "has peculiarities of its own" which distinguish it from all other charges against profits. Present-day economists
are perhaps not quite so unanimous, or its would not have been necessary
for Professor F. W. Ogilvie to say in a recent issue of *The Economic
Journal* that "economists should try to reach some sort of agreement
about rent." But the view that rent is different from every other kind
of expense is still very widely held. The object of the present article is
to show that there is no essential difference between one kind of proper
charge against profits and another; and also, incidentally, that if the
usually accepted economic theory of rent is open to criticism, just as
much may be said against the average business man's conception of
charges against profits generally.

We all know that in the early days of accountancy charges against
profits were limited to actual payments. Because attempts were made to
compute profits at comparatively frequent intervals (usually annually)
it happened that while in the case of some charges the aggregate of actual
payments would approximate more or less closely to the actual expenditure incurred, in other cases the correspondence would be less marked;
and, further, that in some cases very important charges—e.g. depreciation—might get omitted altogether. If one were content to wait until
a business had been wound up before attempting to prepare any account
showing what the profits of that business had been, all the necessary data
might, of course, be obtained from an account of receipts and payments.
It is when one attempts to prepare interim statements computing business
profits that the difficulties begin to multiply. It is only when we seek to
derive the utmost benefit from a perusal of these interim statements of
profit that we find it increasingly difficult to prepare them with sufficient accuracy to serve their intended purpose.

When the whole object of the interim account is to arrive at a figure
of profit that may safely be distributed among the proprietors of the
business without jeopardising its continued success, even approximate
accuracy is quite unnecessary. All that is needed is to arrive at a sum
that may be divided with perfect safety, and so long as the distributions

so computed give satisfaction to those who receive them, any attempt at greater accuracy is obviously superfluous. If, on the other hand, accounts are framed, not merely with the object of enabling periodical dividends to be distributed among shareholders, but also with the object of keeping those responsible for the management of the undertaking informed as to what is going on, clearly a much higher degree of accuracy in computation is called for, and it is probable that even present-day accounting methods are quite a long way off perfection when judged from this higher stand-point.

To turn from the general to the particular, let us consider the incidence of a few of the more important items of expenditure chargeable against the profits of any ordinary business.

Take first the cost of Labour. In a slave-owning community the computation of Labour costs would be just as difficult and uncertain as the computation of machinery costs is under modern conditions; but because ours is not a slave-owning community we find the problem (superficially at least) greatly simplified by the fact that labour has to be hired, and that the wages paid accordingly represent prima facie the cost of the labour. If the reward of labour were invariably based upon the production of the worker there would of course be an absolute correspondence between labour costs and wages paid. But this correspondence hardly ever exists in practice, because even in the case of so-called " productive " labour a certain amount of idle time and short time has to be paid for, in addition to what is paid for work actually performed. Moreover, a considerable amount of the total paid is for supervisory and other similar work which results in no physical output at all. And, yet again, the output, such as it is, may be very intermittent in character. For example, anything in the nature of designing—whether it be designing an engine or the pattern of a wallpaper—is done by persons whose output is most intermittent in quantity, and often exceedingly unsuccessful. Who is going to say what is the correct formula for apportioning such expenditure over a series of accounting periods, which although equal in point of time may be (and probably are) very unequal in point of industrial activity or financial success ?

Passing on to machinery costs, so long as we are content to hire all our plant, the problem here is no more complex than it was in the case of Labour costs, for we have reduced the outlay to a fixed inclusive charge, and our difficulties are limited to determining how that charge should be spread over a period of varying activity and varying profitableness. But if we own our own plant, we are, of course, in effect combining the businesses of a machinery user and a hirer-out of machinery, and we have to ask ourselves whether we shall keep the accounts of the separate departments of our business altogether distinct, or merge them. The latter is, of course, the usual practice even to-day, although the superior results obtained by the former process are beginning to be more generally appreciated. We will come back to this question again later on, but it is time now that we turned our attention to accommodation costs, i.e. the costs incurred in providing our business with the necessary accommodation wherein to function.

As in the case of labour costs and machinery costs, accommodation costs may to some extent at least be simplified by the expedient of hiring ; or, alternatively, we may combine hiring with owning. If and when we hire the outlay is commonly called " rent," but it differs in no wise from the charges payable for the hire of labour or the hire of machinery. As with them, so with rent, the point that has to be considered is whether the actual cost should be distributed purely upon a basis of time, or whether, in order to avoid misleading results, it is not necessary also to take into account the varying quantity and nature of the output. If instead of hiring suitable premises we buy them, as in the case of machinery costs, we have to consider whether we shall treat the ownership of the premises as a separate department for accounting purposes or not. But whether we own or hire, there is nothing about accommodation costs which (to quote Marshall) gives them " peculiarities of their own." They are in precisely the same category as machinery costs, and for the matter of that, it would not be impossible to hire premises and machinery under the same agreement. In industry it is of course not usual to throw in labour as well and charge one inclusive " rent " for all three, but this is precisely what happens when a Chartered Accountant is paid an inclusive fee to provide the registered offices of a limited company together with a secretary and a secretarial staff ; and in the case of London theatres the rent of the premises commonly covers also the cost of the whole of the staff in front of the house.

Having now shown the essential oneness of these different kinds of revenue charges, we may return to the problem of depreciation as applied to machinery costs, which is precisely the same problem as depreciation applied to accommodation charges.

So long as the sole object of keeping accounts was to comply with statutory requirements and avoid paying dividends out of capital, the most that anyone could expect would be that provision should be made for depreciation upon a basis which would recoup wasting capital. For a long time provision for depreciation was thought to be an entirely optional matter, and depreciation itself was even sometimes defined as an amount charged against profits to cover loss, rather than as the loss or wastage itself. But directly we begin to look at the problem from the point of view of a payment made for the hire of certain services it assumes a different aspect, for we then begin to realise that the proper charge will be determined, not by the skill or the good luck of the business man in making the hiring agreements, but rather by the market price of hire at the time the work is actually going on. We shall be able to realise that it is an utter fallacy for a mill-owner to suppose that, because he has been very successful in the past and has been able to write his plant down to zero out of past profits, he can now produce wares which cost him nothing at all for machinery costs. We shall realise that it is a fallacy for a shopkeeper owning the freehold of his business premises to suppose that he can afford to sell his goods at a lower price than a competitor who is paying a fair rental for his. And we shall realise *per contra* that when a business man has made a bad bargain, by paying too much for his premises, his equipment or his labour, he cannot expect to " pass it on " to the customer unless all his competitors have been equally incompetent or unfortunate—which is, of course, unlikely.

Absolute costs are, of course, invaluable to the competent business man, for by comparing them with what costs ought to have been, he is able to judge the degree of success that the management of his business has attained, but in the long run absolute costs can never determine selling prices. While there is any competition left in the world, selling prices will in the long run be determined by what costs ought to have been.

The ACCOUNTANTS' JOURNAL

| VOL. 48 | SEPTEMBER 1930 | . No. 569 |

Popular Fallacies
IX

By LAWRENCE R. DICKSEE, M.COM., F.C.A.

(Emeritus Professor of Accountancy and Business Methods in the
University of London).

THE GENESIS OF WEALTH

If one were to judge at all by appearances it would seem that at the
present time the view is very widely held that all the wealth in the world
is created by the workers of the world—meaning thereby the manual
workers. It may well be doubted whether it is possible for any human
being to " create " anything material : whether under the most favourable
circumstances he can do anything more than alter the form of material
already in existence, and it is quite obvious, of course, that the manual
worker can do nothing without raw material upon which to work ; but,
leaving that aspect of the matter upon one side altogether (and it is, of
course, by no means unimportant), if there were any truth at all in the
dictum that wealth is created by " Labour " with a capital " L," it would
seem to follow that children busily engaged in building sand-castles on
the sea-shore are *pro tanto* wealth producers.

This should suffice to give pause to all who have any respect for Euclid,
and induce them to revise, or at least to amplify, some of their definitions.
Surely " wealth," whatever precise meaning we may attach to that
expression, is not created by unintelligent toil, but rather by the successful
fulfilling of wants or needs. In the most primitive society, by satisfying
the wants and needs of the individual worker ; in a more advanced stage
of society, probably by satisfying the wants or needs of others who are
willing to contribute something in exchange. This seems to raise the age-
long question—Who benefits ? The supplier or the supplied ? And in spite
of what pessimists may say to the contrary, the answer would appear to
be that both must benefit, if such a state of affairs is to be lasting. Sometimes one may benefit a little more than the other, and sometimes a little
less ; but while there may thus be room for differences of opinion as to
whether the benefits are evenly or fairly apportioned, in the long run both
must benefit or the situation would automatically come to an end.

The whole problem of producing wealth has been defined as producing
what is wanted, where it is wanted and when it is wanted, and this seems

to cover very fairly well the fundamental basis of trading operations. Slightly redrafting the dictum so as to make it applicable to industry as well, we may say that it consists of producing the right thing, in the right way, at the right time, at the right price, and at the right place, and it is in these terms that Efficiency has sometimes been defined.

It will be seen that here we are a very long way off the energetic but purposeless production of sand-castles, and further that we have been enabled to travel thus far from this elementary manifestation of undirec- ted energy by the aid of those who are able to see ahead and to contrive, and these are always a very small minority of the world's workers. It is they, and they alone, who enable the unthinking to produce real castles instead of castles of sand. It is the ideas of these, and such as these, that are the real sources of wealth—not perhaps in very many cases of wealth to themselves, for the inventor rarely reaps the full reward of his labour, but of wealth (in the form of lasting prosperity) to those around them.

Comparatively speaking, there is not much to choose between one unskilled labourer and another. There are great differences between one artizan and another, and there are vast differences between the abilities and capacities of those pioneers of human endeavour who are able by taking thought and by contriving to find useful employment for all who care to take advantage of the offer and to pay the price.

From all this it does not necessarily follow that it is the inventor or the business organiser who really *produces* in his own brain the genesis of all wealth. We are only in a position to assert this when we are prepared to prove that the ideas that generate in any human brain really have their origin there ; which may or may not be the case, but certainly has never yet been demonstrated. Without wishing at all to dogmatise upon the matter, I would like to suggest that such a theory seems to me to be upon the face of it somewhat improbable. If the ideas of the inventor were absolutely and entirely his own ideas, one would expect to find some sort of connection between the ideas of famous inventors and the lives of famous inventors, and—to say the least of it—no such connection is obvious. In quite an unexpectedly large number of cases, inventions of importance—whether we judge importance from the point of view of social well-being or from the point of view of producing wealth or giving rise to employment upon a large scale—seem to have been stumbled upon haphazard rather than arrived at as the logical solution of a problem patiently observed and much pondered over. Comparatively few inven- tors have succeeded in making a financial success of themselves, still less of their own inventions. In the majority of cases it has been left to men of a different calibre to turn these ideas, whencesoever they may have come, to real account for the benefit of the human race. Thus, although the idea may appear fanciful to some, it seems by no means certain that these ideas or inventions (which, of course, must always have existed from the beginning of time) ought not to be placed in very much the same cate- gory as the raw materials for which humanity gradually finds a use as time goes on. A very little reflection suffices to satisfy us that the quantity of iron in the world must have been just as great in the Stone Age or the Bronze Age as it is to-day, although as a raw material for humanity to work upon it was useless until the process of smelting the iron ore had been discovered. Electricity is not a modern phenomenon, but no use was made of electricity by humanity even a hundred years ago. It was the investigation of certain puzzling manifestations of electricity in connection with telegraphy about forty years ago that gave rise to the discovery of wireless, and so on.

But we are not concerned in this article with the growth of scientific invention as such, but rather with the question how more effectively is it practicable for us to find out how to do the right thing in the right way, at the right time, at the right price, and in the right place, and—whether we are prepared to give them the fullest possible credit for it or not— the fact undoubtedly seems to be that we have developed as far as we have in this direction mainly through the work done by inventors and business organisers. It is quite certain that, in the past, inventors as a class have not levied a very heavy toll upon the community for such services as they have rendered to it. It is perhaps matter for discussion—a matter open to argument—whether organisers as a class have not succeeded in attracting to themselves the inventor's share as well as their own. But however that may be, if we wish to enlarge the field of possible employment, which is at all times desirable, and was perhaps never more desirable than at the present juncture, this can only be done by offering real encouragement to those who alone are able to provide real employment—that is to say, employment which really produces wealth. So long as there is money to be spent it is of course an easy thing for a Government Department, or for a local authority to spend it in paying wages to workers to construct something which otherwise would not have been constructed, and for which therefore presumably there is no present real need. But a continuous expansion of wealth is not to be obtained by such means as these ; indeed, of the two, it would perhaps be better to spend the same amount of money in building sand castles, for they at least would be destroyed by the incoming tide instead of remaining permanently to disfigure the landscape. If our statesmen are really anxious to find more employment, they should in the nature of things seek it from those who in the past have proved their ability to utilise the services of labour for the benefit of humanity. A tithe of the amount now spent on doles and relief works devoted as a subsidy to those employers who were able to submit reasonable schemes of development would not only produce better results in the immediate future, but would also pave the way by natural means to continuous further developments in the more remote future, because it would be dealing with the problem on the lines along which alone natural development is possible.

Popular Fallacies

X

By LAWRENCE R. DICKSEE, M.Com., F.C.A.

Emeritus Professor of Accounting and Business Methods in the
University of London

RATIONALISATION

If we are to take our newspapers and publicists seriously, there would seem to be a widespread belief that the economic salvation of this country depends entirely upon the rationalisation of our industries. At the same time, there appears to be the widest diversity of views as to what rationalisation really consists of.

Some persons seem to think that rationalisation and wholesale amalgamation are synonymous terms. They rightly stress the importance of standardisation of output, of collective buying, and of the elimination of insane price-cutting; but they overlook the fact that giants have their weaknesses as well as dwarfs, that the tendency is for the overhead expenses of overgrown concerns to go up by leaps and bounds, and—most important of all—they ignore the fact that the larger the business the greater must be the brain that can effectively control it; that to endow a man with authority is not to endow him with either experience or knowledge, that to pay a man a fancifully large salary will not ensure that he is worth that salary to his employers. If a man is really capable of controlling a large busines, as a rule sooner or later he will have a large business to control; but, to say the least of it, it is putting the cart before the horse, first by indiscriminate amalgamation to produce a large business and then to look for someone capable of controlling it.

Probably one of the reasons why so many persons have high hopes of the rationalisation of industry is that it has been widely asserted that rationalisation is the best remedy for unemployment. Against this, Mr. W. L. Hichens—whose experience of rationalisation is anything but negligible—has definitely asserted that " it is not intended as a solution of unemployment." " It is," he says, " no good mixing up the two, as rationalisation may be condemned as ineffective for a reason which does not fit it. It may, of course, aggravate unemployment, but I do not think it will. At the same time it will alter the form of employment." In Mr. Hichens' view, rationalisation is " an amalgamation of businesses doing a similar class of work with the object of obtaining greater efficiency and economy and of correlating productive capacity to demand. It must not be thought that the object of rationalisation is to put up prices. Rationalisation must be distinguished from the trust and the cartel. It is only in so far as it sincerely and honestly achieves its object of obtaining greater efficiency and economy that we shall get good results out of rationalisation." This would seem to suggest that, in Mr. Hichens' view, there is nothing new about rationalisation; that it is really our old friend efficiency under another name; re-christened perhaps on account of the implacable hostility of many trade unions to efficiency, in just the same way that politicians have invented the word "safeguarding" in the hope of avoiding the opposition of other politicians to "protection."

Those who believe in efficiency are not likely to raise any particular objection to its becoming more generally adopted under another name, if by that means its more general adoption can be secured; but, by whatever name it may be known, the really important thing to bear in mind is that while the mechanisation of management is an excellent thing up to a point, like everything else it can be overdone. The successful conduct of business requires a very nice adjustment of a number of different requirements, some of which are essentially antagonistic, and if the balance is not nicely adjusted, a state of unstable equilibrium arises which sooner or later is bound to result in a crash.

It seems safe to say, however, that while slogans and catchy titles undoubtedly have their uses for advertising purposes and propaganda, they contribute absolutely nothing to the real business of life. In this connection, one is irresistibly reminded of the fact that, long before the rationalisation of industry was talked about, the word "rationalisation" was current coin among psychologists. They were not all in precise agreement as to what the term meant (as a matter of fact, there is singularly little upon which psychologists are all in precise agreement), but a fair definition of rationalisation from the psychologist's point of view would appear to be "the manufacturing of good reasons for bad actions." One is tempted to wonder whether this definition was known to whoever may have invented the term "the rationalisation of industry."

The truth of the matter, of course, is that in just the same way that a good constitution is no palliative for a corrupt judiciary, so good organisation is no compensation for effete management. Organisation is the machinery through which management functions, but it is no substitute for management. The whole basis of organisation is the division of labour —the resolving of complex operations into a number of simple (or comparatively simple) processes, each of which is in the nature of things easy of performance as compared with the unresolved whole, and therefore capable of being performed in a satisfactory way by someone of lower attainments. That is to say, it is a question of so arranging matters that comparatively inferior persons, each performing comparatively simple tasks, may be built up into a living organism thus made capable of performing great deeds. But the greater and more complex the organisation, the greater must be the super-brain capable of controlling what is going on, and capable of making those readjustments that are continually necessary to meet incessantly altering circumstances. Organisation without management is a body without a head, and rationalisation—however much persons may differ as to its precise definition—is merely another name for organisation.

To suppose that rationalisation by itself can achieve anything whatsoever is as futile as to suppose that a fleet of battleships devoid of crews could win a naval engagement. Even if some enterprising inventor were able to control crewless battleships by wireless, there would still have to be the human control to direct the wireless impulses.

It is no doubt because we live in an age in which mechanisation has taken such enormous strides that we tend greatly to over-estimate the powers of mechanisation as such. We tend more and more to rely upon State control to get us out of all our difficulties, and to forget that the State is really only another name for ourselves working through a particular kind of organisation. We cease to cultivate individual enterprise as a virtue, and we expect the State to exhibit those very qualities which as individuals we are tending to lose by a process of atrophy. A generation ago, the way that Government Departments were in the habit of conducting their affairs was regarded by business men as a rather grim sort of joke. Now it would almost seem as though some business men thought that the methods of officialdom could with advantage be imported into the market place and the factory. Surely the business man of to-day must indeed be bankrupt of ideas if he thinks that he can learn much from a Government Department or profit much from State interference.

It may, of course, be said that as yet rationalisation has not had time to demonstrate what it is capable of achieving, but this is only true if we pin ourselves down to the word " rationalisation," as distinct from the thing itself. It is now nearly nine years since the principle of rationalisation was applied to the railways of this country, in theory if not in fact. The results have, to say the least of it, been disappointing, chiefly perhaps because our railways have since been run in the interests of the railway employee rather than of the railway shareholder or the railway user. Mr. Hichens has rightly warned us that rationalisation is not intended as a solution of unemployment. As a matter of fact, everything that is intended as a direct solution of unemployment is of necessity bound to increase it, for in the long run the welfare of the employee must necessarily depend upon the welfare of the employer, and the welfare of the employer must necessarily depend upon the quality of the service that he is able to render to the community.

" The game is more than the players,
And the ship is more than the crew."

If we persist too long in regarding the " crew " as more important than the " ship," the time will inevitably come when the ship is a very uncomfortable one to sail in—if indeed it is able to keep afloat at all.

Popular Fallacies
XI

By LAWRENCE R. DICKSEE, M.Com., F.C.A.

Emeritus Professor of Accounting and Business Methods in the
University of London

Trade Cycles

There are still a number of persons, in other respects perhaps quite well
informed, who believe that cycles of good and bad trade follow each
other with approximate regularity at intervals of ten years. At first
glance it might perhaps seem that this belief, however mistaken, was at
least innocuous, but a careful examination shows that, like most superficial views, this particular one is the very reverse of the truth.

So long as people continue to believe that successions of good and bad
trade are due to astronomical causes, they will very naturally regard them
as something quite beyond human control, and according to their individual temperaments will either accept them with varying degrees of
fatalistic resignation or at best will seek to discover whether it is not
possible to make profits in bad times as well as in good times. The fatalist
is, of course, of no use to anybody—not even himself. The " bear " in
certain circumstances may serve a very useful purpose as tending, by
" covering," to steady markets at the time they most need steadying ;
but, of course, no community could exist if it consisted exclusively of
" bears." They may, or they may not, be " the salt of the earth," but even
salt is useless when there are no carcases to be salted ! The object of the
present article, however, is not to discuss the public services of " bears,"
but rather to suggest that trade fluctuations are very largely due to causes
that are within human control, and that a knowledge of this truth intelligently acted upon will go far towards keeping these fluctuations within
reasonable limits.

If we confine ourselves for a moment to the movements of any one
business—no matter what its precise nature may be—we shall find (if it
has been established long enough) that from time to time four entirely
different sets of causes have prevented its profits remaining absolutely
uniform, viz. :

(1) Seasonal variations ;
(2) Variations in the ability and success with which the business is
conducted from time to time ;
(3) Variations in the prosperity of businesses in general in that
particular line ;
(4) Variations in national, and even world, prosperity.

Were it not that the usual practice is still to prepare accounts only once a year, the fact would be much more widely realised than it is that most businesses—one might almost say all businesses—are not equally profitable during every day of the year. In some cases, most of the profits are made during particular days of the week—e.g. over the week-end. In others, they are made mostly in the summer or in the winter. There are probably few businesses that make any profit at all on more than 200 days in a year. To the extent to which profits are subject to seasonal variations they are probably very largely dependent upon favourable weather conditions, which would, of course, not be uniform in every year. These weather conditions are, of course, beyond the control of the individual management; but in every case where it is observed that the profits are earned intermittently and not equally from day to day throughout the year, it will be found that working expenses have to be provided during the 365 days, although they can only be turned to advantage in approximately half that number. This, of course, suggests an inquiry as to how far it is practicable to reinforce a seasonal business by some business of a complementary character, which will be active (and therefore profitable) in the off-season. This is a problem that is probably only rarely capable of complete solution, but it is almost always possible to do something in the direction of reducing seasonal fluctuations.

The second cause of fluctuation in the profits of a business is variation in the efficiency with which that business is being managed. To take a very simple case, if a young man started a business with which he was not very fully acquainted, but was yet able ultimately to make a success of that business, we should undoubtedly find that as he gained experience, so the management improved in character and the profits multiplied; and if the management of the business remained in the same hands until the owner was past his best, the management would tend to become less and less efficient, so that in the course of time the business would probably come to grief. This, of course, is an elementary proposition, and in practice we know it is usual for young people to be supervised, controlled and taught while they are learning their business; and in theory at least " new blood " is brought in and placed in positions of gradually increasing importance, so that the lifetime of a business may, under favourable conditions, be very appreciably longer than the business life of any one individual. But capable " new blood " is not always brought in soon enough, or in sufficiently large quantities, and in some cases men cling to their work long after their best working days are gone for no better reason than that they can think of nothing better with which to occupy their time. But apart from fluctuations in the efficiency of management due to age, it must be remembered that efficiency and age do not always walk in step, and further, that efficiency is a relative term. While business A. is the most efficient of its kind it may be able to command the pick of the trade. But supposing, without any decline upon the part of A., business B. forges ahead, A. will undoubtedly tend to lose customers. Whatever the precise cause may be, during the lifetime of a business there will always be fluctuations in its profits, due to fluctuations in the ability with which it is managed as compared with the ability with which other competing businesses are managed, and such fluctuations are, of course, in theory at least, not altogether outside the control of the management. They are not unavoidable.

The third cause of fluctuation may be described as a contest between commodities rather than between persons. An increase (say) in the popularity of artificial silk is bound to have its reaction upon the cotton and woollen trades. An increase in the popularity of " talkies " has its repercussion upon cinema orchestras, and so on. The moral of this, of course, is that it is well to have more than " one string to one's bow," and like most morals it is very much easier to act on this in some cases than in others. But those who deplore a decline of prosperity owing to the fickleness of public taste would sometimes do well to remember that in all probability they had just as good an opportunity as anyone else of taking up the new commodity, or new idea, which is tending to make their own particular form of activity more or less obsolete. Also, that public taste is itself a manufactured article, and that dying industries are sometimes dying chiefly for want of advertisement and propaganda of the right sort. It would seem, therefore, that fluctuations that affect even a whole trade or industry are not necessarily unavoidable misfortunes as applied to any one particular undertaking. It is quite possible for one business to go forward by leaps and bounds while trade in general is on the down-grade.

Similarly with regard to wider movements, affecting perhaps a whole country. If, owing to altered conditions—as for instance wages, rates, or means of transport—it is no longer possible to manufacture goods in country A. so as to compete upon a world basis with goods manufactured in country B. ; if we are sure of our facts the remedy would seem to lie in the direction of abandoning the manufacture of such goods in country A. and restarting it in country B., or in country C. or D. if either of the latter should be found to offer still more advantageous conditions. The transplanting of an industry from one country to another is, of course, a serious matter, not to be lightly embarked upon ; but it is certainly not impossible, and the objections to it are usually more or less personal. If it is not a case of regarding the crew as more important than the ship, it is at least a case of regarding the captain as more important.

It will be seen, then, that the fortunes of every business fluctuate, and when we come to examine these causes we find that surprisingly few of them are entirely beyond control.

So far, however, we have been assuming the continuity of the business apart altogether from financial considerations, whereas we know that in practice financial considerations usually determine when a new business shall be started and when an old one shall be stopped. In my next article I shall endeavour to show that even these financial considerations are very largely within the control of the individual business man, if only he can disabuse his mind of the absurd belief that general conditions always come from without and never from within.

Popular Fallacies
XII

By LAWRENCE R. DICKSEE, M.Com., F.C.A.

Emeritus Professor of Accounting and Business Methods in the
University of London

GOOD TIMES AND BAD TIMES

As I indicated in my last article, the commonly accepted view is that in the business world there are " good times " when almost anybody can make a profit, interspersed with " bad times " when it is difficult if not impossible to make any profit at all; and that these periods of prosperity and adversity succeed each other at more or less regular intervals, the causes of which are very largely, if not entirely, beyond human control. And I pointed out that this particular fallacy is especially unfortunate, in that it tends to perpetuate a state of affairs which is obviously in the highest degree undesirable and at the same time by no means necessarily unavoidable.

That there must be an essential fallacy underlying this popular belief is shown by the fact that there are much wider differences between the measure of success attending similar businesses under different management than there are between the financial results of any one concern over a number of years. If this fact proves anything at all, it proves that the profits of the individual business are far more dependant upon its management than upon any external conditions, and that therefore unsuccessful results may often be avoided by a change of management or, if not a change of management, then a change of policy. In the present article, however, I propose to approach this matter from a slightly different angle, and to suggest that cycles of " good " and " bad " business—whether in the case of individual concerns or of trades (or trade) generally—are very largely unreal, in the sense that they are commonly brought about by charging against the profits of so-called " lean " years, losses which ought really to have been charged against the profits of boom years; that is to say, they are brought about by insufficient attention to the all-important question of adequate reserves.

Let us take the case of any ordinary business house at the opening of a boom period! It is, we will say, properly equipped, provided with adequate capital, and endowed with an organisation capable of carrying a given volume of business which we will call capacity X. When the orders coming in from time to time are just sufficient to fill capacity X, that concern will be operating to the best advantage in all respects; but as the boom proceeds and orders increase, the position becomes increasingly disadvantage-

ous. To refuse to work beyond capacity X would be to make one's competitors a present of some at least of one's customers, and therefore of
one's goodwill, with the result that when orders fall off we should find
ourselves in the position of not being able to keep up to capacity X. Moreover, every successful concern must necessarily be also in the long run a
growing concern ; the undertaking that insists upon remaining stationary
is expecting to remain alive without movement—which is, of course,
impossible. Accordingly, every effort must be made to keep pace with the
ever increasing flow of orders.

For a time this may be possible by introducing improved methods of
operation and by working overtime, but sooner or later it will be found
only possible to compete with an ever increasing flow of orders by enlarg-
ing equipment. If steps be taken to enlarge equipment at this particular
juncture, it will be found that the additional capital outlay is being
expended at a time when prices are unusually high, and when therefore
the cost of what is required is unusually large. Even assuming the necessary expenditure can be financed upon a satisfactory basis, capital
expenditure upon a large scale cannot be incurred wisely without very
careful consideration and constant attention, and the time when the
management is being " snowed under " with orders is not the most favourable time for it to divert its attention from the business of the day to the
consideration of problems connected with capital extension. It therefore
follows, almost as a matter of course, that capital extension incurred under
these conditions will be incurred under disadvantageous conditions, and
that while it may seem remunerative at the moment, it may very well
prove to be unremunerative later on. Indeed, it must of course be unremunerative later on unless it is possible to establish permanently an
increased demand for one's output sufficient to cover the increased
capacity, which may now be represented by $X + Y$.

While all this is going on, it is almost certain that the former control of
the financial side of the business is being relaxed. It is becoming increasingly difficulty to get through the day's work in the day, and that being so,
as every reader of *The Accountants' Journal* will know, the financial and
the accounts side of the business is likely to be the first to fall into arrears.
Unwonted activity, and the appearance of great prosperity all round
induce a form of mental intoxication which makes it increasingly difficult
to insist upon reasonable precautions. Credit limits are allowed to expand,
new work is undertaken first and the question of making adequate financial arrangements to enable it to be carried through is postponed until a
more convenient season. Because prices are rising, stocks are accumulated
well ahead of current requirements. Probably no increase is made in the
personnel of those acting in a supervisory position, with the result that
control gets weaker and waste crops up at every turn. And if these tendencies are noticed at all, it is thought that they are unimportant because the
profits of a greatly increased volume of business *must* be sufficient to carry
them and leave a handsome margin to the good !

Now, as everyone knows, weeds grow much more quickly than choice
flowers. If once control is relaxed, the consequent leakage will sooner or
later be sufficient to swallow up profits, however large the profits may seem

to be. The inevitable result of such a state of affairs as has been indicated —as history has shown time and again—is the bursting of the bubble. To a rapidly increasingly extent it is found that business houses which have been relied upon fail to meet their obligations, and the repercussions of these losses extend over a very wide area. There comes a sudden check in the receipt of orders—and particularly of orders from those who beyond all question will be able to pay for the goods—because while everybody buys ahead who can afford to do so when prices are rising, so as to be able to obtain what they want at a minimum price, directly they fear that they may be left with an inconveniently large stock of goods on their hands they cease buying, and endeavour to reduce stocks rather than to increase them. In order to meet maturing obligations, some are compelled to dispose of stocks at a sacrifice. This at once tends to reduce the value of the stocks held by others, and so we quickly get the whole reel of events rewinding. Assets which were thought to be free assets are found to be frozen assets ; credit is paralysed and failures are frequent.

The whole of this state of affairs has been brought about because, in times of great activity, those in control were too busy to exercise control effectively and too intoxicated with apparent success to exercise control judiciously. That is to say, the slump is directly and solely caused by mistakes made during the previous boom.

But after the first panic has subsided, and after the most inefficiently managed concerns have been wiped out, those that survive are able to take stock of their surroundings in a chastened mood. They may not perhaps be prepared to admit that the position is entirely due to their mis-handling of the boom period, but they will at least realise the imperative need of setting their house in order; of stopping leakages; and of rebuilding an organisation that has collapsed through overwork . And, as this feeling becomes general, it will be recognised that lean times, like fat times, do not last for ever, and so the survivors will set to work to rebuild their fallen fortunes.

But it is a most difficult thing to get young people to visualise that which they have never experienced, and thus it is a true proverb which says that "You cannot put old heads upon young shoulders." One must have been through a war, or a financial crisis, and come out alive upon the other side to appreciate its true significance. Thus, while the same individual is rarely caught twice in two successive slumps, because the management of business houses is a shifting personnel, a business house that has been through one slump is not for that reason immune from all financial troubles in the future. It may not be precisely true to assert that these financial crises recur with each new generation of business managers, but there is certainly far more reason to suppose that they are due to the collective mistakes of those in control of big business than that they are due to sun-spots or bad harvests, or any other purely external cause. And beyond all doubt they could be greatly mitigated if it were more widely realised than they are, at least to no small degree, due to causes which are internal—and therefore preventable.

Popular Fallacies
XIII

By LAWRENCE R. DICKSEE, M.Com., F.C.A.

(Emeritus Professor of Accountancy and Business Methods in the University of London)

OVER-PRODUCTION

I have already drawn attention in these articles to the fallacy of supposing that the deliberate curtailment of output can possibly increase the wealth of the world. This fallacy or economic heresy (whichever one prefers to call it) is, however, so widely held that I may perhaps be excused for returning to the attack, and especially to its bearing upon the very important subject of stock control.

If a commodity is not readily saleable, and its price falls below the cost of production, it is often said that there is " over-production " of that commodity. Very often, however, what has actually happened has been that a certain body of habitual consumers have lost their previous buying power, or diverted it into other channels. Thus, owing to a bad harvest, a farmer may have to curtail his expenditure upon implements and even fertilisers ; but the consequent lack of demand for these latter commodities is not caused by over-production, but by a shrinkage of effective demand. The need for them is just as imperative as it would have been in the case of a bumper harvest, and it cannot really be said that there is over-production until the amount produced is in excess of the real need, as distinct from the effective demand.

Similarly, if a person of limited means (and which of us has unlimited means?) suddenly launches out into a relatively large expenditure upon wireless sets, gramophones and the like, he will necessarily have to curtail his orders to his tailor and perhaps other tradesmen. These latter will feel the pinch caused by the diversion of effective demand from one class of commodity to another, but the need for proper clothing remains precisely where it was before. It is a significant feature of the present moment that while almost everybody is complaining of bad trade conditions, the yield from the entertainments tax is greater than it has ever been in the history of that impost.

On the other hand, it is, of course, an elementary proposition that it is the function of producers to produce that which is wanted. This, indeed, might almost be said to constitute the whole art of the trader. But the function of the trader is not thus purely negative. In addition to supplying that which is wanted, he should have the vision to foresee that which ought to be wanted, and the ability to create a demand for it. It seems probable that not a little of the present trouble is due to a lack of this particular kind of vision. Further, it should be borne in mind that the trade of the world is not really financed by gold, or even by money, so much as by credit, and that credit is based on character—that kind of character which may be slow in entering into commitments, but which when it does can be depended upon as being both able and willing to meet its engagements. When there is a deterioration of national character there is a corresponding decline in national credit, which must inevitably lead to a decline in prices.

Passing on to the question of stock control, which perhaps at first sight may seem to have no bearing whatever upon so-called over-production, it may be pointed out that this has only become an effective force upon a large scale in quite recent times, although its theoretical advantages have been known for a generation or more. The essential idea of stock control is that, by keeping proper records in suitable detail, it may be possible for a business man to make himself acquainted in detail with the normal movements of his stock, and thus in course of time build up data that will enable him to determine the precise quantity of each kind of stock that it is necessary for him to keep in order to meet the demands of his customers, allowing for the fact that some kinds of stock can be replaced at much shorter notice than other kinds of stock, and therefore need not be ordered so far ahead of actual requirements. The advantages of this kind of knowledge are, of course, manifold : in the first place, the amount of capital locked up in unsold stock is reduced to a minimum ; in the second place, the risk of loss through the deterioration or the obsolescence of stock is reduced to a minimum ; in the third place, the risk of running altogether out of stock of any particular commodity—and thus for the time being losing trade, and possibly also goodwill—is reduced to a minimum ; and in the fourth place, the general effect of a detailed consideration of stock requirements will often lead to the conclusion that a quite unnecessary variety of articles is being stocked, and that very drastic economies may be effected along the lines of standardisation. All this is, of course, very true ; but every change has its repercussion.

The natural—and indeed, of course, the expected—result of instituting any effective system of stock control is to lead to the conclusion that the present stock is unnecessarily large, and that great advantages may be attained by its reduction, more or less drastic according to circumstances. This means that stock which is now regarded as redundant has to be disposed of, probably at a sacrifice. But if the trader were immediately to place orders with his suppliers for the replacement of all stock thus disposed of, he would, of course, be as far off as ever from a reduction of stock. The first effect, therefore, of systematic stock control, so far as the supplier of goods is concerned, is for him to experience a falling off of orders from his customers. This state of affairs will, of course, not be permanent. When stock has been reduced to minimum requirements, replacement orders will again be determined by sales, but in the meanwhile the supplying houses will experience a very appreciable slump in orders which will tend to pull down wholesale prices ; and even when the volume of orders returns to normal, which may not be for very many months, these orders will tend to flow along different channels, representing an increased demand for the standardised commodities that are retained in stock and a total cessation of demand for those articles which have been rejected under the trader's scheme of stock standardisation and simplification.

It would be highly interesting to know (if one could get to know) to what extent this trend of events is responsible for the fact that, for some little time past, wholesale prices have been falling out of all proportion to any reduction in retail prices. In some occupations, naturally the effect of stock simplification has been very much more marked than in others, and the effect would of course be most noticeable in luxury and quasi-luxury trades. But the tendency towards stock simplification is probably much more widespread than is generally supposed, and even where it is non-existent, or of relatively little importance, there is still the factor of stock reduction—a process which is still going on—to account for a falling off in effective demand, which is popularly supposed to be the same thing as over-production.

It is a significant fact that this so-called over-production usually becomes apparent only after some large-scale destruction or over-consumption of wealth, which has deprived former buyers of their former buying power, or after some drastic change in public taste which has caused buying power to be diverted into other channels. It is, however, a question whether at the present time stock control is not being overdone in some quarters. Of course, it goes without saying that the essential problem of the trader is how to conduct the largest possible business with the smallest possible stock ; but if stock be too mercilessly reduced, especially in the matter of variety, the tendency will be for the customer to restrict his purchases to his absolute needs ; that is to say, to curtail *his* buying orders. And thus stock control—like everything else—can be overdone, and may thus defeat its own ends.

The ACCOUNTANTS' JOURNAL

VOL. 48   MARCH 1931   No. 575

Popular Fallacies

XIV

By LAWRENCE R. DICKSEE, M.Com., F.C.A.

(Emeritus Professor of Accountancy and Business Methods in the
University of London)

THRIFT

When we read two statements that are absolutely contradictory, our
first impression probably is that one or the other of them must be wrong ;
but a little further consideration may perhaps suggest to us another
alternative—namely, that both of these contradictory statements are
equally fallacious.

Two very precise statements upon the subject of thrift, that have
recently been made by men who might be supposed to be authorities
upon the subject, have given rise to the above reflection. Mr. J. M.
Keynes is reported to have said " Whenever you save 5s. you put a man
out of work for a day," and almost simultaneously Sir Hugh Bell is
reported to have said " the best way to spend money now is to save it."
It would indeed be difficult to find two statements upon a simple issue
more utterly opposed to each other, and the curious thing is that neither
statement seems to stand alone ; each has its supporters. For instance,
even among bankers, Mr. Goodenough seems to have ranged himself
upon the side of Sir Hugh Bell ; whereas Mr. McKenna comes forward in
support of Mr. Keynes. One naturally expects, of course, to find politicians in opposite camps enunciating widely divergent theories with an
emphasis which is only exceeded by their confidence ; but one does not
like to think that bankers are really talking politics when they ought to
be talking business, or that economists are talking politics when they
ought to be talking science. As I have said before, it is quite impossible
that both these opposing views should be correct ; but it is, on the other
hand, not impossible that they should both be fallacious.

If we are to approach the matter seriously, and to disregard mere
rhetoric, we may well ask ourselves in the first place what is meant by
" saving." In one sense, of course, the man who keeps his money in his
pocket, or in a box, or who buries it in the ground, may be said to be
" saving " it ; but it will save confusion if we describe this particular
process as " hoarding." The effect of hoarding is to postpone the exercise
of the right which money confers upon its possessor, of acquiring goods or

services in exchange. The right is not relinquished, but merely postponed, and may be exercised at will on some more convenient (or inconvenient) future occasion. In the meanwhile hoarding does no good to anybody.

But under modern conditions, a man who " saves " does not "hoard"— or, at least, not to any appreciable extent. What he does is to deposit his money with a bank (or otherwise lend it to some person or institution) so that he still possesses the same right that the hoarder would have had, of using it for his own purposes hereafter. But in the meanwhile, this right, instead of remaining latent, is merely transferred. The money does not go out of circulation, and it is only possible to suggest that the community might suffer from this particular form of saving on the assumption that bankers, and those to whom they in their turn lend money, are less able to spend it advantageously than the original depositor. Most persons have a more or less fixed idea that they are entitled to do what they like with their own money, but there are probably few persons so self-satisfied as to imagine that they are better able to spend it to the public advantage than *anybody* else. To say that " whenever you save 5s. you put a man out of work for a day " is the merest nonsense, and mischievous nonsense at that. To say that everyone who can save 5s. ought not to hoard it, but to invest it with someone who can use it wisely until he wants to spend it later on, is, of course, another story altogether.

If there had been more thrift in the past, there would be less unemployment to-day. Twelve years ago, people were so intent upon spending war gratuities and accumulations of munitioners' wages that it was for a time quite impossible for production to overtake demand, with the result that the higher level of prices (inevitable during the war, at a time of real shortage) was continued so long that most people seem to have thought it had come to stay, and many productive concerns changed hands upon a capitalisation based upon this essential fallacy. That is to say, history repeated itself, and gave us yet another illustration of a spurious prosperity based upon the reckless spending of capital, as distinct from the spending of income. When the capital was spent the fictitious demand petered out, and prices would undoubtedly have fallen in sympathy, had they not been maintained partly by the combination of trade unions, partly by a very natural disinclination on the part of holders of stocks to write them down and dispose of them at a loss if by any means that could be avoided. As Mr. Wiggin, the head of the Chase National Bank recently stated : " It is not true that high wages make prosperity. Instead, prosperity makes high wages. When wages are kept higher than the market situation justifies, employment and the buying power of labour fall off." Within limits it is possible for combination to postpone this inevitable reaction, but only in the way that a high wind may delay the turning of the tide. Sooner or later the inevitable must happen.

One of the most obvious uses of high wages is to enable wage-earners to tide over periods of unemployment, which are as inevitable as the seasons although less regular. It is because thrift has ceased to be accounted as a virtue that workers who have been drawing good wages for years seek unemployment benefit the moment they are out of a job ; and it is for this reason that, after so many years of unexampled prosperity, there are at the present time some ten million unemployed workers in the United States of whom one million are said to be upon the verge of destitution.

If everybody had thrown thrift to the winds, there would be no conceivable chance of any of these unemployed persons every being employed again, for there would be no fund out of which they could be financed during the inevitable period of waiting until that employment became reproductive, in the sense of producing something capable of being sold and turned into money.

For this reason, huge schemes involving capital expenditure of vast sums are—and must necessarily be—the most unsatisfactory way of attempting to relieve unemployment ; for they are just the schemes which postpone to the remotest possible date the moment when any return may be expected that will reimburse those who have financed the undertaking. Only wealthy combinations can afford to undertake capital expenditure upon a vast scale, and only they can afford to do so out of their surplus resources.

By way of conclusion to this article, I should like to quote the following comments of a well-known City financier who, however, prefers to remain anonymous. " Dr. Samuel Johnson on one accasion said that a defect of a gifted contemporary was that ' he never clarified his notions by filtrating them through other minds.' This is, indeed, an outstanding defect of the text-book economists of our Universities. Adam Smith, the founder of economic science, had a unique opportunity (of which he availed himself to the full) of passing his ideas through the minds of prominent business men in Glasgow at a time when Scotland was developing international trade. But since then, especially in recent years, they have, with notable exceptions, wandered far astray. Economic theorists should nevertheless be able to fulfil a useful function, though business men do not attach much weight to their pronouncements nowadays. They have an opportunity of taking a leisurely and wider survey of one business in relation to other kinds of business, and of one country in relation to other countries, which the average business man usually does not possess. But unfortunately, instead of building up their theories upon a basis from observation of business facts, they are much too apt to adopt the *a priori* method of pushing forward hastily formed generalisations and theories, and then occupying themselves in selecting facts and rearranging statistics which will bolster up their preconceived notions. The business man is perhaps apt to be utterly impatient with the slender grasp of practical problems shown by the theorist, who may nevertheless at times have something of value to impart ; while the theorist is too often so much in love with his preconceptions of what should be the case that he has little patience to glean humbly of the fruits of the experience of men who have spent their lives with credit and success in a particular trade or industry, but who do not trumpet forth their individual experiences, beliefs and exhortations from the housetops, or from their modern equivalent the B.B.C."

The ACCOUNTANTS' JOURNAL

| VOL. 48 | APRIL 1931 | No. 576 |

Popular Fallacies

XV

By LAWRENCE R. DICKSEE, M.Com., F.C.A.

(Emeritus Professor of Accountancy and Business Methods in the
University of London)

TRUSTEES FOR DEBENTURE HOLDERS

One of the most widespread fallacies at the present time is that
debenture-holders are better off when there is a trust deed charging the
assets which constitute their security in favour of trustees than they are
in cases where there are no trustees for debenture-holders, and the charge
is given in favour of the debenture-holders direct.

Where there are no trustees, each debenture-holder receives one or
more debenture bonds, ranking *pari passu* with other bonds forming
part of the same issue, setting out the property charged, and, *inter alia*,
the circumstances under which the principal moneys secured thereby
become repayable, and providing for the appointment of a receiver by
any debenture-holder at any time thereafter in the event of a default in
the repayment. Even in cases where there has been no actual default
within the terms of the debenture issue, and when, therefore, it is not
competent for a debenture-holder himself to appoint a receiver, the mere
fact that the debenture-holders' security is "in jeopardy" is sufficient
ground for bringing a debenture-holders' action in the Chancery Division
of the High Court, and upon being satisfied that the security of the
debenture-holder really is in jeopardy, the Court will appoint as Receiver
such suitable person as may have been nominated by the plaintiff
debenture-holder, subject to the usual affidavit of fitness. In such cases,
accordingly, it is possible for a dissatisfied debenture-holder to take that
prompt action which may be essential for the preservation of his interests,
without the inevitable delay and uncertainty of getting all the debenture-
holders together and getting them to agree upon a common policy. The
matter is essentially one between borrower and lender, and a dissatisfied
lender who has cause of action cannot be jockeyed out of his rights because,
perhaps, other lenders may wish to adopt a more lenient attitude towards
the borrower.

When, however, the charge upon assets which constitutes the debenture-
holders' security is not given to the debenture-holders themselves, but to

trustees supposed to be acting upon their behalf, the position is altogether different, for in that case the individual debenture-holder has surrendered all his rights in favour of trustees whom he has not appointed and cannot dismiss, and his sole remedy if dissatisfied would be to bring an action against them for breach of trust, which would never be worth while even in a flagrant case unless the debenture-holder's investment was a very substantial one.

Trustees for debenture-holders are nominated by the directors of the company—i.e. by the borrowers, not by the lenders. They are no doubt in the great majority of cases persons of untarnished reputation, but there is no body of case law that clearly defines their duties, and no text-book that even remotely bears upon the matter, with the result that when it is deemed desirable in the interests of the company to make some rearrangement of its finances, the trustees for debenture-holders seem sometimes to consider themselves less as the guardians of the secured creditors of the company than as parties occupying a position of benevolent neutrality, quite willing to fall in with any scheme which seems upon the whole to be in the best interests of the company—that is to say, of the borrowers rather than the lenders. It is true that the powers of these trustees are not unlimited ; but they may be, and not infrequently are, used to persuade the requisite majority of debenture-holders to agree to a scheme abrogating some of their rights, when it is in the highest degree unlikely that such a scheme would have been accepted, but for the weight of the debenture trustees' influence.

There is, of course, the safeguard that such schemes as these require the approval of the Court before they become effective. But where the requisite majority of debenture-holders (some of whom are perhaps very large holders of ordinary shares in the company) have approved the scheme, and where it is cordially recommended for adoption by the trustees for debenture-holders, it is hardly to be expected that any individual debenture-holder for a few hundreds, or even thousands, of pounds would incur the expense and risk of appearing individually to oppose the scheme. And in the absence of such opposition the approval of the Court is, of course, a foregone conclusion.

There can, it is thought, be little doubt that during the past few years many capital reorganisation schemes to the disadvantage of debenture-holders have been carried through in this way, which would have been quite impracticable had there been no trust deed, and no trustees for debenture-holders. In a recent case, holders of 4 per cent. debentures were persuaded by their trustees to exchange them for 6 per cent. debentures upon a basis that provided them with only a very fractional increase of income, with the certainty that if, and when, the new debentures were paid off they would receive only about three-quarters of what they would have been entitled to receive under the old arrangement. And there was nothing whatever in the scheme to prevent the company from reconstructing the moment the scheme had been carried through, for the sole purpose of making such a profit upon redemption. At the same time, the security of the debenture-holders was " watered " considerably by the issue of a large block of similar 6 per cent. debentures to creditors who were previously unsecured.

In another comparatively recent case, where the trustees for debenture-holders had in hand the investments of a sinking fund representing about 20 per cent. of the entire issue, they recommended the debenture-holders to allow these investments to be returned to the company, and to agree to a moratorium as regards the payment of debenture interest.

Cases might be multiplied, but enough it is thought has been said to show that in many cases the position of an individual debenture-holder is not one that secures him against loss in the event of the borrower company becoming unsuccessful ; and in some cases at least trustees for debenture-holders, instead of acting up to their name, and using all their powers for the protection of debenture-holders' interests, seem to think that they owe a duty to the company from whom they derive their appointment at least as great as that which they owe to their cestius que trust.

Popular Fallacies

XVII

By LAWRENCE R. DICKSEE, M.Com., F.C.A.

(Emeritus Professor of Accountancy and Business Methods in the University of London)

FATIGUE

Closely allied to the question of monotony which I discussed in my last article is the question of Fatigue or, as it is usually called, Industrial Fatigue. There was a time when fatigue on the part of the worker would have been regarded by some at least as merely another name for laziness, and there was also a time when our scientists would have scoffed at the idea that inanimate things such as metals could suffer from fatigue ; but to-day we know rather more about the subject, although we are probably still very far from knowing all that there is to be known.

It would seem that there are two kinds of fatigue, physical and mental ; but it is at least arguable that there is yet a third kind, viz. spiritual fatigue. All have points of similarity, but each has its own distinctive features. Physical fatigue in living bodies—i.e. muscular fatigue—may be described as a state of physiological dis-repair. In just the same way that machinery may be clogged by dirt, the muscles are clogged by the waste tissues which have been used up in the processes of muscular exertion. In the healthy body, only time is required to secure complete recuperation, for the living body does its own running repairs ; but the process may, of course, be assisted by external means, such as hot baths, massage, &c.

No one quite knows the cause of fatigue in metals, but it is supposed to be due to some derangement of the molecular structure, possibly akin to the difference between a metallic body when first magnetised and then de-magnetised. Like muscular fatigue, time alone is necessary to secure complete recovery ; but, at present at all events, there does not seem to be any artificial means of hastening the process of recuperation.

As regards mental fatigue, properly understood this is a blunting of the senses (or some of them) owing to sustained concentration. With young people, fatigue follows very quickly upon sustained effort ; but with practice, the length of time during which concentrated effort may be put forward effectively tends to increase, and modern endurance tests by air-men and others seem to show that so long as the real need for sustained effort is recognised, and relaxation would obviously be attended by serious consequences, the human brain is capable of accomplishing far more than is ordinarily required of it even in times of stress. Like most other things, it is partly a matter of natural aptitude, partly a matter of training, but mainly a question of forgetting oneself in the work that one is doing. The natural remedy for mental fatigue is, of course, sleep ; but within limits a change of occupation will serve the purpose.

Tiredness is frequently confused with fatigue, but it differs from fatigue in that it is a purely subjective state. No one is tired unless he thinks he is. Anyone who thinks he is tired is tired. Some people were born tired. Whereas the fatigue is a blunting of the senses owing to sustained concentration, tiredness is rather an inability to concentrate effectively. It is therefore practically indistinguishable from boredom—a state in which the mind insists on wandering from the work it ought to be concentrating upon, and of thinking instead of anything and everything else under the sun.

As I pointed out in my last article, where the work is of such a repetitive character that it can be, and is, performed automatically by the subconscious mind, it is far better that the conscious mind should be occupied with something altogether different, and something pleasurable, rather than with nothing in particular. Even those who have a quite undeveloped order of intelligence find it very difficult to think of nothing in particular for any considerable time on end, and the result is that unless they can contrive something to occupy their thoughts pleasurably they will roam about from one topic to another, and thus the worker will tend to exist in a chronic state of boredom. This is likely to be the ultimate goal of the industrial employee who " tends more and more to live in two different planes," unless he has sufficient ingenuity (or originality) to be able to devise something useful and pleasant to think about, and so keep his mind occupied while he is engaged upon purely repetitive work. If he can take an interest in what he is doing, it is of course all the better ; but if his work fails to grip his attention, he must either find something else to occupy his attention, or else inevitably he will be bored. Time will seem to stand still. He will be always tired, and think that his work is unduly exacting, whereas in fact it is not exacting enough.

But, as has already been stated, fatigue is an entirely different thing, and the important thing to remember about fatigue is that it may—and very often will—overtake the worker who does not feel tired. So long as the worker takes a living interest in his work, he will feel no fatigue ; but the fatigue is there all the same ; and, whether the worker knows it or not, it is impairing the efficiency of the work as well as the efficiency of the worker.

Some years ago, some very interesting experiments were made, to see whether any connection could be established between industrial fatigue and industrial accidents, and the general trend of statistics worked out over a very large number of cases was that in any work period there was a tendency for accidents to be rather more frequent than the average during the first half hour or so of the spell, after which the percentage dropped rapidly to something appreciably below the average, and then tended to creep up to a maximum which was reached about half-an-hour before the end of the period, when it again dropped. These results seem to show that there is less efficiency (and therefore less immunity from accidents) at the commencement of a spell of work, before the worker had " got into his stride " ; but thereafter the risk of accident tends to increase as fatigue becomes greater. But when the end of a working spell is in sight, the prospect of a rest has, so to speak, a rejuvenating effect, enabling the mind to overcome the weakness of the flesh.

Further experiments have shown that, as a rule, if the said period of uninterrupted work be shortened, the accident curve never rises so high, and that the advantage of increasing the number of rest periods, or " breaks," is greatest where the work has been of the most exacting character, whether mental or physical. The prevention of avoidable accidents is, of course, a matter of very considerable importance in itself, but at the moment we are concerned with it merely because there seems to be a very clear connection between accidents and fatigue, and as it is practically impossible to measure fatigue in itself, it is very useful to be able to measure it indirectly through the medium of accidents—or their equivalent in the office, mistakes.

Every factory is obliged by law to keep a record of the accidents that occur. It would perhaps be a good thing for clerical efficiency if every office was obliged to keep a similar record of mistakes. It would then probably be realised more generally than is at present the case, that long hours and overtime do not make for efficiency, and that continual overtime is an infallible sign of bad management. The correction of mistakes represents a very appreciable addition to the time occupied in performing any kind of work ; but, apart from that, it is not always practicable to correct a mistake, in the sense of entirely eliminating its consequences. Freedom from error is therefore a far more important ideal in the office than mere speed of operation, and undoubtedly one of the simplest ways of reducing mistakes to a minimum is by keeping working spells as short as may be, and wherever practicable arranging that no one worker shall be performing exactly the same kind of routine work for more than half a day at a time.

In just the same way that an engine will race its heart out if there be no governor to restrain it, so the willing worker needs to be safeguarded against undue strain. In a short distance race, the competitors can, of course, go " all out " all the time ; but in a long distance race they must conserve their forces, and should always have enough left in hand to be able to make a final spurt if necessary. But life is a much more long distance race than any sporting event, and it is the duty of office managers—who, after all, take the place of pace-makers—to see that the pace set is one that can be maintained. If the worker can rely upon the pace-maker, he can safely concentrate upon his own particular job ; but if he has to do the manager's job as well as his own, it will not be altogether surprising if his own work suffers, because here we seem to come into contact with what I have called " spiritual fatigue "—a state in which the worker has lost heart, because he feels that there is no one looking after him—that the whole world is against him. There is no cure for spiritual fatigue, save a complete change of heart, which as a rule can only be brought about by an entire change of conditions.

Popular Fallacies

XVI

By LAWRENCE R. DICKSEE, M.Com., F.C.A.
(Emeritus Professor of Accountancy and Business Methods in the University of London)

ROUTINE WORK AND MONOTONY

One of the commonest fallacies at the present time is that modern industrial methods, as represented by mass production and the extensive use of machinery, make it impossible for the worker to take any interest in what he is doing. Indeed, this is asserted so often, and by so many different writers, that the worker would be almost compelled to believe it to be true, if he were in the habit of reading literature of this description. There is, of course, no particular reason for supposing that the average worker is a very diligent reader of technical works, but it is nevertheless unfortunate that this particular fallacy should be so insistently cultivated, for we are all inclined to be influenced by continual reiteration and very much too prone to assume that whatever is is inevitable.

Originally, the word monotony had reference to speaking on an absolutely uniform pitch ; that is, without any of those inflections which give life and soul to the spoken word. The term is also applied by artists (only it is then called " monotone ") to an absence of colour contrast. In that case it does not, of course, mean without light and shade, but that the work is executed in a single colour (usually black) upon a contrasting surface, not necessarily white. In each case the underlying idea of the word is a deliberate reticence, which is very suitable to some subjects, but rather apt to induce a certain sombreness of outlook, which, however suited it may be to special occasions, is certainly not always desirable.

As applied to industry, work is said to be monotonous when it exhibits a continual sameness, as when the individual worker is continually doing the same thing time after time. If the repetition consisted of a series of lengthy complex operations, each exactly alike, the idea of monotony would not obtrude itself, for in that case there would be variety in each separate unit ; but as the units are shortened and simplified the process inevitably tends in the direction of monotony. Monotony may thus be better described negatively, as the state existing when there is a failure to appreciate the existence of variety, than it can be (positively) as the effect of recognising the existence of continual sameness.

Now if there is one thing more certain than another, it is that there are not, and never were, two things in this world precisely alike. Anyone who supposes that he is engaged all day long in the performance of purely repetitive duties stands self-convicted of a want of observation. The faculty of observation tends of course to become atrophied as conditions of life become more secure. Under primitive conditions, when one is surrounded by potential dangers, those who wish to survive must perforce train their observation to a very high pitch of efficiency. If we are searching the undergrowth for snakes, we are probably very much more observant than we should be if we were merely looking for botanical specimens ; but if we are searching for anything at all, we shall see many things that will be quite invisible while we are looking for nothing in particular.

It requires no very high degree of scientific training to realise that no single square inch of grass is the same as any other square inch of grass, and that each square inch exhibits an infinite variety which not even the most powerful microscope is able to exhaust. A girl who spends her working hours placing little dots of synthetic cream upon a continuous procession of chocolates passing under her hands upon an endless band may think that all these chocolates are alike, and that her work is monotonous. If there were the possibility that even one in a hundred of these chocolates might turn round and bite her if she failed to place the blob of synthetic cream exactly in its centre, her whole attitude towards her work would be changed. She would not be likely to call it " monotonous " any longer. The spice of danger would undoubtedly have given it an added interest.

For years past, of course, factory inspectors have been doing their utmost to eliminate all possible risk of danger to the worker, and in consequence they have to a very large extent made it unnecessary for the worker to take a real interest in his (or her) work. But because it is no longer necessary, it does not follow that it is now impossible. It simply means that those who want to be unobservant may, to an ever increasing extent, be unobservant without risk to themselves. They are no longer obliged to take an interest in what they are doing, and therefore—being what they are—they rarely do.

This fact is very well expressed by the writer of an article on " Psychology and Modern Industry " in the current number of *The University*. " The modern factory hand," the writer says, " is working under infinitely better conditions than the craftsman ; and though he may be unable to take much interest in his actual occupation, he may be keenly interested in the pay it brings him and in the conversation of the man on the next machine. And there is a further point of difference. The craftsman's work was his whole life : he had no other interest. Whereas the industrial employee tends more and more to live on two different planes. His real life goes on outside the factory. During his working hours he is often little more than a wage-earning automaton—his mind, possibly, active, but its activities having little or no connection with what he is doing." This particular extract may perhaps give the impression that the writer is framing an indictment of the way the modern factory hand does his work. That, however, is not so. The general trend of the article as a whole is merely to state facts, and it is not impossible that the author has altogether failed to realise what these facts imply.

The truth would seem to be that there is a great deal of work now being done by wage-earners which, if it could not be equally well performed by them in their sleep, can at least—and is—being performed by them while their minds are functioning on an altogether different plane. It is no longer necessary for them to be constantly on guard lest some accident overtake them, with the result that they become more and more detached, until a stage is reached when the output is secured by the machine rather than by the machine-minder. The social welfare enthusiasts come along, and tell us that the work has become so monotonous as to be " soul destroying " whereas, properly understood, there can be no such thing as monotony because there is no such thing as uniformity.

But although it is perfectly true in theory that there can be no such thing as monotony, because there is no such thing as a continual series of events each exactly alike, there will *seem* to be monotony wherever, owing to a want of imagination, or a failure to appreciate the differences between a series of events following each other in quick succession, an impression of sameness is formed rather than a just appreciation of continual differences. To a very large extent, this can be avoided if the worker can be induced to take an interest in his work ; or, if not in the actual work that he is performing, in the materials he is operating upon, or in the uses to which the finished article may hereafter be put. But when the objects follow each other in very quick succession, this becomes increasingly difficult.

Many persons find that it helps them to get to sleep if they can visualise a flock of sheep following each other through a gate, because they picture each sheep exactly like all the rest. But if, like the shepherd or the shepherd's dog, each sheep appeared to them to possess its own individuality and to be absolutely unlike all the rest, this particular method of inducing sleep would fail altogether. If, and when, the worker is able to look at his work with the seeing eye with which the shepherd or the shepherd's dog regards his flock, there will be no impression of monotony, and no inducement towards sleep.

But in some cases this is, of course, a counsel of perfection, and when, owing to the speed with which the various objects pass under the eye, it is impossible to stimulate the observation or imagination sufficiently to observe subtle differences, the alternative is, of course—rather than to think of nothing at all—to divert the thoughts on to some other plane altogether. And this will be quite possible in such cases, because in such cases the routine work has by practice become almost automatic. What is the most suitable alternative plane must, of course, necessarily depend very largely upon the individual worker. I may mention, however, in this connection that in my young days, when I had to do a good deal of checking additions (which, as every reader of *The Accountants' Journal* knows is purely routine work) I found that I could work more quickly, and more comfortably, if at the same time I extemporised tunes. If I was working alone I would either hum or whistle them ; but when I was not alone, and this was of course impracticable, I would hum them mentally. Whether the tunes so improvised had any musical value or not was, of course, immaterial. They served to keep my mind pleasantly occupied while I was performing purely routine work ; the important point, I take it, being that they prevented my mind from wandering in a desultory fashion from one topic to another, which invariably leads either to boredom or to a disastrous relaxation of attention upon the routine work itself. Any manual worker who can sing at all can sing at his work without the work suffering, but it is very doubtful whether manual workers can discuss their grievances while at work without the work suffering.

Popular Fallacies

XVIII

By LAWRENCE R. DICKSEE, M.Com., F.C.A.
(Emeritus Professor of Accountancy and Business Methods in the
University of London)

RULES AND EXCEPTIONS

A few months ago a group of railway men in London, feeling themselves aggrieved, organised what they called a " Work to Rule Strike." The movement failed to secure the official countenance of the men's Union, and accordingly proved unsuccessful ; but what we are concerned with is not the merits of this particular labour dispute, but the system under which such a method of seeking a redress for grievances was possible.

A " work to rule strike " differs from an ordinary strike in that the men, instead of refusing to work at all, insist upon carrying out their work according to the letter of their instructions, with the result that conditions sooner or later become chaotic, and the work suffers—if, indeed, it is not absolutely brought to a standstill. There is nothing very original about the idea of a " work to rule strike." As a matter of fact one upon a much more extensive scale, and of much longer duration, occurred on the Austrian railways more than twenty years ago. From the point of view of the worker such a strike has this important advantage over an ordinary strike, that it enables the worker to make himself throughly unpleasant to his employer without any cost to himself. There are some, no doubt, who think that it is not quite " cricket " for a worker to seek to obtain the advantages of a strike without being willing to suffer the privations that a strike involves ; others take the view that, whatever the circumstances, an employer has no right to expect employees to do more than to obey instructions, and that if the result should be great confusion, or even absolute chaos, the fault rests with those who have framed the instructions rather than with those who are punctiliously carrying them out. From the point of view of the scientific organiser there can be little doubt that the latter is the sounder view of the two.

In the days before people realised that organisation called for ability as well as authority, it was a common thing to hear those in responsible positions say to those under them " I do not pay you to think," or words to that effect. If that is to be taken as the keynote of organisation, of course, it necessarily follows that it is the duty of those in subordinate positions to obey their instructions to the letter, without troubling to consider what the consequences of obedience might be. It is no doubt a recognition of this somewhat obvious fact that gave rise to the proverb

" There is no rule without an exception "—a highly convenient phrase which enables the responsible person to pass on the blame to his subordinates whenever things went wrong. But those in authority can hardly expect to have it both ways : either rules are made to be kept whatever happens, or those in charge of operations must be trusted to use their judgment as to how far general instructions apply to any particular case, and how far any particular case calls for exceptional treatment which must be improvised to meet the special occasion. The object of the present article is to discuss this question ; to consider how far routine should be rigid, and to what extent it must be elastic.

It goes, I think, without saying that in every organisation there must be some uniformity of procedure ; otherwise it would be impossible either to localise responsibility or to dovetail a series of operations which combine to form a completed work. Moreover, if each separate worker were to be left to perform the task allotted to him according to his own ideas of what was necessary, the result would in many cases fall very far short of what that worker was capable of achieving under proper guidance. Again, each problem outside the experience of the individual worker would have to be laboriously considered and solved ; and apart altogether from the waste of time involved, the individual worker might or might not be capable of arriving at the best solution of a problem, new perhaps to him, but by no means necessarily unusual in the experience of the business as a whole.

For these reasons, long before organisation was approached scientifically, it became the custom for each business to formulate methods and usages to which individual workers were expected to conform. Such usages might or might not be identical in different concerns carrying on a similar type of business. They might be—but probably were not—reduced to writing, but they represented the standard instructions as to how work was to be done in that particular house, and newcomers were expected to make themselves familiar with these instructions.

But because the whole problem had been approached not scientifically but empirically the standing instructions were never more than general. They were not framed so as to apply to every case that might arise, but loosely drawn ; applicable doubtless to the majority of cases, but not to all. Hence the comfortable phrase " There is no rule without an exception," rendered even more smug by its variant " The exception proves the rule." Haphazard arrangements upon these lines may be quite sufficient to ensure the measure of uniformity which is necessary to produce coherence under normal circumstances, but they leave untouched the problem, how to determine when the general instructions are no longer applicable, and when a special procedure must be improvised to deal with a particular case. This perhaps calls for a higher degree of discrimination than the average employee possesses, and certainly calls for a higher degree of discrimination than is necessary for the performance of his ordinary work. It tends also in the direction of allowing unusual cases to be dealt with according to the inclinations of individuals, with the result that there is a lack of uniformity in dealing with these unusual cases, even if (as time goes on) they become increasingly frequent, and ultimately perhaps not unusual at all! There is, of course, also the risk that an individual employee may fail to recognise the exceptional nature of a particular case, and accordingly treat it according to his general instructions, which are unsuitable; and there is also the risk of the employee who wishes to make things difficult preferring to work upon the lines of general instructions even when they do not apply, rather than to take the risk of initiating new methods on his own responsibility.

It is not, of course—and never will be—possible to mechanise the science of management, but to an ever increasing extent the attempt is being made to substitute a standardised routine for loosely drawn general instructions. That is to say, to make such instructions less general and more comprehensive and particular.

In just the same way that Parliament has the power to repeal laws as well as to make them, so in business management power must be reserved to modify the routine from time to time as circumstances require, or even to declare some particular thing outside the operations of routine altogether. But if confusion is to be avoided, such supreme powers must always be reserved to the supreme head, and the need to exercise such powers will depend mainly upon the skill and care with which the routine itself has been formulated. If routine is to be really worthy of its name, there can be *no* exceptions to it. The mere fact that exceptions occur shows that what has been promulgated is not really routine but some sloppy counterfeit. The essence of routine is that every conceivable variant has been thought of in advance and provided for. If this be done, there can be no exceptions left. It is only in this way that thinking can be centralised. It is only in this way that it is practicable to say that all thinking shall be centralised, and that those who do the work are "not expected to think" but merely to obey. The great advantage of routine planned upon these lines is that, because all possible variants have been foreseen and provided for, the time never comes when the clerk is faced with a problem upon which his standardised instructions give him no guidance whatever. So faced, the clerk, if left to himself, will doubtless handle the problem in the way he was accustomed to do before the routine was established; so that as time goes on, more and more of the former discarded practice will be resumed, and the new routine will fall ever lower in repute and usefulness. We shall find that our routine, which we had thought so adequate, is in practice only being used in quite simple cases, and that all the difficult cases are being handled in the old bad way.

It is, of course, easy to say that every conceivable variant should be foreseen before a routine is formulated. In practice, this is not so easy, because new variants are always being evolved. We shall never reach the stage when further development in this or any direction is impossible; but what we can do is to consider our problem carefully and in detail in the first instance, and not merely in outline, and we can stipulate that all exceptional cases (i.e. cases not provided for in the routine) shall be reported to us at the earliest possible moment. If and when it is practicable to arrange for them so to be reported before they are dealt with, that will enable us to enlarge our routine before anyone has had an opportunity of dealing with that particular kind of case in what we consider to be not the best way. But sometimes even this would involve more delay than is practicable. In that event, we must necessarily leave the man on the spot to decide what is to be done at the moment ; but such cases should always be reported with the least delay possible, and it should be for the centralised mind to decide whether the improvised methods adopted in this particular case are to be accepted as part of the enlarged routine, or what better methods are to be added to the routine to meet similar cases as and when they arise in the future.

When exceptions arise, they must be dealt with by exceptional means, and commonly they will be too urgent to be dealt with otherwise than by the man on the spot according to the best of his ability. But such cases should be reported and dealt with forthwith, otherwise an ever increasing crowd of exceptions will grow up round our routine which are not being dealt with on any approved method, and are by no means necessarily being dealt with on any uniform method at all. The great thing to bear in mind in all cases, however, is that the fewer the exceptions the better has been the planning of the routine. No properly planned routine ought to cause serious trouble, simply because it is literally adhered to.

DIMENSIONS OF ACCOUNTING
THEORY AND PRACTICE

An Arno Press Collection

The American Association of University Instructors in Accounting. **Papers and Proceedings of the American Association of University Instructors in Accounting.** 1916-1925

Baily, Francis. **The Doctrine of Interest and Annuities.** 1808

Beckett, Thomas. **The Accountant's Assistant.** 1901

Blough, Carman G. **Practical Applications of Accounting Standards.** 1957

Bray, F[rank] Sewell. **Precision and Design in Accountancy.** 1947

Brief, Richard P., editor. **Dicksee's Contribution to Accounting Theory and Practice.** 1980

Brinton, Willard C. **Graphic Methods For Presenting Facts.** 1914

Brooks, Collin, editor. **The Royal Mail Case.** 1933

Burns, Thomas J. and Edward N. Coffman, editors. **Ohio State Institute of Accounting Conferences: Collected Papers, 1938-1963.** 1980

By a Chartered Accountant and William A. Vawter Foundation on Business Ethics. **The Etiquette of the Accountancy Profession and The Ethical Problems of Modern Accountancy.** 1927/1933

Carey, John L. **Professional Ethics of Public Accounting.** 1946

Cerboni, Giuseppe. **Primi Saggi Di Logismografia Presentati All' XI Congresso Degli Scienziati Italiani In Roma.** 1873

Cleveland, Frederick A. **Chapters on Municipal Administration and Accounting.** 1909

Cocke, Sir Hugh. **A Summary of the Principal Legal Decisions Affecting Auditors.** 1946

Cotter, Arundel. **Fool's Profits.** 1940

Courcelle-Seneuil, J.G. **Traité Élémentaire de Comptabilité.** 1869

Daniels, Mortimer B. **Corporation Financial Statements.** 1934

DeMond, C.W. **Price, Waterhouse & Company in America.** 1951

Devine, Carl Thomas. **Inventory Valuation and Periodic Income.** 1942

Dicksee, Lawrence Robert. **Business Methods and the War** with **The Fundamentals of Manufacturing Costs;** and **Published Balance Sheets and Window Dressing.** 1916/1927, 1928

Dicksee, Lawrence Robert. **Business Organisation.** 1910

Dicksee, Lawrence Robert and Editor of the Accountant's Library. **Fraudulent Accounting** and **Fraud in Accounts.** 1909/1924, 1925

Edwards, J.R., editor. **British Company Legislation and Company Accounts, 1844-1976.** 1980

Ficker, Nicholas Thiel. **Shop Expense.** 1917

Goldberg, Louis. **An Inquiry Into the Nature of Accounting.** 1965

Green, David, Jr. **Accounting for Corporate Retained Earnings.** 1980

Greene, Catharine De Motte. **The Dynamic Balance Sheet.** 1980

Hain, Hans Peter. **Uniformity and Diversity.** 1980

Hawawini, Gabriel A., and Ashok Vora, editors. **The History of Interest Approximations.** 1980

Hepworth, Samuel Richard. **Reporting Foreign Operations.** 1956

The Herwood Library of Accountancy. 1938

The Institute of Chartered Accountants in England and Wales *Library Catalogue, 1913.* 1913

The Institute of Chartered Accountants in England and Wales **Library Catalogue, 1937.** 1937

Het Internationaal Accountantscongres, Amsterdam 1926. 1927

Johnson, H. Thomas, editor. **System and Profits: Early Management Accounting at DuPont and General Motors.** 1980

King, George. **The Theory of Finance.** 1882

Langenderfer, Harold Q. **The Federal Income Tax: 1861-1872.** 1980

Leake, P.D. **Commercial Goodwill.** 1921

Leautey, Eugene and Adolfe Guilbaut. **La Science Des Comptes Mise A La Portée De Tous.** 1889

Levy, Saul. **Accountants' Legal Responsibility.** 1954

Lubell, Myron Samuel. **The Significance of Organizational Conflict on the Legislative Evolution of the Accounting Profession in the United States.** 1980

Marchi, Francesco. **I Cinquecontisti.** 1867

Merino, Barbara, editor. **Business Income and Price Levels.** 1980

Norris, Harry. **Accounting Theory.** 1946

O'Neill, Michael T., editor. **A.P. Richardson: The Ethics of a Humanist.** 1980

Parker, R.H., editor. **Bibliographies for Accounting Historians.** 1980

Parker, R.H., editor. **British Accountants: A Biographical Sourcebook.** 1980

Perera, M.H.B. **Accounting for State Industrial and Commercial Enterprises in a Developing Country.** 1980

Previts, Gary John. **A Critical Evaluation of Comparative Financial Accounting Thought in America 1900 to 1920.** 1980

Rich, Wiley Daniel. **Legal Responsibilities and Rights of Public Accountants.** 1935

Richardson, A[lphyon] P[erry], editor. **The Influence of Accountants' Certificates on Commercial Credit.** 1913

Roberts, Alfred R., editor. **Selected Papers of Earle C. King.** 1980

Saliers, Earl A. **Principles of Depreciation.** 1915

Schiff, Michael, editor. **The Hayden Stone Accounting Forums 1962-1967.** 1980

Schmalenbach, Eugen. **Dynamic Accounting.** 1959

Scovell, Clinton H. **Cost Accounting and Burden Application.** 1916

Sprague, T[homas] B[ond]. **A Treatis on Life Insurance Accounts** and **A Treatise on Insurance Companies' Accounts** 1874/1911

Stacey, Nicholas A.H., **English Accountancy 1800-1954.** 1954

Stamp, Edward, G.W. Dean, and P.W. Wolnizer, editors. **Notable Financial Causes Célèbres.** 1980

Staubus, George J. **An Accounting Concept of Revenue.** 1980

Taylor, R. Emmett. **No Royal Road.** 1942

Todhunter, Ralph. **Institute of Actuaries' Text-Book of the Principles of Interest, Life Annuities, and Assurances, and Their Practical Application.** 1901

Wells, Murry C., editor. **Controversies on the Theory of the Firm, Overhead Allocation and Transfer Pricing.** 1980

Wildman, John R. and Weldon Powell. **Capital Stock Without Par Value.** 1928